THE GEORGE M. BEDINGER PAPERS

Heritage Books by Craig L. Heath:

*Georgia, Alabama and South Carolina Papers
Volume 1V of the Draper Manuscript Collection*

South Carolina Papers, Volume 1TT of the Draper Manuscript Collection

The George M. Bedinger Papers in the Draper Manuscript Collection

The Illinois Manuscripts, Volume 1Z of the Draper Manuscript Collection

The Mecklenburg Declaration

The Virginia Papers, Volume 1, Volume 1ZZ of the Draper Manuscript Collection

The Virginia Papers, Volume 2, Volume 2ZZ of the Draper Manuscript Collection

The Virginia Papers, Volume 3, Volume 3ZZ of the Draper Manuscript Collection

The Virginia Papers, Volume 4, Volume 4ZZ of the Draper Manuscript Collection

The Virginia Papers, Volume 5, Volume 5ZZ of the Draper Manuscript Collection

The George M. Bedinger Papers in the Draper Manuscript Collection

Transcribed and Indexed by

Craig L. Heath

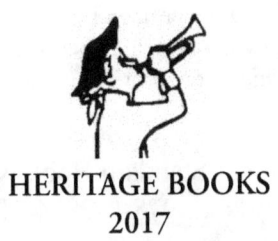

HERITAGE BOOKS
2017

HERITAGE BOOKS
AN IMPRINT OF HERITAGE BOOKS, INC.

Books, CDs, and more—Worldwide

For our listing of thousands of titles see our website at
www.HeritageBooks.com

Published 2017 by
HERITAGE BOOKS, INC.
Publishing Division
5810 Ruatan Street
Berwyn Heights, Md. 20740

Copyright © 2002 Craig L. Heath

Copyright © 2001 in Great Britain and Northern Ireland
by Craig L. Heath

The right of Craig L. Heath to be identified as transcriber of this work has been asserted by him in accordance with the Copyright, Designs and Patents Act 1988.

All rights reserved. No part of this book may be reproduced or transmitted in any form or by any means, electronic or mechanical, including photocopying, recording or by any information storage and retrieval system without written permission from the author, except for the inclusion of brief quotations in a review.

International Standard Book Numbers
Paperbound: 978-0-7884-2071-9

INTRODUCTION

"Maj. George Michael Bedinger (1756-1843) was born of German ancestry in York County, Pennsylvania. At the age of six he removed to the neighborhood of Shepherdstown, Virginia, where he enlisted (1775) in Col. Hugh Stevenson's company of sharpshooters, which joined the Continental army before Boston. Continuing in volunteer service, Bedinger participated in the battle of Germantown, and brought supplies to the army at Valley Forge. In 1779 he joined a company setting forth for Kentucky, where they reinforced the Indian-harassed pioneers at Boonesborough; later in the same year, he was appointed adjutant in Col. John Bowman's regiment, and participated in the latter's unfortunate campaign. Returning to Virginia, Bedinger rejoined the army, being present at the siege of Yorktown, thus escaping the Battle of Blue Licks. Again in Kentucky (1783-85), he explored the Green River country, finally making his permanent home in the new community at Lower Blue Licks. Thence, after taking part in St. Clair's campaign (1791), he was sent to the state and national legislatures.

"His papers consist of personal recollections written by Bedinger or taken by Draper from his verbal dictation, affidavits of services, land warrants, and letters from his descendants." [Quoted from *Descriptive List of Manuscript Collections of the State Historical Society of Wisconsin* (State Historical Society of Wisconsin, Madison, 1906)]. A fuller description of the contents of these papers, gathered as Volume 1A of the Draper Manuscripts in the collections of the State Historical Society of Wisconsin, is given in *Guide to the Draper Manuscripts*, by Josephine L. Harper (State Historical

Society of Wisconsin, Madison, 1983).

Access to the contents of the Draper Manuscripts has been facilitated by the above *Descriptive List* and *Guide* and by documentary publications and calendars and their indexes prepared from portions of Draper's collection, as well as by the availability of the entire collection on microfilm. Nevertheless, obstacles to research in this important historical resource have remained, owing to its sheer size (491 volumes of largely handwritten documents and notes) and the lack of an index to most volumes. It is to help remedy these difficulties that the current printed transcription and index to the George M. Bedinger papers has been undertaken. It is hoped that further volumes in this series will follow.

NOTE TO USERS

This transcription of the Bedinger papers was made from the 1980 microfilm edition of the Draper Manuscripts, Volume 1A. Portions of the documents in this volume are illegible or poorly legible, owing to fading or staining. Where illegible, these portions (whether single words or entire passages) are indicated by ellipses (...); some effort has been made to interpret poorly legible portions, but the original manuscript or microfilm copy should be consulted for verification. Some documents in this collection are incomplete, breaking off at the end of a page; in some cases, only the first page of a document is included. All text in the 1980 microfilm edition is included in this transcript. In addition, pages 135, 136, 188, and 189, missing from the microfilm edition, have been included in this transcript. However, the transcript should be viewed as an aid to use of the manuscript, rather than a replacement or substitute for it, and users are urged to consult the original manuscript or the microfilm in parallel with the transcript.

Draper frequently edited his own notes, sometimes heavily. Words and passages were crossed out and replaced, sometimes by writing between the lines. In most cases, the replacing text was merely a rewording of what had originally been written, and is reproduced in the transcription in place of the crossed-out text, which is omitted. In the relatively few cases where additional information is contained in lined-out text, this is included in the transcription.

Page numbers, stamped on the pages of the original manuscript, are indicated in brackets at the beginning of the text for each page in the transcript. Owing to the variability in length of text on the manuscript pages, no attempt has been made to correlate page breaks in the transcript with those in the manuscript. It has at times been necessary to rearrange pages in the transcript to preserve the continuity of the narrative. Likewise, blocks of text were sometimes marked by Draper for insertion at another location in the manuscript; these insertions have been made according to Draper's instructions. To enhance readability, the cross-examination sections of depositions have been put into a uniform question-and-answer format.

The spelling, punctuation, capitalization, and grammar used in the original manuscript have been preserved so far as feasible. Dashes have generally been replaced with appropriate punctuation.

The Table of Contents reflects Draper's division of the manuscript into sections; the section titles are generally Draper's own, modified in some cases, and with titles added when not supplied by Draper. Some sections in the table have a brief description of the section's contents, added in small typeface after the title; these were supplied by the transcriber for the reader's convenience. The order of items in the table follows that in the transcription, and may differ somewhat from the order in the microfilm edition where pages have been rearranged as explained above.

The Draper Manuscripts are owned by the State Historical Society of Wisconsin. The cooperation of the Society in the production of this volume is hereby gratefully acknowledged.

TABLE OF CONTENTS

Note from GMB, Lower Blue Licks, Ky., July, 1843 1
    Death and burial of Col. Joseph Swearingen. GMB's resignation and service in state legislature. Military career of Gen. Wm. Darke. Military career of GMB. Deaths of Benoni Swearingen and Maj. Henry Bedinger. Location of land in Madison Co., Ky.

Poem, "Thy Spirit, Independence" 2
Ancestry of GMB
Education of GMB 3
Estill's Defeat 4
First Courtship and Marriage 5
The War of 1775 5
    Enlistment in Stevenson's company. Farewell barbecue. Song, "That seat of science, Athens". Reunion in 1825. March to Boston. Military engagement on Staten Island. Imprisonment of GMB's brothers on prison ships. Battles of Piscataway and Germantown.

In 1778 12
In 1779 12
    Expedition to Boonesboro.
Incidents at Boonesboro, 1779 15
Amusing Incidents 16
Siege of Boonesboro, 1778 19
Bowman's Campaign of 1779 19
    Abortive attack on Shawnee Indian village and retreat.
Events of 1779-1783 31
Trips to the Green River country
    First, 1784 32
    Second, 1784 37
    Third, 1785 39
    Last, 1785 39
Death of Capt. Nation 53
The Piankeshaws 54
Addenda, Green River Trip, Spring of 1785 55
Lynn's Staion — No-Linn, &c. 55

Death of Walker Daniel	56
Bear Incident, Spring of 1779	56
Events of 1787	57
Defeat on Little Sandy	57
Intended Trip to the Pacific	60
St. Clair's Campaign	61
Political offices held	62
Van Swearingen	63
Kenton & the Indian Canoe	64
Orr's Campaign of Spring of 1791	64
Extract of letter from Henry Bedinger, Feb 27, 1792	65
Advises against trip beyond the Mississippi.	
Affidavit by GMB, Nov. 28, 1787	66
Concerns James Rumsey's scheme for constructing a steamboat.	
Miscellaneous Scraps.	67
Michael Rudolph, Maj. Zeigler, Gen. St. Clair, Col. Wm. Darke, Gen. Adam Stephens, Col. John Holder	
The Defenders & Hunters of Boonesboro, 1779	69
Williamson's Expedition to the Muskingum, 1781	69
Piomingo — St. Clair's Campaign	70
The Lower Blue Licks	70
The Late James Rumsey	71
Acknowledgement by Congress of Rumsey's role in invention of the steamboat.	
The Harpes	73
Act for relief of Christiana Tully	
Wabash Expedition of 1786	74
Logan's Expedition of 1786	74
Maj. G. M. Bedinger's Writings	75
Military career of Col. Wm. Oldham	
Military Career of George M. Bedinger	80
Affidavits of George M. Bedinger for pension application	
1834	82
Feb. 1835	85
Oct. 1835	89

Bowman's Expedition	97
Affidavits of George M. Bedinger for pension application	
Dec. 28, 1835	99
Jan. 25, 1836	107
Letters from George M. Bedinger relative to pension application	
Feb. 15, 1836 (addressee not stated)	115
April 19, 1836 (addressee not stated)	117
June 13, 1842, to a dear friend	121
June 18, 1842, to a dear friend	123
Deposition of Ralph Morgan, 1815	130
Letter from George M. Bedinger, June 26, 1842, to a dear friend	134
outlining part of his military career.	
Peter Fisher's Deposition	138
relative to GMB's military career.	
Deposition of George M. Bedinger, at age 78	140
outlining part of his military career.	
Estimate of crop yields from farm	140
Depositions of George M. Bedinger, at age 78	141
Military careers of GMB and Peter Fisher.	
Letter from George M. Bedinger, June 4, 1785	145
in support of land claim on Muddy Creek, Ky.	
Claims of James Gates, Joel Walker, and George M. Bedinger	147
to tracts of land on Muddy Creek, Ky., with accompanying documents, Dec. 28, 1779	
Depositions relative to land claim of George M. Bedinger on Muddy Creek, Madison Co., Ky.:	
Joseph Proctor, June 8, 1815	150
Thomas Warren, June 8, 1815	155
Evan Watson, June 8, 1815	159
William Briscoe, June 8, 1815	159
David Lyntch, June 9, 1815	160
William Cradelbough, June 9, 1815	166

Thomas Lamb, June 9, 1815	167
Samuel Gilbert, June 9, 1815	167
Green Clay, June 10, 1815	170
Laurance Thompson, Feb. 13, 181	174
Ralph Morgan, June 8, 1816	179
David Lyntch, June 8, 1816	182
Nicholas Proctor, June 14, 1816	187
Oswald Townsend, April 15, 1817	196
William (or James) Berry, April 15, 1817	201
Samuel Estill, April 24, 1817	203
Thomas Warren, April 25, 1817	210
John Crooke, April 25, 1817	219
John Williams, April 26, 1817	221
David Lyntch, April 26, 1817	222
Aquilla White, Aug. 19, 1817	228
Thomas Townsend, Aug. 19, 1817	232
John Gass	235
David Lyntch, Aug. 28, 1817	236
Questions placed to Banta by J. Wicklif	241
Questions placed to Mr. Warren	242
Instructions of Mr. Wicklif	243
Walker & Martin: questions	245
Letter from Col. Edwd. Carrington to George M. Bedinger, Dec. 21, 1789	247
Authorizes making of contracts for land at mouth of the Cumberland.	
Letter from J. Swan to George M. Bedinger, July 7, 1790	248
Authorization for land settlements.	
Letter from M. Rudulph to George M. Bedinger, Nov. 18, 1792	249
on sundry military affairs.	
Endorsement of M. Rudulph by George M. Bedinger, Nov. 1792	252
Letter from M. Rudolph to George M. Bedinger, Feb. 19, 1793	253

Notice from George M. Bedinger to Andrew S.
  Hughs   253[2]
  relative to lawsuits involving William Whittamore.

Broadside to voters of Bourbon, Nicholas, Mason,
  and Bracken Counties, Ky., July 25, 1829.   254
  George M. Bedinger justifies his reentry into politics after
  more than twenty years.

Broadside to voters of the Second Congressional
  District   255
  relative to candidacies of George M. Bedinger and Judge
  Beatty for Congress.

Letter from Henry Bedinger to George M. Bedinger,
  Sept. 1832   256
  Statement on military service of George M. Bedinger.

Statement by Henry Bedinger, July 1834   260
  relative to military service of George M. Bedinger.

Letter from Henry Bedinger to George M. Bedinger,
  June 25, 1835   262
  Family news.

Political address   266

Letter from George M. Bedinger to Walker Reed,
  Dec. 16, 1842   266
  Request for legal help in preventing condemnation of land.

Letter from D. P. Bedinger to Lyman C. Draper,
  Sept. 13, 1847   267
  on deposition of Jesse Hodges relative to Bowman's
  campaign.

Letter from Lyman C. Draper to D. P. Bedinger,
  April 2, 1848   269
  about Maj. John Finley.

Recollections of George M. Bedinger taken down
  by B. Drake, Sept. 13, 1839   271
  Childhood memories; Bowman's campaign and retreat;
  death of Black Fish; service with Orr's company on Ohio
  River; service with St. Clair's army; dispute over command in Gen. Wayne's army; political career in Kentucky
  legislature and Congress.

Declaration by George M. Bedinger, Jan 26, 1836   301
    Summarizes his military service for pension application.
Interrogation by the War Department   307
Deposition of Jesse Hodges, Jan. 7, 1836   309
    relative to military service of George M. Bedinger.
Deposition of George M. Bedinger   311
    giving character references.
Map of the Blue Lick Battle Ground   312
Deposition of Robert Pogue   313
    relative to his military service, for a pension application.
Deposition of Gen. James Ray   314
    relative to family and military service of Robert Pogue.
Deposition of Elizabeth Thomas   314
    relative to military service of Robert Pogue.
Speech of Hon. A. R. Boteler, Jan. 25, 1860   316
    Discusses strategy for defeating John Sherman as Republican nominee for Speaker of the House, incident at Harper's Ferry, the Helper book, plea for reconciliation of Northern and Southern states, argument against abolition, reminiscence of expedition from Virginia in 1775 to the rescue of Boston.
Letter from Henry Bedinger, March 16, 1846   324
    Historical notes on Bedinger family, Gen. Wm. Darke, Capt. Abraham Shepherd, and Gen. Wood.
Letter from George Wm. Ranson to Lyman C. Draper, May 3, 1887   325
    Request for George M. Bedinger's papers pursuant to writing an account of his life.
Interesting jubilee   326
    Commemoration of 1775 barbecue.

THE GEORGE M. BEDINGER PAPERS

[p. 1]
**From Maj. Geo. M. Bedinger, Lower Blue Licks, Ky.
July, 1843.**

Col. Joseph Swearingen died Aug. 9th, 1821, after a five days' illness with a bilious attack — buried on the 10th with the honors of war.

Majr. Bedinger resignd. the last of Feb. 1793 ... member of Assembly in the Fall of '94. Also representative in '92, probably elected in the Spring. Was a State Senator the close of 1800 & early in 1801.

Gen. Wm. Darke com'd. a brigade in the Fall of '94 against the Penna. insurgents, & Col. Joseph Swearingen a Regt. Was a candidate to represent _____ Co. in the Va. Legislature. ... Died in 1801 in Jefn. Co. Va. about 25th Novr. after 60 days illness.

Maj. Bedinger comd. a company at the siege of York, served also as Adjutant, in Lt. Col. Wm. Darke's regt., & a short time as Brigade Major in Brig. Gen. Edward Steven's Brigade: Served 3 mos. under Capt. Wm. Morgan as a Lieut., in Col. Chs. M. Thurston's regt.

Benoni Swearingen died 30th March, 1798, after a long & painful illness. Maj. Henry Bedinger died at the residence of his son-in law, Col. Devenport, in Jefn. Co. Va. on the 14th May, 1843, in his 90th year.

Located 400 acres on west fork of Muddy Creek (in Madison Co. Ky.) in May, 1779.

[p. 2]
Thy Spirit, Independence, let me share,
Lord of the Lion Heart, and Eagle Eye,
Thy steps I follow, with my bosom bare,
Nor heed the storm that howls along the sky."

Ancestry of Maj. G. M. Bedinger (July 3d '43)

His grandfather Adam Biedinger, who was the youngest son of a numerous family, was born & raised in the village of Dorschel, in the Principality or Lordship of Lichtzstein, in the Province of Alsatz, near the city of Strasburg. Adam was married there, & had four sons, Nicholas, Henry, George Michael, & Peter. Sometime in the year 1736, himself with his wife & family emigrated to America, landed at Philadelphia. Maj. Bedinger's father, Henry, was then aged about 8 years, & the second son. The family resided a few years near the Susquehanna in Lancaster County, whence he removed to Conawaga, a branch of the Susquehanna, a new settlement forming in York County, Penna., where he obtained and improved a handsome tract of land on which he resided to the day of his death. He was principally raised there, when about twenty two years of age he married Magdalene, aged about 18 years, the daughter of Christopher Schlegel, a neighbor residing on Plumb Run. The newly married couple resided within a few miles of their respective parents for about nine years, had six children there, to wit: Henry, born 16th Oct. 1753, married to Rachael Strode, 22 Dec. 1784, and died May 1843. 2d Elizabeth, born 28th April, 1755, married to Abel Morgan, died 1st June 1829. 3d. <u>George Michael</u>, born <u>10th Dec... 1756</u>, married Dec. 25th, 1786, at Shepadstown Va. to a ~~wealthy young widow Sarah~~ Miss Nancy Keene, who died the next year; 2d marriage to Miss Henrietta Clay, in Bourbon County, Ky. 11th Feb. 1793, then 17; 4th & 5th Christian & Christina died in infancy, 6th Danl. born 11th January 1761, married to Sarah Rutherford, died 17th March 1818; then 7th Anna Maria, married Col. Abraham Morgan; 8th Jacob;

[p. 3]
9th Sarah, born 29th March 1768, married Benoni Swearingen & died 7th Feb. '92, nearly 24; 10th Solomon — the four last born in Shepardstown, then Frederick, now Jefferson Co. He removed here in the Spring of 1762, sold his plantation in Penna. & removed. While residing in Shepardstown he kept a public house a portion of the time; & died 23d January 1772 leaving 8 children to the care of his widow, all of whom grew to maturity & married except Solomon, who died a bachelor at Norfolk in 1808, in his 38th year.

The Revolution had a considerable effect even on the surname of the family. Both Major Bedinger's father & grandfather, spelt their surname

Biedinger, & pronounced it Bie-ding-er. Since then it has more Anglified, & is now universally spelled Bed-in-ger, pronouncing the g in the third syllable soft, as jer. The Schlegel family surname has been revolutionized to simply Slagle, & so pronounced.

During the year 1774, Maj. G. M. Bedinger learned the waggon making business — his mother was anxious to have him learn a trade — buit a shop & got tools, worked but six months when the man hired to learn him the trade, enlisted in Dunmore's war; but with the six months apprenticeship he made a waggon. Was of great benefit to him in settling Ky., & even enabled him to apply his mechanical skill in the erection of saw & grist mills on the Licking just above the Blue Licks.

Education of George M. Bedinger

When the family removed to Shepardstown in the Spring of '62, the children could not speak English. Went to German school, & some to English school. Henry & Daniel were very smart scholars, George M. not quite so apt — more of a turn for manual labor, in the woods & in the field, & rather taciturn.

[p. 4]
Estill's Defeat.

James Berry & Irwin were wounded in the action; David Lynch escaped uninjured. The whites got the first fire. The tree under which Estill was killed, was a large one: The creek across which they fought, which was shallow there, was not more than 15 paces wide. Lt. Miller was sent to the Indian rear, cleared himself & did not return: Miller was blamed very much.

Sometime in July 1779, three men from Va. were at Boonesboro, wishd. to locate good land, a young Calloway went with them to the waters of Elkhorn. When within a few miles of Boonesboro on their return on the trail up Howard's Creek Calloway advised them to leave the path for safety. They scouted the idea; they didn't fear Indians & boasted ... their bravery. Calloway left them. When within 3 miles of Boonesboro, & in ambush opposite to a five acre field of corn (known as Bush's Settlement, abandoned two or 3 years before & grown over with cane & reclaimed that year, which covered the corn right preemtion of ten persons, Bedingers company of emigrants were fired on by a party of Indians. Two were taken, one if not both of whom were wounded, & the other, one Smith, escaped & came dashing & halloeing into Boonesboro (lost his overcoat in his flight). Capt. Jas. Estill, with Bedinger, Holder, young Calloway, & some dozen others seized their rifles & dashed off, first failing to get Smith to accompany & show them the spot. When they reached the spot it was near night; no Indians were to be seen, some buffalo tugs & other small articles lay scattered around, & some slippery elm bark, wh. they generally carried with them for use in case of wounds. It was asceretained that the Indian party, from the several hiding places they had occupied, were about 21 in number, had eaten & destroyed cucumbers in the corn field. It was deemed prudent to return, being too week to venture pursuit & too near night, & there was danger that they might be intercepted. Their little party comprised the effective force of Boonesboro, & they cd. not hazard too much. It was ascertained the next morning by the spies that the Indian party had evidently not gone more than one or two hundred yards from where they had attacked Smith & his two comrades, & had chosen a well selected position to waylay any pursuing party, wh. they knew pretty well wd. follow; & had Estill's once got into the trap, but few men cd. have escaped.

[p. 5]
Maj. Geo. M. Bedinger
First courtship & marriage

The year 1786, in Va. became acquainted with the widow Keene & her several daughters; the widow was wealthy. ~~No particular intentions~~ but Nancy, ~~a fine maiden~~ and an able, & intelligent & industrious young lady, one day met Maj. B. at his sisters, Mrs. Abel Morgan's where it is presumed she merely happened by accident, when Major B. casually remarked that he must soon leave for Ky., upon which the fair girl half intimated, that she shd. like to live in that famed El-Dorado of the West. Nothing of the kind had previously passed between them; the Major frankly said his surveys demanded his immediate attention in the Green River country & a considerable time would be requisite to complete them, & he could not think of asking any one to share with him the privations & dangers incident to a residence in a rude cabin in the wilderness. Her feelings got the better of her accustomed prudence: "I would rather" said she, "live in the back woods with the man that I love, & hoe corn, than to remain & enjoy all the comforts of weath in Old Dominion." "Well, then," said the Major, "we will be married on Christmas day" but a few days distant. Quick work — were married accordingly. The following Spring Maj. B. was taken sick & confined Seven months with the nervous fever, & had scarcely recovd. when his wife sickened & died in Octr., greatly to his loss & grief, leaving him an only daughter.

The War of 1775

When the war broke out, the two young Bedingers Henry & Geo. M. enlisted for a year in rifle company of Capt.

[p. 6]
Hugh Stevenson; another company was embodied in the neighbod. of Winchester, in Frederick Co., some twenty five miles distant, under Danel Morgan, afterwards so famed in the war. Stevenson's company numbered 100 men, young & athletic & famous sharp shooters with their rifles. This company was honored with a barbecue at Stevenson's or rather <u>Stinson's</u> Spring, in the neighborhood of Shepardstown a little southwest of the town, a large, clear spring surrounding wh. was a lovely grove. Here the barbacue was given by Col. Wm. Morgan & others their neighbors. Aplenty of meats & cake. A large number of the people of the neighborhood collected — men women & children. It was something new — & with some it was a painful parting.

In the company were some men of talent; one

of the number wrote a song to be sung on the occasion, & all joined in singing it:

1st.   That seat of science, Athens,
And Earth's great mistress, Rome,
Where now are all their glories!
We scarce can find their tombs:
Then guard your rights, Americans,
Nor stoop to lawless sway,
Oppose, oppose, oppose, oppose
The landing of the tea.

3d.   Far from a world of tyrants,
Beneath the western sky,

[p. 7]

We formed a new dominion,
In the land of Liberty,
The world shall own their masters here,
Then hasten on the day,
We'll shout & shoot, & shoot & shout,
For brave America.

4th.   We led fair Freedom hither,
And lo the deserts smiled,
A paradise of pleasure,
Just opened in the wild;
Your harvest, bold Americans,
No power shall snatch away,
~~Preserve, preserve, preserve, preserve your rights~~
Then let's huzza, huzza, huzza
For brave America.

5th.   Some future day shall crown us,

> The masters of the main,
> By giving law & freedom
> To the subjects, France & Spain,
> And all the isles & oceans spread,
> Shall tremble & obey
> The laws, the laws, the laws, the laws
> Of North America.

2d. Proud Albion bowed to Caesar,
And numerous lords before,
To Picts, and Danes, & Normans,
And many masters more,
But we can boast, Americans,
We've never fell a prey,
Preserve, preserve, preserve your rights
For brave America.

[p. 8]
At the close of the barbacue, it was proposed that ~~as the company were about to march out in defence of their liberties~~ the survivors of the company present, if successful in the mighty struggle in wh. they were about to engage, should that day fifty years meet again on that spot & commemorate the interesting event. The mutual pledge was quickly interchanged, & then followed the touching parting scene of the little patriot band with their wives, their kindred, their sweehearts, and friends. It was the 10th June, '75.

To complete the incident: The 10th June, 1825, was the time for the semi-centennial meeting. Maj. Bedinger looked forward with interest to its approach, mounted his horse & Started from the Blue Licks; called on the venerable Gen. Sam Finley at Chillicothe, and Wm. Hulse near St. Clairsville, two of Capt. Stevenson's company, but both regretted exceedingly they were too feeble to think of undertaking such a tedious journey. Maj. B. pursued on, & when he reached Shepardstown he found only his elder brother, Maj. Henry Bedinger, prepared to join him in the appointed Jubilee. Beside Finley and Hulse, it was ascertained that there were three others of their old companions in arms yet surviving: Judge Robert White, of Winchester, in an adjoining county, had a short before been struck with a paralytic stroke; Dr. Garrit Tunison, then residing in New Jersey, & Peter Haines, in Jefn. Co. Va., were unable to attend. The two old veterans met, a splendid dinner was prepared for them, a company of artillerymen from Shepardstown joined in the celebration, an appropriate oration was pronounced, & the old veterans, by special request, sung the song "That seat of science, Athens", & some other of their old war songs.

[p. 9]

To return: When Stevenson's company was in readiness to march, Danl. Morgan sent word that he wishd. Stevenson to tarry a few days that they might march together to Boston. He waited accordingly, when he learned with surprise that Morgan's object was to gain time, steal a march on Stevenson, & have the honor of being the first to reach the army near Boston. Stevenson hurried on through Lancaster, Reading, Bethlehem (where they were kindly entertained by the Moravians), thence on to Easton, through Jersey, to

Peekskill on the Hudson, to Hartford, on to Boston. Morgan had reached there just before them. Washington had but a few days previously joined the army. It was now early in July. The siege of Boston cont'd. The next Spring, Stevenson's company were of the party that took possession of Dorchester Heights & fortified in the night. It was a great nights labor. The enemy, not daring to attack the Americans, evacuated the city; not, however, without receiving some brisk cannonading from the rebels in Dorchester which injured some of the British shipping. After the evacuation, the riflemen were ordered to New York, & Stevenson's company with a portion of Otho H. Williams' were stationed on Staten Island. A party of British from Adminal Howe's fleet near Sandy Hook had come to a large spring on Staten Island for a fresh supply of water; when Bedinger with his comerades cut off 13 British from their boats, & took them prisoners, besides killing & wounding others on board the boats.

Expecting a general engagement, & desirous of participating, Maj. Bedinger remaind a short time after the expiration of his term of enlistment in June, but finally left for home, & hearing that the subject of Inde-

[p. 10]
pendence was to be called up in Congress on the 4th July, made extra exertion, & reached Phila. in time to hear that immortal document proclaimed to the people.

Returned home; see scraps of Majr. B. In Nov. 1776, his brothers Henry & Danl. were taken prisoners at Ft. Washington. In the action, his brother Henry then comd. a company, heard a Hessian captain, having been repulsed, spoke to his riflemen in his own language to follow his example & reserve their fire until close. Bedinger, recognizing his mother tongue, watchd. the approach of the Hessian officer, & each levelled his unerring rifle at the other; both fired, Bedinger was wounded in the finger, & ~~the same ball~~ passing cut a lick of his hair. The Hessian was shot through the head, & instantly expired. Capt. Bedinger's young brother Daniel, in his company, then but a little past 15, shot 27 rounds, & was often heard to say after discharging his piece, "There, take that, you buggers!" His youthful intrepidity & gallant conduct, so particularly attracted the attention of the officers, that though taken prisoner, he was promoted to an ensigncy, his commission dating back six months that he might take precedence of the other ensigns of his company. These two brothers remained prisoners — the youngest, but a few months, & the elder nearly 4 years — both in prison ships, with the most cruel treatment, in filthy holds, impure atmosphere, & stinted allowance of food. With such treatment it was no wonder that but eight hundred out of the 28 hundred prisoners taken at Ft. Washington, survived. During the captivity of his bro. Henry, Maj. B. wd. ~~sometimes work as if to earn~~ by labor, loans at different times, & the property sold wh. he inherited from his father, to procure money to convey to the British commissary of prisones, to pay his brother Henry board. Then he was released from the filthy prison ship, limited on his parole of honor to certain limits at Flatbush, decently provisioned &

better treated; & it is pleasant to add, that the British officers having charge of these matters were faithful in the proper application of funds thus placed in their hands. Maj. B. made many trips on this labor of fraternal affection. This, with his attention to his mother & family kept him from regularly serving.

[p. 11]
in the army. But he, nevertheless, wd. make short tours of service, viz:

After the expiration of his 1st years service, went to his uncles company at Amboy, stayed as a volunteer some little time with him, & had volunteered to attack a British vessel but the vessel left the coast before the plan was executed. Then went on to Phila. & heard Dec. of Ind. read, went on home, was prevented from joining any again that year; see scrap.

In Jan. 1777 went under Capt. Wm. Morgan, a Lieut. to N. J. — battle of Piscataway in March. Thruston's regt. & others were placed to 'cut off' supplies & prevent plundering parties, should fight the British met & distressed them. The British that winter wintered at Brunswick & had not yet left their winter quarters; it was pretty near Brunswick. After the repulse & retreat, & all left except Maj. Bedinger, ~~one Wm. Morgan & relative of the captain's~~ & two of them, who remained & fired upon the advancing foe; in open view, Maj. B. was picking & tightening his flint, & finally the three intrepid soldiers were compelled to leave the field, & fled through the woods & regained the American troops. Several Americans were killed, & others wounded. Capt.

Willson & a Mr. Shields were among the latter. The British over shot, & with their cannon balls made considerable havoc among the tree-tops. There ground was then covered with snow, & a very bitter cold day.

After Brandywine, Maj. B. & Benoni Swearingen, who subsequently married sister of his, voluntarily joined Washington, & took part in the battle Germantown, in Gen. Adam Stephens division. In the midst of the heavy smoke, a couple of horsemen with the American dress rode up saying, "For Gods sake don't fire, you are killing our own men"! Gen. Stephens immediately ordered the

[p. 12]
right wing to fall back a short distance out of the smoke, & then stand. This was evening; & for this he was suspended, Maj. B. thinks unjustly. The two horsemen, as was it turned out, were British, & resorted to that ruse-de-guess. Maj. B. & Swearingen were in the attack on Chew's house, in the earlier part of the action; indeed, Maj. B. was around & in the neighborhood of Chews well nigh all day. Commenced the march the afternoon of the 3d Oct. & all the night previous to the battle kept the troops moving slowly, & the night after were pretty well fatigued. Marched 19 miles gaining to Germantown. Back after the battle of the 4th Oct. Col. James Wood, was so well pleased with Bedinger & Swearingen, that offered them a subaltern place, which they kindly declined, saying that their mothers were widows & their assistance was requisite at home, but whenever

danger threatened they wd. again fly to their country's rescue. Col. Wood gave them certificates of having signally distinguished themselves at the hard fought battle of Germantown.

In 1778

The Army was not engaged (I think) in '78, & Maj. B. was, except when on missions to convey means for his brothers benefit, where pay, in continental money was too depreciated to be of any service. Built a house for his mother. Carried in the winter clothing, blankets &c to <u>Valley Forge</u> & remained there some days.

In 1779

On the 1st March, Majr. Bedinger, Col. Wm. Morgan & his son, Ralph Morgan, Maj. Thomas Swearingen & his brother Benoni, John Taylor, John Strode, James Duncan, John Constant, Saml. Duree, & two negroes belonging one each to the Swearingens, left Berkley County Va. & started for Ky, via Powell's Valley, & Cumberland Gap & thence the old Trace on to Boonesboro. It is necessary to state, in order to get a better understanding of the events in this connection, that Boonesboro

[p. 13]
had been in constant apprehension from Indians loitering around the Fort. They were reduced to great strait — the men few, nor could they risk any great hazard, as the life of each was too precious & their families too dear. Stratagem had

to supply the place of greater strength. Each night a horse was placed a proper distance from the fort with one his hind feet securely fastened to the root of a sapling, & three good marksmen in ambush near by. One night a small party of Indians, seeing the horse made up towards him, but half suspecting the rat in the meal tub, they cleared themselves & thus narrowly escaped. These Indians remarked to their fellows, that the Long Knives must be fools to think of catching them like so many beaver. A white prisoner, who heard the remark, soon after escaped & reached Boonesboro, where he related the circumstance.

Not relishing the dangers & hardships of the new settlement, a party of some ten or twelve with Captain Starns at their head, left Boonesboro about the 6th April, on their abandonment of the country. Boone nor Calloway were at the Fort; Holder was chief in command. The folks in the garrison had entreated Starns & his party not to leave them, thereby greatly weakening their defensive force & exposing them to yet greater dangers. These entreaties were fruitless.

As was subsequently ascertained, that when Starns left, the Indians, still hovering around, divided their party; some twenty or 30 followed on the trail behind Starns & must have kept along pretty close up, while the smaller portion of Indians remained around Boonesboro. Soon after midday, of about the 6th April Bedinger & his party, & when within some fifteen miles of Boonesboro, very luckily missed the path & wandered along through the thick tall cane perhaps half a mile before again falling into the trail, & but a short

[p. 14]
distance before striking the path it was observed that the horses snorted & appeared very much alarmed; & when they struck the trail, they discovered the fresh tracks of a party of some 30 or 40 persons altogether, picked a broken bow, & saw other signs of Indians. They were fully convinced a party of Indians going South had passed along the trail while they had lost their way & were groping their way through the cane. Seeing no Indians, Bedinger's party pursued on until near dusk, when within 6 miles of Boonesboro, they were about camping some one proposed that they shd. for safety go a little off the trace & sleep without fires; whereupon Col. Wm. Morgan, who had seen some service as well under Braddock as duty in the war, dryly remarked that "They need not trouble themselves so much, for they wouldn't die until their time came." The others not wishing to be thought cowardly, did not call the Colonel's philosophy in question. Their horses were made fast to the surrounding saplings, a goodly quantity of rich, juicy cane cut & placed before them; a large bright fire was soon struck up, & having partaken of their simple repast, they nestled down in their blankets before the cheerful blaze. The next morning, they arose & had proceeded but a few rods when to their astonishment, they discovered where an Indian party, seeing the large fire in the night & the party & horses so boldly encamped on the trail, had evidently mistaken extreme carelessness for stratagem, & gladly shunned the distrustful spot.

 Bedinger & his companions soon reached

Boonesboro to the infinite gratification of the inhabitants. The loss of their late companions was now fully replaced, & this was a sufficient cause for extravagant expressions of joy. With Holder were some 15 or 20 men only; & next

[p. 15]
in point of influence to Holder at this time was Capt. David Gass & Capt. James & Col. Samuel Estill. Bedinger & his party learned that on the ... night of the day preceding, Saml. Estill & one other guy went out to see if they discovered any Indians, about sun-set & but a mile or two from the Fort they espied the Indian party of some 15 in number & dodged into the thick cane, the Indians scattered in pursuit; one passed within a few paces of Estill, who lay crouched with his trusty rifle ready for use. Estill felt confident that the Indian looked him boldly in the face, but most probably he did not; at all events the tawny warrior bounded away, & both Estill and his comrade reached the Fort in safety. This Indian party was doubtless, the one that so cautiously shunned the camp of Bedinger's party that very night on their way, most likely, to join their fellows in the pursuit of Starnes' party.

Not more than two hours after the arrival of Bedinger & his friends, Jacob Starnes, a young man, a son of the captain, came in with the melancholy tidings that his father's party were attacked the night previous some twenty or 30 miles from Boonesboro, and all save himself had doubtless fallen a prey to the Indians. Some few others were subsequently said to have escaped under cover of the night; but, at best, it was a most dismal massacre. The two successive escapes of Bedinger & his party were very justly considered singularly fortunate, while some thought they saw in them a most striking providential interposition.

Incidents at Boonesboro, 1779

Bedinger & all his companions, save ..., together with Capt. John Holder, went out early in May & commenced

[p. 16]
preparing for raising a crop of corn, at Bush's settlement, as indicated on the 4th page of 1st sheet. See depositions — that either Bedinger or Benoni Swearingen marked out a claim on ... Creek "May 4th 1779" & so cut the date in a tree.

Amusing Incidents

Among the new comers that came to Boonesboro this season was a simple hearted fellow who knew little of the back woods or its wild inhabitants. When out one day near the Fort, some waggish companions pointed out to him a polecat with the assurance that it was a young cub. Wishing doubtless to distinguish himself in the way of some daring exploits, he made a dash at young bruin intending to make him his prisoner. It is hardly necessary to add, that he of the white & black spots suddenly & effectively worsted his adversary to the infinite amusement of the company present. Subsequent experience added to a genuine love of daring made this simple hearted recruit one of the bravest & best of hunters & Indian fighters in the country.

Boonesboro could boast of no better defender, or more successful hunter, than White. Yet he had his failing; his lack of sufficient prudence, & his careless & unnecessary exposure of himself to danger was deemed more thoughtless than foolhardy. John Cradlebaugh, a noble fellow, as cautious as he was brave, seeing White and another of the garrison wending their way of a summer afternoon to bathe in the river, concluded he would see if he could not, by a little stratagem, put a stop to this heedless imprudence. ~~Siezing his gun~~, Soliciting the aid of a fellow hunter, with their guns and blankets, and a small quantity of paint, made their way to a ford up the river, crossed — he daubed their faces with paint & adjusted their blankets in good Indian style, & stole upon the their unsuspecting comrades bathing in the stream near the north shore. A little rustling sound

[p. 17]
among the bushes attracted the attention of White & his companion, who looked with stupid amazement upon the supposed Indians. Whenever Cradlebaugh wd. level his rifle, White, with the quickness of a wild duck, would make a quiet splashing in the water, & swim towards the southern shore; White, when he cd. stand it no longer, wd. rise to the surface to take breath, & Cradlebaugh's threatening rifle wd. again cause him to seek safety beneath the river's surface. In this way White finally reached the southern shore, & his comrade, filled with the greatest consternation, swam the stream, but so weak was

he from fear that in ascending the bank, he fell backwards; and had they been actual Indians, neither White nor his fellow would have escaped. The garrison expressed their doubts whether White & his comrade saw any Indians. Yes I did, said White; one even had eyes like Cradlebaugh! The garrison was greatly alarmed, & a party went out in pursuit. Cradlebaugh & his friend washed the paint from their faces & secretly returned to the ... in time to join in search of the Indians. For a long time Cradlebaugh & his comrade kept the secret.

White, who was one of the best hunters in the Fort, & often brought in more than his share of meat, finally lost his life on a hunting tour north of Ky. river.

The men in the garrison were divided into hunting squads 4 or 5 in each. Bedinger Thos. & Benoni Swearingen Ralph Morgan & John Haweson formed one party. This party on one occasion left the Fort singly just at the dusk of evening, crossed the river a short distance above; where they by preconcert met & went on a few miles & camped without fire. The next morning a fine young buffalo crossed their rout, & it was proposed that it be shot to provide meat, for their breakfast. Maj. Thos. Swearingen reproached them for their boyish conduct, that their scalps would surely be the forfeit of their rashness as Indians were around; & that they ought to exhibit more self denial and fortitude, act like men. "Well Brother Tom," said Benoni Swearingen: "I'll tell you what it is; we'll see who the <u>boys</u> are, & who evince the most fortitude, for you shall be the first to say when we shall slay & eat."

[Here it shd. be remarked, that the hunting parties never made it a practise to kill game until

[p. 18] near night, then pack & return by night to the Fort.] The third day rolled around & no buffalo. A fine deer temptingly passed in their way, and Maj. Swearingen could stand it no longer & very readily ordered it to be shot. They scarcely gave it time to die ere its hide was off, a little fire hastily kindled in some low, concealed place, & a delicious repast quickly prepared; & if a scanty supply of parched corn meal, their only article of provision (save a little salt) they usually carried with them from the Fort, yet remained, it sufficed to make a real banquet. Except that allowance of the parched corn meal, they had eaten nothing for three days; as might be expected this meal, simple as it was, relished mighty well. That evening they succeeded in killing a noble young buffalo. Waile one or two dressed it, the others stood guard. In fifteen minutes they were ready for starting, each with about 100 lb. clear of bone, placed either in a bag brought from the Fort or one made of the buffalo hide — a hide usually made two — hastily stitched together with tugs, swung across the horse; then taking the ridges started for Boonesboro, perhaps 15 miles distant. The great danger was in nearing the Fort, for they knew from the 2 or 3 deserted fresh Indian camps they had seen, the distant reports of their guns, & other fresh signs, that there were different parties prowling about, & on the North side of the Kentucky opposite to the Fort were high cliffs, on which the Indians could secrete themselves &

watch the movements in the garrison — for they steal up some unfrequented way & got into the gate ... the sentinels discovered them.

These hunting parties were sometimes about day and night by tho' generally not for ..., & wd. ramble off many miles. Hodges, on one occasion, killed a buffalo at the Lower Blue Licks in the summer of '79, packd. 200 weight of choice pieces of meat on a strong horse & tho' 40 miles from Boonesboro, he made his way & reached the Fort in safety.

One day John Bankman requested Bedinger & Jas. Berry to go with him to catch his horse, & had proceeded but half a mile passing outside a cornfield, wh. lay adoining the river above the Fort, when they were immediately fired on by a party of Indians in ambush, three balls pierced Bankman through the heart, Bedinger & Berry dashed into the cane at different points & escaped unhurt. Bankman's body was brought in, stripped of his entire scalp.

[p. 19]
Siege of Boonesboro, 1778

Maj. B. was told that it was old John South that was wounded in the heel at the breaking up of the conference, prior to the seige. And it was near Henderson's house where the ditch was dug inside the fort to counteract the subteranean ditch of the French & Indians outside. That Calloway, not Smith, was the man whom Boone represented as the Superior commander, when the Indians wished to surrender, or something of that sort. Thinks that Col. Boone, Squire Boone, John South Sr. & a nephew of the same name, Col.

Calloway, & Capt. Gass, perhaps the other Boone, & perhaps one of the Proctors went out to hold the Treaty or conference. The Indians remained 10 or 11 days. During the siege, the Indians wd. march up in good order, & demand a surrender, promising good treatment. Prior to the siege, Boone had returned; the Fort was repaired; horses & cattle brought in with corn & fodder to supply. There was but one well in the Fort to furnish water, & the supply was scanty & had to go on short allowance. When targets were fired upon the houses, water scant, took some old gun barrels, converted them into squirt guns. Such was the the ready invention of necessity, & such their success in thwarting the designs of the enemy.

Maj. Bedinger brought out fully a quart of apple seeds, gave them to old Mark, a negro of Estill's, to raise trees upon ... He made a fine nursery, & tho' Bedinger got none, they were a great benefit to the county.

Maj. Bedinger, when at Boonesboro, was appointed commissary, to deal out salt brought up from N.C. for the settlers, & keep an account of it. A drove of hogs was in the woods, the originals brought out by Boone, now so wild that even the wolves dared not attack them; now & then one was killed by the hunters & brought in, placed in the commissary's hands, salted & placed in the old "ware-house" & kept for use when the supplies of fresh meat shd. fail.

Bowman's Campaign of 1779

Started about 1st of June, & continued about 4 weeks. Holder commanded a company; not over 20 or 25 belonged to Boonesboro, the remainder in neighboring stations, if any then settled. Marched to Lex-ington, thence on to mouth of Licking. When near the mouth, one of the party rambled off to hunt, & while clambering a hill, discovered a buffalo below him, & in attempting to run, fell, when the hunter, desirous of performing some valiant exploit, ran up bounded upon its back, & with his knife he actually killed the animal. This hero of a hunter was greatly complimented by the troops.

[p. 20]
At the place of rendezvous, at the mouth of Licking, beside other troops were a party of some 70 from the Falls of the Ohio, under Col. Wm. Harrod. They belonged near Red Stone Old Fort on the Monongahela, & had visited the country to locate lands down the Ohio. On their way up from the Falls, they had visited Big Bone Lick & had brought a large quantity of the bones of the Mastodon or mammoth in a canoe, which they designed carrying to Pittsburg. It was the presence of these men in the country, whose aid could be secured, that chiefly led to the expedition.

Bowman had also reached, by another rout. But a day or two elapsed & the necessary arrangements effected, the little army took up its line of march, up the valley of the Little Miami. Soon after commen-cing the march, Maj. Bed-inger was introduced for the first time to Col. Bowman, who, having heard that Bedinger had seen service to the eastward, desired him to act as Adjutant and Quarter Master, to which he readily consented.

During the march, and when pursuing a trail in Indian file, they passed a rattlesnake by the side of the path unobserved, & the man who brought up the rear was bitten by the reptile, & sent back to the boats, with wh. a few men were left to guard, & ordered to go back down to the Falls. No Indians were seen. When within 8 or 10 miles of the Indian town, & near the close of day, a council was held to determine upon the mode of attacking the town. The troops were divided into three parties: one under Logan, another under Jas. Harrod, & the third under Holder. Logan with his men & Wm. Harrod's company was go to the left of the town, Harrod with Bowman to the right, & Holder in front, take their respective positions as early in the night as they could reach, & between Logan's & Harrod's command a space to be left through which for the Indians, when roused from their cabins by Holder's party, to escape; it being deemed the better policy to suffer them first to get out of the town & then fall upon them, rather than completely surround them & compel to keep their cabins or take to their council house, from which, as the sequel proved, they might make

[p. 21]
a successful stand. These arrangements made, the march was resumed with proper care & secrecy. Each party posted itself as originally designed: Logan on the left between the town and the Miami, Harrod on the right, & Holder directly in front of the town in the high grass.

It was early in the night when the town was

reached & the several designated positions occupied. All was quiet until about midnight, when an Indian came runing in on the trail the troops had pursued. He had evidently, when out hunting, or something of the kind, discovered the signs of a large army invading the country & directing their course toward the Shawnee town of Chillicothe on the Little Miami, & was then on his way to give the alarm. As he neared Holder's party, puffing & blowing, & seeming to suspect or discover the trap into which he was running he suddenly stopped & made a kind of interrogative ejaculation, as much as to say "Who's there?", when one of the party by the name of Ross shot him, upon which he gave a weak, confused yell, & falling to the ground Jacob Stearns (who escaped a few months before when his father was defeated at Boone's Trace) ran up, scalped & tomahawked him. By this time the town was aroused to a sense of their danger; the dogs set up a great noise & the squaws with cries & whimperings were heard to say "Kentuck! Kentuck!" Finding themselves surprised & their town surrounded, they fled in disarray to the large council house near the center of the town. [Holder's party laid close & still a short time, giving time for some 6 or 7 of the Indians to come out and ascertain the cause of the alarm, who approached cautiously with the arms recovered & one behind another & sufficiently near Holder's party, cocking their guns, the noise of wh. was heard by the Indians who stopped, when they were fired upon & fled, leaving some blood behind.] In the hurry of the moment, Holder's men rushed into the town, killed a few dogs, & may have shot

Indians; where the Monongaheleans set up a confused hallowing, within plain hearing of the council house, saying "if there were any prisoners with the Indians, they had better flee; ~~as they intended to kill them all~~ that the Kentuckians were ... & all that remained in the council house wd. all be killed in the morning " [It shd. be remembered that among the troops were several who had been prisoners with the Indians & understood their language, sufficiently well, at least, to comprehend whatever Black Fish said to his warriors; & he spoke in a a very sonorous manner, exhorting them to remember that "they were men & warriors; that they must fight & be strong; that their enemies, who had invaded their firesides, were merely Kentucky squaws, and his braves could easily whip them." To all this they would subscribe by a kind of simultaneous & rapidly spoken guttural affirmative, very much like "ye-aw, ye-aw, ye-aw" etc.

Portions at least of Harrods & Logan's men since the plan of attack had been so changed by circumstances,

[p. 22]
now run into the town. Occasional shots were interchanged, but the most were busily engaged in searching the deserted cabins, from which their occupants had so suddenly decamped that they carried nothing with them. The articles of plunder consisted chiefly of silver ornaments, of which a large number were found, together with a goodly quantity of clothing, & lastly, a fine scarlet vest & a double-barreled gun of Simon Girty's recognized by a soldier along, who had

but recently been a prisoner with the Shawanoese. It was during this scene, or probably at its close, that Logan attempted the moveable battery. While these things were progressing the Indians in the Council house seemed busily employed in cutting port holes until near day light.

"A man or two were wounded" says Maj. Bedinger, & perhaps with Logan. About this time, a negro woman came running from the council-house to Logan's party on the left, pretending to have made her escape, but very evidently sent by the Indians purposely to deceive & frighten their invaders. She represented that Girty was at the Pickaway town (some 8 or 10 miles distant, perhaps,) with a hundred of his Mingoes & wd. soon arrive. This intelligence, notwithstanding the evidence of stratagem it bore upon its face — for Girty's scarlet vest & rifle had been found, & he was very likely himself in the council house — spread among the troops; & the chicken-hearted among the whites Mononga-heleans, who did not exactly relish the idea of fighting, were not slow to magnify the number of the expected reinforcement of the enemy under Girty, & in this way the one hundred soon reached to the terrible number of six hundred. While all this was transpiring, the negro woman, who had been unmolested, secretly disappeared; another evidence that hers had been an errand of deception.

This sacking did not continue long. Nearly all left, & went to hunting up Indian horses outside the town; while a little party of 15, among whom were Maj. Bedinger, Jesse Hodges, Thomas & Jack South, & one or two of the Proctors had screened themselves behind a large oak log not over 40 paces from the council house, & there awaited the approach of day break, after wh. for several hours frequent shots were exchanged by the respective parties. ~~& the log seemed to be pretty closely watched by the Indians & here they lay nearly 5 hours after daylight.~~ While this little party lay thus awaiting patiently a vigorous support from their friends, they were doomed to disappointment. There was some firing from some cabins on the left, from Logan's party; but nothing like concerted action. Wm. Hickman, who had served with Bedinger at the seige of Boston, & who, by-the-way, was strongly suspected of

[p. 23]
having stealthily killed a man below Pittsburg during Dunmore's War, while peeping around the corner of a cabin to the left of Bedinger's party, was shot through the head & died instantly. He remarked the previous evening that he had a presentiment then that he shd. be killed in the expected attack in the morning.

Bedinger's little band continued to lay close behind their rude & uncertain breastwork. The log, & it was an oak, was something over two feet in diameter, & lay a little up from the ground, but the grass & weeds grew thickly beneath and around it. Had the Indians known it, they might have killed the entire party by directing their fire <u>under</u> the log; as it was, whenever a Kentuckian would venture to expose himself to get a more satisfactory shot, several instantaneous cracks from the enemy's port holes would tell how closely they watched the old oak log, and the every movement of those screened behind it. Several were already killed though repeatedly cautioned by Bedinger to avoid exposure. Tom South, who lay directly to the right of Bedinger, eager to get an effective shot, ventured to take a preliminary peep, Bedinger had scarcely exclaimed "down with your head", when South was shot in the forehead & with a single groan fell down partly upon his side. His young brother John, or Jack, as he was familiarly called, then a lad of about 17, who was on Maj. Bedinger's left, was affected at the fate of Thomas & shed some tears, & asked Bedinger if he could not place his brother in a position in wh. he could die easier. This could not with safety be done but he expired in a few minutes after. By this time seven of the fifteen behind the log were killed besides Hickman at the corner of the cabin, and still the survivors awaited a regular & combined attack from their friends. But they hoped in vain. About nine o'clock, Col. Bowman made his appearance partly behind the hill, on horseback some 200 yards to the right of Bedinger's party, & waiving his hand exclaimed, at the top of his voice: "Make your escape! Make your escape! I can bring no one to your assistance!" Bedinger then said to his seven surviving companions, that he would take the lead & they shd. dodge in oblique directions, with a quick zig-zag movement, and in this way make for a few scattering trees some sixty or 70

[p. 24]
yards to the left but still within reach of the en-

emy's fire. It was discovered that the Indians had comprehended Bowman's orders, & a few were scattering out of the council house; no time was to be lost. Bedinger started, jumping through the grass, frog like, first in one direction, & then as suddenly in another, sometimes siezing a shrub violently to aid in throwing him to some opposite and distant point, & the while balls whistling past, around him like so many hail, but being strong and remarkably active in his zig-zag movements singularly enough he escaped them all & reached a good sized tree, behind wh. he made a few moments rest. Upon looking around, he was surprised to see that none had followed his example; but, it must be confessed after all that they acted wisely, for by this time, & it was all the work of a moment, the Indians had discharged their rifles, & before they could reload the whole party were beyond their reach, without receiving so much as a single shot. The retreat was as successful as it was singular. Just before leaving the log, ~~Bedinger~~ espied his old friend Ralph Morgan behind a tree to the left, fighting single-handed on his 'own hook'; every now & then the Indians from the council house pay him their respects, & make the bark fly merrily from the tree behind wh. he was posted; Bedinger called out to him that he was needlessly exposing himself, ~~until others should come join him~~ & had better get out of the way of danger.

When Bedinger & his little band reached their friends partly behind the hill, within long rifle shot of the council house, in a confused mass,

[p. 25]
& some distance still further to the South, were some three hundred horses, guarded by a large number of men. [Jesse Hodges deposition will tell of the number of horses.] Bedinger ordered the men to form in a line of battle just behind the brow of the hill, which with here & there a tree, served as a protection: he ... were to make a stand & check the Indians who were advancing at a distance, sheltered behind the scattering trees, & firing upon the Kentuckians. Not more than a fourth of the men could be got into the line, & as the others were scampering off out of harm's way, these could not be expected long to expose themselves; & while here & there some brave spirit would venture a chance fire upon the distant foe, the more timid would every now & then dart off singly and in squads, until after a short lapse of time when the remaining few, seeing the foolhardiness of attempting to maintain their ground unaided & unprotected, sought their safety in flight. Bedinger, who as Adjutant, and in the absence of any apparent movement on the part of Bowman, had assumed the command & formed the line, was not a little mortified at the needless consternation that seemed to pervade the troops; he had hoped to have made a stand & defeated the enemy in open battle. When the last of the line commenced retreating he fortunately found his horse, mounted & moved on with the fugitives. Soon overtook his old friend & companion-in-arms at the siege of Boston, Wm. Oldham, who had been with Morgan's riflemen in the disastrous attack on Quebec & the same who was subsequently killed at St. Clair's defeat.

Consulted with Oldham, & then ordered the officers to form their respective companies in single file, Logan's command to the right, Harrod's to the left, & Holder's in the center, and about 30 paces apart; with orders for Holder's line, when the word "halt" was given, to divide & the rear half to fall back & close the rear, while the other portion were as quickly to close the front, thus forming a hollow square. This order was effected, & the men formed about a mile from the hill. In this order the three divisions moved on rapidly, with an Indian but seldom seen or heard & certainly they did no execution. Some three, or four, or five miles were gained, & a creek (less in size, probably, than Cesar's. wh. they subsequently followed) easily forded on foot — for nearly all were on foot; when Bedinger, who was in the rear, on reaching the elevated ground, looking back perceived a shaking among the tall grass & herbage on the flat on the opposite side, & soon after, of the enemy, some were seen to make demonstrations of crossing the creek, ordered a halt, some 40 or 50 rods south of the stream; Holder's company, according to previous understanding, closed the front and rear. Until now the drove of horses with a

suitable guard for their protection, had been driven in front; separated frequently from their colts, no small neighing was kept up. They were now placed within the hollow square. The ground for making a stand was very judiciously chosen, elevated, and a sufficiency of trees & fallen timber for the protection of the men. There had evidently been a small windgale & some of the fallen trees were piled upon each other, affording in many instances very desirable shelter from the enemy's fire. The men were ordered to shelter themselves as well as they could, compatible with the design of a hollow square: some accordingly tried, while others screened themselves behind the fallen timber.

As the troops halted, one Elisha Bethiah, who belonged to James Harrods company & had been badly wounded in the thigh the night attack on the Indian town was now in front & favored with a good horse, concluded he would choose to risk his chances of escape alone, rather than hazard himself, already wounded as he was, in another fight with the Indians. He dashed off, and just at the moment the enemy had gained the front & four of them pursued Bethiah. His horse proved that his rider had not overestimated his good qualities, & soon outstripped his pursuers. That night the wounded man, fatigued & not a little exhausted, selected some suitable spot, dismounted, fastened the horse's rein to one of his wrists, with perhaps some protection between himself & animal, laid himself down, & Sleep was soon upon him. When he awoke the next morning, he was alarmed to find his horse gone. In horror of his situation rushed upon him ~~thoughts~~ far away in the wilderness, he knew not where, save that it was in the enemy's country, destitute even of the commonest food, & utterly unable to walk! While thus in despair brooding over his misfortunes, his horse came up to him; doubtless at home he had been <u>tolled</u> to the habit; & Bethiah, with a joyous heart, mounted his good steed & continued on his way. In due time he reached Harrodsburg, recovered from his wound, & often used to allude, with grateful feelings, to this instance of singular sagacity in his horse, in returning to the aid of his helpless master.

It was now about half past ten o'clock in the forenoon. The firing & yelling of the Indians were first heard in front & soon all around, with the low & distinct voice of Black Fish heard first in one directon & then in another, encouraging his braves, repeating in substance the speech he made them at the council house, adding "that, as they now had the ~~Long Knives~~ Kentuckians surrounded, they must have them all, not suffer one to escape." And wherever the well-known voice of their beloved War Chief was heard, their hearty responses & reiterated whoops would make the words resound again. Their number was small, it could scarcely have exceeded fifty; but their deficiency in numbers they remedied as well as they could by resort to stratagem & greater activity. While one ...Black Fish, the life & soul of his people, was exhorting his warriors to "be strong and fight, load well & shoot sure" in another direction a little squad would feign to have killed some unfortunate Kentuck & raise with their shrill voices their accustomed scalp yell, alike to encourage their friends, & strike terror to the hearts of their foes. The Indians were careful not to show or expose themselves, but would creep up as near as they could with safety, fire, & then skulk away to reload & renew the zig-zag fight. Whenever the Kentuckians, on the other hand, fancied they saw the trembling of some distant cluster of bushes, or luxuriant bunch of tall grass, peradventure really nodding to some passing breeze, they would fire upon the suspected covert. This singular & irregular contest which lasted nine hours, was comparatively blowless; the Kentuckians, without positive evidence, claimed to have made several effectual shots, & lost, it is believed, some one or two killed, & perhaps as many slightly wounded. It was now past sundown. Bedinger went to Col. Bowman, and said, in substance, "As the surrounding enemy seemed to be increasing in numbers, and redoubling their zeal with their success, and as our men were sinking under fatigue and hunger, it was necessary that a vigorous effort should be made to disperse them." Col. Bowman, who seemed disheartened, replied "Do as you please; I don't know what to do." Bedinger added, "We must rush upon them on foot with tomahawk in hand, advance

[p. 27]
rapidly, dodging as we proceed & in this way we shall avoid the enemy's fire, then with ours reserved, we can dash upon them and force them to retreat." Accordingly Bedinger some other officers called out "Come, boys, let's rush on, with tomahawk in hand & reserved fire, & leading the way, a party of 40 or 50 of the boldest of the men followed, and made for the well known voice of Black-Fish, not then more than 40 or 50 yards off. In this well-planned charge, Black Fish was mortally wounded; the Indians were seen hurriedly to place their fallen chief upon a horse, with a faithful warrior mounted behind him, and then fled towards their town. It

was observed that B. Fish was dressed in a beautiful white shirt richly trimmed with broaches & other silver ornaments, & from white prisoners who subsequently escaped or were killed, it was ascertained that the brave Shawaone chief expired as he entered his town. Though an enemy as he was, we cannot but admire the intrepid bearing and self-devotedness of the brave and eloquent, but unfortunate Black Fish.

[p. 28]

The retreat was now resumed ~~near by was a creek, perhaps the one they had crossed near the battle, took~~ at dusk, & within 4, 5, 6 ms struck Cesars Creek. This, tho bearing a little to the right of their rout, was taken as a guide for a considerable distance, sometimes following along downstream on its banks, & at others along its bed knee-deep in water: All who wished were mounted upon the horses taken from the Shawnees. Maj. Bedinger, while riding his own horse, soon after the march recommenced & before reaching the creek, got his hat brushed off by the branch of a tree, jumped off, and feeling around for it in the dark, someone coming up behind gave the horse a little rap to make him step aside, when he took fright & broke away, carrying off saddle, bridle, camp kettle & blanket; the distant tinkle of the kettle as it came in contact with brush or trees, told but certainly that the horse was beyond reach. Maj. Bedinger plodded along on foot through brush and briars & nettle, & lagged behind somewhat. The party halted a short time, but then fearing lest the Indians should be reinforced & follow in pursuit, they soon resumed their slow & weary retreat. At this point Maj. Bedinger got a poor sharp-backed excuse of a horse, without saddle or blanket, & jogged on with the others. While sitting sidewise upon his horse, the animal suddenly jumped one side & threw him off backwards down a little ravine, but luckily escaped with a few knocks & bruises. Thus the retreat continued; it was a meandering rout that they pursued. They suffered exceedingly from hunger, nor did they venture to hunt the following day; the fear of an attack from a pursuing foe, to recover their horses, was enough to impel them forward, & as quickly as possible to leave the enemy's country. The second night, worn down with fatigue and hunger, they ventured to take a little repose; and it was but little, then up, and on for the land of Ky. Early the ensuing day they reached the long wished-for Ohio, crossed just above the mouth of the Little Miami. Maj. Bedinger was careful to place several sentinels in the rear, to guard against surprise; one of these, Thornton Farrow, saw an Indian dog at a distance, which was considered, at the time, satisfactory evidence that the Indians, not being able to collect together a sufficiently formidable army in time for pursuit, had sent a few spies to see that their invaders had actually left the country. Bedinger and the sentinels were the last to leave the enemy's shore.

The army now felt more at ease, moved on some three or four mile in the rear of the elevated hills skirting the river,

[p. 29]
reached a fine large spring; here a halt was made. Hunting & fishing soon supplied the camp, these with rest soon gave new life and vigor to them all. They were once again in a land of plenty, where pea-vines, wild clover, & wild rye, furnished abundance of food for the half-famished horses. It was now agreed to have a sale of the horses & other booty, & then make an equal division of the amount realized. The conditions were simply these: a credit of a year; the captains were to keep the accounts with their respective companies, & when it shd. be subsequently ascertained that any one had bid in property exceeding the amount of his dividend, he was to pay the surplus; & this excess to be given to such as had fallen short of theirs. The theory was very pretty, & all seemed well pleased with it; and, excepting such horses as had been stolen from the settlement, identified by their owners present, or kept in reserve for the proper claimants, the sale commenced. Some of the finest horses were struck off at fifty or sixty dollars, but generally much less; and a pound of silver trinkets would bring some twenty dollars. Thus went the large drove of horses, the silver ornaments, clothing, and other articles. The Monongaheleans, who seemed to figure prominently in everything save fighting, were far from being modest in the ~~sale; certain it is they got their full share~~ number of their bids, or the amount of property they purchased. The result was, scattered as were the purchasers from Red Stone Old Fort to the Falls of the Ohio, & thence to Boonesboro on the Kentucky, no collections were ever made; or if made, never accounted for

to those who had a right to expect them. The spring were Bowman's party camped, and where the sale took place, is to this day known as The Horse Camp Spring.

Thus ended the celebrated campaign of 1779; a campaign, it shd. be remarked, the real history of which has been but imperfectly understood. Made at so early a day, & not as fortunate in its results as some of its successors, it is not strange that its true character

[p. 30]
should have been misconstrued or undesignedly misrepresented. Bowman, when too late to retrieve his error, seems to have felt keenly the miscarriage of the expedition, & given himself up to despondency and inaction. Nor is it at all certain, that he should be made the scape goat for the failure of the enterprise. The numbers engaged were amply sufficient, the officers confessedly brave and experienced; & withal they reached the Indian town entirely undiscovered, they evidently found less than its full quota of warriors there, & the plan of attack seemed proper & judicious. And notwithstanding all these auspicious circumstances, superadded to their great superiority in numbers, the campaign was well nigh a total failure. The Monongahelians, upon whose aid so much reliance had been placed, seemed to have engaged in it more from motives of plunder than patriotism. They were the first to disobey express orders, and set up a noise when they shd. have remained silent; they were the first, after the cabins had been sacked, to seize upon & magnify the foolish story of Girty's pretended reinforcement,

thereby engendering a panic among the troops, who abandon the immediate vicinity of the town; & it appears highly probable, & perfectly in character, that they shd. be foremost in searching for horses, foremost in not fighting, & foremost in the retreat. Their desire for gain was sufficiently manifest at the sale at the horse-camp spring. With such a body of almost demi-savages, whose pernicious examples were but too contagious, is it to be wondered at that Bowman, chagrined & disheartened, should ride up & call out to Bedinger's little band behind the memorable oak log, to make their escape, for he could bring no one to their assistance; not that he would not, but truth extorted the confession, that he could not?

There is still another feature in the case worthy of notice. When the hope was expressed to Bowman during the outward march that at least the

[p. 31]
women & children that might be taken shd. be spared, some of the Monongaheleans, slipped in their notions about such matters with "No! indeed; kill them all, the d__m savage! We are ordered to destroy the heathen off the land; & as for these little Indians, if not killed, they will soon be big ones!" Such were the men, very like, who two years after went out from West Penna. under Col. David Williamson & butchered in cold blood the unoffending Moravian Indians on the Muskingum. Of such doubtless were the men from that same region of country, who, by their timid, ... dastardly conduct contributed in no small degree to the defeat & misfortunes of the

ill-fated Crawford in 1782. At all events, it was the conviction of Maj. Bedinger & others on the expedition of Bowman that had the Monongaheleans not have been along, the result would have been more creditable, but with them defeat was preferable to victory; for an indiscriminate massacre, as with the Moravians would doubtless have followed success, & an eternal disgrace would have attached to the campaign of 1779.

Events of 1779-1783

In November, 1779, Maj. Bedinger left Boonesboro for Virginia. After his return, as usual, he was busily employed at his widowed mother's, or taking money to the army for the benefit of his brother Henry at ... prisoner with the enemy. In the autumn of 1780 he went on a trip with a team to the High Hills of Santee in S. C., with supplies for the army. At that day there was no small danger attempting such a trip through the Carolinas during the famed Tory ascendency; it was was a war of extermination between the Whigs and Tories. Thus passed 1780.

In the Spring of '81, raised a company, joined Lt. Col. Wm. Darke's reg't, was at the siege of Yorktown, acted as Adjutant, & some little as Brigade Major in Ed. Steven's Brigade.

The Green River Trip, 1784

Returned to Kentucky in the fall of '83 by the river rout, landing at Louisville. a large company came through the wilderness road, perhaps ... of wh. he was appointed leader. Staid at Strode's* Station & at Boonesboro, & was busy attending to land claims. The next Spring went to the Falls of the Ohio, intending to go thence into the Green River country in western Kentucky to locate lands for himself & others. A large number of surveyors, 30 or more, were to meet 1st April at the Falls, & proceed thence into the Green River country to run off the continental State line military bounty lands. Having crossed Ky. River at Leestown

*Doubtless his old friend who came to Ky. in 1779, John Strode. LCD

[p. 32]
& had proceeded westward but a few miles when he met Jacob Myers, an honest old Dutchman just from the Falls, & asked him if the surveyors had met, & were prosecuting their surveys. "Oh, no!" said honest Jacob, "a number of obstickles hash represented themselves, & they hash reclined." And so it proved; Indians were in the country, & it was thought too hazardous an undertaking, & the design was for a season abandoned. Bedinger, not thus to be foiled in the accomplishment his object, determined that alone and unaided, he would explore the country between Green & Cumberland rivers. Accordingly he left the Falls of the Ohio, went first to Col. Thos. Marshall's surveyor's office in Fayette County, where he met Lewis Fields, a young man of his acquaintance, some 18 or twenty years. Fields endeavored to dissuade him from going alone, holding out his ... should he be snake bitten in the wilderness, or if killed by the Indians, no one would know his fate. That night they slept together, & next morning when ... Bedinger was about to take his leave, Fields finding his entreaties useless, was promp-

ted by his generous disposition to say, if he had single extra shirt he would go along rather than see his friend undertake so dangerous a trip alone. Maj. Bedinger observed he had a shirt he could spare him, but added that he could not ask him to make so great a sacrifice particularly so since it was out of his power to make him adequate compensation. Having nothing especially to engage his attention, & partaking freely of the prevalent spirit of daring and adventure, Fields decided at once to accompany his friend Bedinger. They struck ... in the country near the present Elizabethtown, reached Hanley's Station near the head of Seavern's Valley, some 50 ms. from the Falls of Ohio went on struck Green river, crossed, were proceeding down several miles to the mouth of of Big Barren, when plenty of very fresh Indian sign were discovered which caused them to push on hastily to the mouth of Barren, swam over to the south bank, & it being twilight, they concluded to secrete themselves in the high grass on the margin of the stream. An Indian party who had followed on their trail, soon reached the opposite bank, their dusky forms were but faintly seen through the approaching darkness but their low

[p. 33]
earnest conversation was distinctly heard, though not understood. Bedinger and Fields, though excessively annoyed with musketoes, lay close & maintained the greatest silence. In a little time their pursuers disappeared. The next day, while exploring near an mouth of Little Muddy creek, just at the junction of Big Barren with Green

river, Fields, he being a little ahead, suddenly exclaimed "Bedinger, I'm a dead man!" Not suspecting the cause, & hearing no report of firearms, Bedinger concluded in the excitement of the moment that an Indian had crept up & had shot Fields with an arrow, & snatched his gun from his shoulder. "I was snake bit", said the young man, in extreme pain & agony. Siezing a stick, Bedinger made an effort to kill the reptile, when the stick broke in his hand; and using his knife with a single stroke severed the head from the body, before the reptile had time to repeat its deadly stroke or get out of the way. It was of the large moccasin species, fully four feet in length. Fields complained of great pain in a few moments his whole frame was affected, even his tongue began to swell, his wound was a severe one, just above the knee, a bandage was drawn tightly around the leg ... to prevent the poison from spreading, and ... and Bedinger bound a portion of the yet writhing reptile upon the wound ... powder & slippery elm & butternut bark, served in turn to dress the ... Fields begged Bedinger not to abandon him to his fate. ~~Bedinger told him~~ "Be now no trouble on that score; he would stick by him to the last." It was now near night, & thinking it more secure from the Indians than where they then were, Bedinger proposed to carry Fields over the river. It had rained considerably that day, & the river was commencing to rise; this derternined Bedinger to effect a passage that night, found a fording place, water ... deep, first carried over their two rifles, & then upon his shoulders conveyed his friend across the stream, & a little distance in the cane &

struck up a fire. After a while, hearing the report of guns, perhaps a rifle a couple of miles down the river, & believing it proceeded from the Indian party that ... for evidence, Fields expressed a strong desire that Bedinger would go & see them, as they were known to be skillful in cases of that kind. He took his gun & started, anxious to do anything that would hold out a hope of alleviating the sufferings of his companion. Night shortly overtook him, & being cloudy it was pitch dark; the croaking of the frogs along the river again was his only guide. Sometimes he would find himself in a tree top, at others in a quagmire

[p. 34]
or foul of a rock or tree, & on one occasion as he approached unseen a small cave that put up from the river he fell down some twenty or thirty feet into the sand & water below. Very fortunately he escaped unhurt, but his rifle was somewhat injured; however scrambled up & proceeded on his benevolent but weary pilgrimage. Progress, under such circumstances, was extremely slow, & as several hours had been consumed, he considered some two or three miles must have been gained, & set up a loud hollowing, begging if white men were within hearing they would answer him, as his companion was badly snake bitten & in great distress; & if Indians, he both desired peace & their kind assistance. Though often repeated, no response was heard; though he always after used to think that the Indian party must have been near by, but fearing it was stratagem of a stronger party of whites, studiously

remained silent. At length, failing at his object, he commenced his return, alone, painful & uncertain, & progressed as well as he could. The night was now far spent, & supposing he must be somewhere within hearing distance of Fields, he commenced hollowing, but no reply. He wandered on, when all at once just before him, he caught a glimpse of what appeared to him of some one silently extinguishing the dying ... of a camp fire; as though an enemy, wishing to avoid discovery. Expecting every moment a foe to advance upon him, Bedinger for some time maintained a death like silence, though with his gun the while ready for action; but seeing no movement, he finally advanced to the spot, and was surprised to find his friend Fields extended on the path. He had fallen into a kind of stupor, consequent upon pain & fatigue, & when aroused from it, he said he had a faint recollection of hearing a noise, but supposed it the howling of wolves.

Something like three weeks were spent at this place. The little camp was made as comfortable as a temporary occupation would justify; they were at least protected against stress of weather. Provisions, they had none: a supply of fish or meat, the only resort of the woodsmen, was all important. Their amunition, too, was getting scarce, and must needs be carefully husbanded. Bedinger with his rifle on his shoulder went to the river, & attempted to shoot fish, only at first making no allowance for the curvature of the water, would overshoot & miss his aim; he subsequently, however, learned the secret, had no difficulty after in killing fish whenever he desired. But the amunition was getting to scarce to warrant their longer continuing to rely upon fish for their food. Maj. Bedinger bent his course to a lick a mile or two off on the southern bank of the Big Barren where

[p. 35]
he succeeded in killing a fine buffalo calf, swung the hind quarters, weighing together some 70 or 80 pounds, across his back, without dressing them, & had scarcely started on his return when a yellow wolf of the largest kind, hearing the report of a gun, came up to share the game. The wolf followed pretty close behind Bedinger, & ran around him keeping at a distance, but a load of powder at that time would have been poorly expended for a worthless wolf. He finally took a back trail & disappeared.

Having returned to camp while some of the men were caring for ... broiling upon the embers... underwent the customary ... of jerking with a view to its preservation. The ... made of ... curing or jerking meat, whether buffalo, bear, deer, or elk ... simply this: erect a scaffold by placing iiin a ..., in an upright position, four forked stakes some five or six feet in heighth across the top of these place two parallel poles, & transversely a number straight sticks or splints two or 3 inches apart, upon which to place strips of meat an inch or even less in thickness weighing from half a pound to a pound ... then raise a smoke on the ground beneath, & on days ... rainy weather or as a protection against night dew a blanket or skin would be stretched overhead. A day or two would suffice, when the combined process of ~~smoking and~~ ... would ... complete, and the meat pronounced jerked. A little sprinkle of salt ~~seems to expedite~~ would lessen the amount of smoking requisite as well as add greatly to the relish & flavour of the ...; but in early times it was seldom the woodsman could command a sufficiency of salt ~~for this purpose~~ to warrant so great a luxury.

It was early in June, the jerked meat exhausted, & Fields partially recovered, that they concluded to start for the settlements by proceeding slowly; & in crossing streams or high pieces of ground or when Fields would become weary, Bedinger would carry him upon his back, & both their rifles. Hunger compelled them to seek for meat; & in a valley they discovered a drove of buffalo. "Be careful, Fields, to aim between the horn the ear, where the skull is thinnest, & the ball will best take effect; remember we've only 4 charges left." "Yes, yes", said Fields, as he crept along from tree to tree, & shortly fired. "Thank God", he exclaimed, as he saw the buffalo fall to the ground, "we are safe!" As Bedinger came running up, the

[p. 36]
animal, probably hit on the thick forehead impenetrable to ball, & only stunned for the moment, recovered himself & bounded enraged towards Bedinger, who fired & dodged to the left, while the buffalo dashed on to join the drove ahead. Not relishing the idea of getting thus tricked out of their buffalo, Bedinger ran & got another shot at the same animal, but provokingly

enough lost him after all their care and anxiety. But a single charge of powder remained, & with this Fields made an ineffectual shot a turkey. Nothing daunted, they pursued their rout, aiming for Severn's Valley. On one occasion, seeing a piece of buffalo hide upon a bush, which had evidently been stripped off by white or Indian hunters several months therefore, Bedinger proposed that, parched up as it was, they might roast it upon some coals, & make it answer in place of better food. Fields couldn't second it, & a day passed on; but the same day came across a small live terrapin, stripped off its shell, & roasted it nicely. Bedinger was as averse to touching the terrapin as Fields had been to the dried buffalo hide. It was a rich treat, and full well did Fields relish it. He had well nigh eaten it all, when Bedinger's hunger brought him to it; he tasted, and was angry with himself that he had tasted no sooner! Fields mended rapidly, while Bedinger, from long exposure & exerting himself in carrying his sick friend, began to decline. Worn down with fatigue and hunger they neared the settlement of Jacob Van Metre, within two miles of Henley's Station. Fields, now the strongest, went ahead and reached the house a while before his companion, & when Bedinger arrived a fine bowl of mush & milk was in readiness for him; & though cautioned to eat at first but a _very_ little upon a weak & empty stomach, he really thought he gave good heed to the caution; but so it was, he transgressed one of Nature's laws, & she inflicted the penalty. After recruiting a few days, they proceeded on to the older & denser settlement. Lewis Fields, than whom few men were more kind or generous-hearted, subsequently married & did well, and as an evidence of the estimation in which he was held by the people among whom he lived, it is sufficient to remark that they invested him with the office of High Sheriff of [Hardin] county.

[p. 37]
2d Green River Trip, 1784

After but a short respite at the Falls of Ohio Maj. Bedinger, with his chain & compass, a supply of amunition, a Depy. surveyor's appointment from Col. Rh. C. Hudson's Va. State Line Military Land Office, commenced sometime in the summer his second trip to the Green River country. In Severn's Valley he secured the assistance of George & Jack Berry, one King & one Nelson. Went down the valley creek with a canoe, & thence down No-Linn to Green River. Recent heavy rains had swollen the stream, & beaver were seen here & there posted upon logs or the many ... of the water & seeing the approach of the party would dive making a peculiar flap with their broad tail upon the surface ... in every direction. George Berry had traps already, & caught some of these animals, the pelts were retained for their fur, while the tails, trowel shaped & weighing from one to two pounds, were salted & jerked to be carried on the return into the settlements, where they bid up a liberal price for these as an article of exquisite luxury.

They landed at the upper part of the Big Bend of Green River within the limits of the present county of Butler & there commenced the surveys.

They were not annoyed by Indians ... trip. One little incident occurred here worthy of notice. It was near the end of a drizzly day, when the party struck up a fire near the mouth of a large cave in a hill side near the upper neck of Big Bend. A little parched corn meal brought in the canoe, with some broiled fish or venison, furnished a supper fit for a lord or lady, and then perhaps as they sat around at night near the fire, some good lively songs from the Berrys, with the interchange of their respective hairbreadth escapes and adventures ~~they had severally made in the wilds of the west~~, would close the events of the day. Bedinger bethought himself that the cave at hand would make a very acceptable bedroom & expressed his intention of bestowing on it his patronage, as furnishing at least a shelter from the rain.   George Berry had given it careful examination, & had his fears lest some overhanging rock might fall and bury him beneath its ponderous weight; & though his name was <u>Berry</u>, he didn't particularly relish the idea of a such burial; beside, there might be snakes in the dismal place, & he couldn't sleep there, no how. Bedinger with more pluck, entered the cavern and with his trusty rifle beside him, he laid himself down upon his rocky bed for the night, and slept soundly; a feather would scarcely have made it softer.   When he awoke the next morning, curiosity led him to examine the apartment

[p. 38]
more minutely. The room in which he slept was nearly circular, some eight or ten feet in heighth, & fully fifteen feet in width. Though rather dark

in the back part of the cavern, he discovered an aperture about three feet wide, leading apparently still further into the earth; he had scarcely entered it when a large fat bear, alarmed at this unceremonious invasion of his domicil, dashed suddenly by him, not, however, without something of a squeeze in effecting the passage. Bedinger gave the alarm; his comrades, who were busying themselves outside, siezed their rifles & shot the retreating foe as he emerged from the cave. His weight could scarcely have been less than three hundred ~~pounds~~, & a right smart chance of first rate jerky he made. A portion of the cured bear meat was kept upon the scaffold where jerked, with the hide securely spead over to protect it from the pilfering buzzards, while the party went on down Green river ~~and up Big Muddy Creek~~ to continue the surveys. They returned after an absence of a couple of weeks, but were sorely disappointed to find their bear jerky missing.

 Surveying lands and exploring the country employed their time until autumn had considerably advanced. A short time before returning to the settlements, Maj. Bedinger one day while near the mouth of Muddy River, heard the tinkle of a bell, & soon discovered that it proceeded from a fine young horse on the opposite bank of Green river. He mounted a log astraddle & attempting to swim over with a little bag of salt in his mouth the currant in the stream whirled his log over & plunged him into the river, and the salt being soluble of course he lost it all ere he reached the shore. With some difficulty he caught the animal, stripped the bark from a pawpaw & made a bridle, mounted & entered the water. The horse was rather averse to stemming the currant & when partly over, & in a jumping fit, broke the bark bridle, returned, and bounded away through the woods & bushes; Bedinger clung to her back, crouching forward to avoid being swept off by the limbs of the trees. He succeeded in his purpose & finally stopped the alarmed animal, & considered himself fortunate in escaping with divers scratches and bruises. A stronger bridle was readily fabricated, & the horse soon reached the opposite bank in safety. A bark saddle with corresponding stirrups was the result of a little ingenious industry; upon this the camp blanket was folded & placed, wh. completed the preliminary arrangements for the journey to the settlements. With his rifle slung behind him, & his compass in front, Maj. Bedinger set out alone; while the Berrys, King, and Nelson, in the canoe, with their peltry & beaver tails, took the water rout to the Severn Valley country. In due time all reachd. the settlements. The horse advertised etc.

[p. 39]
3d Green River Trip in 1785

Early in the spring of 1785, Maj. Bedinger made a short surveying trip on Paw river & its tributaries. Shot an enormous buffalo, the largest he ever saw, & as it fell it barkd. a tree: the cheese anecdote, & early in the summer again set out on an exploring trip to the Green river country, acompanied by John O'Bannon and another person. As they passed to the western Bank of Green river they saw Indian signs plenty

& had to be continually on their guard. One night they selected for their camp Deer Creek where the banks were high confident that they were in the neighborhood of Indians. Bedinger having a small bear skin knap-sack containing a few land papers of value for safety bent down a sapling & fastened his knap-sack upon it and let it ... up, then silently lay themselves down in the tall grass, and were ... on guard against surprise. Some time in the night they heard the half suppressed growl of a dog, and a whispering ... in the Indian tongue; knowing full well that an Indian band were stealing above them, they all at once sprung down the bank, dashed over the creek & escaped, Maj. Bedinger had not time to secure his knapsack. Several days elapsed. When they returned to the spot, with papers torn up & scatterd apart.& at no great distance ... they discovered the knap sack hanging upon a bush, & in it the dear ...

Last trip to Green River

About the 20th Sept. 1785, Maj. Bedinger with three other surveyors, & Capt. Mayo Carrington of Va., an officer appointed by the continental line to superintend the military surveys, & a servant with him. Each surveyor had two chain carriers, a marker & hunter, making in all twenty two in the party. They struck Green river just above the confluence of Rough Creek, in which they caught a fish. The water was found too high to ford. All looked to Bedinger, as he was so well acquainted with the country, to be their leader. He twice crossed the river on horseback, & three times swam it in succession, before all their surveying & camp equipage were rafted over. The water being cold, this exposure brought upon Maj. B. the rheumatism, from which in the end he suffered greatly. They proceeded on to Tradewater creek, which flows west & falls into the Ohio. They located the most of their surveys on Tradewater, and some few on Livingstons creek which empties — disembarques — itself into Cumberland. On Paw creek a northern fork of Tradewater, they

[p. 40]
found abundance of beaver, trout wild geese & ~~crane~~. At this there seemed to be no buffalo in that region of country; but beaver & deer were there. Some of the party proposed to tear away a portion of a beaver dam and when the beaver during the night, would attempt to repair the breach, to watch & kill them. The sagacity of the beaver enabled them to float logs along slyly with the currant, with their bodies submerged & push with their noses, & carefully place them in the rupture & as carefully fill the interstices with dirt. All this was done so secretly, that though closely watched they were unobserved. The party felt a little sheep next morning when they found they had been outwitted by the cunning beaver, & the dam completely repaired.

Same day, after some of the hunters reported that they had discovered a camp of eight Indians on the northern bank of Tradewater some 5 miles from its mouth. Bedinger's party were on the opposite side of the stream, not more than half a mile off. All was motion in the camp, and several were for surprising and attacking the Indians forthwith. To this Bedinger strongly objected, saying they had but seven guns in the party, & moreover to attack the Indians would, in his opinion, be equivalent to abandoning their surveys for the season; for the Indians would thenceforward, with such reinforcements as they could command, would so annoy them, to say the least of it, that a continuance of the surveys would be out of the question. As it was then night, he proposed that they should camp without fire, to avoid discovery, & the next morning he would join any one on a friendly mission to the Indian Camp. Captain Carington heartily acceded to all this, & said he wd. be the man to accompany his friend Bedinger. The night passed away. The messingers of peace started on their errand, Bedinger, with the muzzle of his rifle in his hand & the breech thrown carelessly over his shoulder, taking the lead, & Carrington without a gun & a little distance behind him. The men were cautioned to keep out of sight, but sufficiently near to lend their aid in case of necessity. It was after sun-rise as Maj. Bedinger crept up slyly & neared the shallow

[p. 41]
ford directly him and the Indian camp. But two warriors and a squaw were there, & they did not observed Bedinger's approach until he had commenced fording the creek, when they jumped from the camp fire & snatched their rifles. Bedinger saluted them kindly with "How do you do, how do you do, brothers!", and being in no fighting attitude, the Indians returned the

complement with "how do you do brother", & then in a very friendly way shook hands. Bedinger said he was hungry, & asked for some food; when the squaw immediately set herself about broiling some bear meat upon the coals. Carrington now came up. One of the Indians was Captain Whitenday, the leader of the party; they were Delawares, & the others of his band had gone out early that morning hunting game. They informed Captain Whitenday that their "great father", General Clarke at the Falls of Ohio, had sent them to ask their Indian brothers to come in and make peace. By this time the whole surveying party had made their appearance, which at first seemed to alarm Captain Whitenday. All who desired were now served with bear meat, & the most of the men soon after went off down the creek. Wishing to show the Indian captain some mark of kindness, Capt. Carrington gave him a good saddle which his servant was carrying on his back, the captains horse having shortly before given out; Carrington told Whitenday that he might have the horse too, and explained where he would find him. Captain Whitenday, not backward in generosity, gave Carington in return several dressed deer skins, which moccasined the whole party. Bedinger and Carrington took their leave, with the promise on the part of Captain Whitenday, that he would go & make peace with Gen. Clarke.

While the surveyors still kept in the country locating lands six or 8 days after this interview, they ran out of provisions; & hearing the report of guns down toward the mouth of Tradewater, several miles off Bedinger mounted a horse &

started off alone in that direction. He came close upon Captain Whitenday's band without

[p. 42]
discovery, rode up in a friendly manner & greeted them with the usual salutation of "how do you do, brothers!" While some seemed friendly, Whitenday, evidently in liquor, spoke out angrily. "You dam lie! One dam rogue!" Bedinger suspecting he had not found the horse Carrington had represented, took a piece of paper, marked out the Tradewater & its junction with the Ohio, & then drew the figure of a horse, on one of its forks. Captain Whitenday evidently satisfied with this explanation, remarked "Maybe so, you one big cap-pa-tin, maybe so you one dam lie; me look & no find him; but me look again, then no find him, then me go steal good hoss, may be so two." Bedinger told him that he must not steal from his white brothers even if he did not find the horse, for that would create mischief, but come to him, & he would pay him for the horse. Whitenday was, by this time, in a pretty good humor, commenced introducing himself and friends to the Major, striking his breast, said "Me Cap-patin Whitenday. This, Poweder; this, Inning Corday; and this, Foudnee, Captain Buck's son, he young Buck; besides these, one or two others were formally presented to their white brother. During this interview Bedinger had held his horse by the reins; now, in the act of fastening him to a sapling, Powder, whose face was blackened, came up and took hold of the bridle, when Bedinger snatched it out of his hand; thereupon he went away silently & sat down on a log a

distance. After a while Powder took from his head a rimless and topless hat, & walked up to Maj. Bedinger proposing "come, swap"; the Major declining, Powder immediately snatched it, but Bedinger as quickly recovered it. Upon this Powder seized him by the shoulder, but as quick as thought the Indian found himself sprawling upon the ground. The Indians let up a great laugh, and none seemed to participate in it more heartily than Maj. Bedinger himself. Powder again retired to the log, handled his rifle rather suspiciously, but sulkily kept his seat without apparently daring to use it.

Captain Whitenday again addressing himself to Bedinger, proposed that they smoke the pipe of peace; a few whiffs were taken

by each, When Whitenday said, presenting him some whiskey in a tin cup, "Come, drink him all up"; Bedinger declined. The Indian captain, still persisting, said "if you don't drink, I'll kill you"; so saying, he drew his knife, & presenting the point, in a back-handed way, to Bedinger's bosom, he doubled up his fist as if to strike the end of the handle & drive the blade to his heart. The Major with apparent unconcern took the cup, and without seeming to notice the menace of Whitenday, carelessly passed it on to some one near by, when the chief, unobserved, withdrew the knife, and stroking Bedinger slightly upon his breast, said with much emphasis, "You big cap-pa-tin"; and, smiting his own breast, added with an air of pride, "Me big cap-pa-tin too!" "You White men," he continued, "kill good many praying Delawares on the Muskingum, but me no mind that none, for me kill white men, too, so many", indicating by his fingers, fifteen; "and for this," continued the chief, "me made big cap-pa-tin".

(Captain Whitenday was inquisitive to know what so many white men were doing so far from the settlements? "Oh," said Bedinger, "some have come to see the country, and visit their friends at the French Lick on Cumberland" (now Nashville). 'What,' said the chief, doubtingly, "all dose got friends at the French Lick!" Just then discovering the end of an ivory scale sticking out of Bedinger's pocket, and perhaps half suspecting its object, suddenly pulled it out and asked eagerly "What dis for?" Bedinger, tho' taken somewhat by surprise, ~~was rather at a loss for a plausible answer, but~~ ventured this explanation: "Oh, its a rule, to make lines so I can talk on paper to my friends in the settlements." This all seemed very plausible to the old chief.)

At this juncture, as one Edward Rice and an Irishman were approaching us from a small island within sight. Whitenday commenced shaming them: "You squaws. You afraid, you squaws. You run away, you squaws." "Yes," said Rice, "we were afraid of <u>whiskey</u> last night." Bedinger knew this Rice very well; the latter, according to a previous understanding had come down with a few supplies for Bedinger & his party, and in return they were to survey a tract of land for him. The evening previous the Indians had darted out from the dusky shore with their canoes above and below him, & completely hemmed him in. Rice and his Irishman, ~~were taken prisoners and then~~

the Indians examined — finding it useless to attempt an escape, made a virtue of necessity, were glad to meet their brothers, saying Gen. Clark was desirous of making peace with all the Indian tribes, & they had been sent to convey his wishes to the Delawares. Tho' this seemed satisfactory, yet Captain Whitenday could not resist the temptation of seemed to think the plunder in

[p. 44]
the canoe unquestionably his own; and at once asked for whiskey and salt: the one to preserve his body, the other his meat. A jug of the 'fire water' was soon produced, and by evening Whitenday and his band were pretty well intoxicated and the fell spirit of destruction had come upon them. The squaws had succeeded in hiding some of the guns & knives but Rice and the Irishman sought safety by returning to the little island in the stream. They had returned to camp to get their guns.

Bedinger enquired of Rice if he had brought any flour; he replied in the affirmative, but thought it prudent that Whitenday's consent to taking it away should first be obtained. The old chief said he might have part of it; upon which the white men went down to the canoe. Rice enquired of Bedinger if he wd. venture to take a pound or two of salt wh. he had sewed up in a cloth, & which the evening before he had successfully secreted from the Indians. Hardly any risk was too great to secure so desirable an article as salt, and accordingly, when some five & twenty pounds of flour were put in a bag, the little wallet of salt was placed near the center. By this time the ever watchful eye of Whitenday discovered what he thought looked rather suspicious, came down to the

[p. 45]
canoe, and commenced feeling nimbly with his fingers the outside of the bag, but very fortunately did not happen to detect the salt; its discovery, under the circumstances, might have cost them their lives. Bedinger now took his leave of the Indian party, shaking hands with them all accompanied with a friendly 'farewell' to each, and last of all he went to Powder, still sitting upon the log as surly as a bear, and not giving any indications of extending a parting hand, Bedinger seized and shook it heartily. Then mounting his horse, with a wary eye upon his friend Powder who, he feared, might have reserved this opportunity to shoot him, dashed into the bushes and was soon lost to view.

They continued surveying until early in December, when the season was so far advanced as to admonish them to leave for winter quarters. Situated as they were, the consequent exposure to cold and wet weather, Maj. Bedinger became almost helpless with the rheumatism first induced by swimming Green River. The camp at this time was on the border of a small pond in the cane, a few miles back from the Ohio, and in the region of country between Tradewater & Cumberland. Maj. Bedinger was unable to leave for the settlements, and one of his chain carriers, John Stovall, volunteered to remain with him, while the remainder of the company started on their return by the way of the French Lick. Capt. Carington, upon bidding his friend Bedinger adieu, had nothing else to give him but a green baize shirt; & even this was peculiarly acceptable to one in his destitute situation. ~~with a scanty supply of clothing pretty well nearly work thread bare at best & his camlet jacket some garments even worn even to strings, while for the cheerless winter now was rapidly approaching. Moccasins with dry leaves. Wild goode cut.~~ Before their departure, the hunters had killed a fine fat bear, & left a goodly share with Bedinger & Stovall. It may here be added, that Carington & his party suffered greatly before they got in, several of them were badly frost bitten. They reported they had left Bedinger good as dead, & that he could never survive etc.

Here, far away from friends and the comforts of life, with approaching winter and a cheerless prospect

[p. 46]
before him, was Maj. Bedinger left in the wilderness, worse than alone, as the sequel will show for his companion was a heartless and treacherous man. They were illy prepared for the severity of the season; each with a buckskin hunting shirt and breeches, & instead of the seams being regularly stitched, they were tied with from a half to an inch and a half apart, with the knots outside, & the ends sometimes dangling down. Opposite the knee & hip joints, for instance, the tyings would be pretty close together, while along the thigh and below the knee there was less occasion for their frequency;

& strings supplied the place of buttons. In addition to these very necessary garments, Major Bedinger wore under his hunting shirt, a camlet jacket that seen its best days, his baize shirt, an old Revolutionary cocked hat, and a good pair of buckskin moccasins; and with dry black or white oak leaves as a substitute for socks, would complete the picture. (It should here be added, that when their moccasins were once frozen, it was necessary to keep them so, in order to prevent the leaves within from becoming wet and uncomfortable.) And as perfectly in character with the oddity of the Major's cocked hat, let it be observed that Stovall was ensconced in a curiously fashioned cap, not by any means the most graceful in its fit, produced simply from skinning the carcass of a large wild grey goose; this, with the feathers and down exposed to the weather, and strings to fasten beneath the chin, presented altogether as singularly ludicrous an appearance as perhaps ever graced a hunter's head since the days of Nimrod the mighty. Add to this, a long unshaven beard on a naturally ugly countenance, with powder horn and shot-pouch properly adjusted, with belt, and knife and rifle, and we have John Stovall pictured to the life.

They continued in their sequestered camp in the cane-break some two or three weeks; as they had plenty of meat, it was thought prudent for Stovall not to venture out, for Indians were still in the country. A blanket streached upon poles sheltered them from the storm, while a good camp-fire served the double purpose of cooking their bear meat & keeping them warm. A little camp kettle, a pint tin cup, and a spoon or two of hickory bark or buffalo horn: to these and the tomahawk axes the ever needful bullets, his rifle, wh. also ... the duties of a razor. While Maj. Bedinger was thus

[p. 47]
confined in camp, he one day observed a lonely paroquet on a sapling under which they had camped, which he soon perceived had a broken wing and could not fly. After a little the bird fastened its bill in the bark & streached its legs to their utmost capacity, secured a good foot hold with its claws, then loosen its bill & re-fasten it between its feet, when it wd. again let itself down as before, and in this descended to the ground. The poor bird seemed hungry, and commenced picking up some grape seed & bits of meat which lay scattered around; & apparently conscious of its comparative helplessness, it slowly wended its way to Maj. Bedinger, who had the while been intently watching its movements. As the paroquet came near enough the Major extended his hand and kindly smoothed its feathers, fondled it; it seemed exceedingly fond of these attentions it would come down daily & sometimes repeatedly the same day if tolled by food during their stay.

Still afflicted with rheumatism and having heard on some former occasion that the Indian treatment was simply to take a cold bath, Major Bedinger determined he would make the trial cold & freezing as the weather then was, he went to the little pond but a few yards off, and plunged himself into it, and when he came out, so cold was it, that the water as it ran down to the ends of his hair, would freeze and form little knots. His wardrobe re-adjusted, the re-action upon the system, together with a good toasting before the bright blazing fire, would produce a warmth and comfort, to be attained in no other way. The first experiment was so satisfactory that it was often repeated, and followed with the most gratifying improvement.

During their sojourn in camp Stovall's wickedness of heart and rascality of character began gradually to develope themselves. He one day carried off & secreted Maj. Bedinger's tomahawk, and then suggested the idea that the Indians had crept up and stolen it. When they left, as he did not take it, the inference is, he intended sometime to pass that way again when he could easily possess himself of it. Sometimes he would, unsolicited, recount

[p. 48]
his successful roguries, and by obscure allusions or dark inuendo would hint the commission of deeds that well might vie with the fiendish boastings of a gray-haired buccaneer. "You must be a grand rascal, indeed, if the half of all you intimate be true," would be the reply of Bedinger; which would excite from Stovall a low chuckling laugh. These things very naturally gave Maj. Bedinger not a few misgivings respecting his personal safety, but circumstanced as he was, weak, dependent, and lonely, he could only keep an eye on the alert, and make the best of his situation.

Maj. Bedinger had recovered so rapidly that about Christmas they concluded to commence the return for the Falls of Ohio. With some of the remains of their bear meat, they set out on the dreary journey. On the waters of Little river, a tributary of Cumberland, they succeeded in killing an unusually fat buffalo cow, and while Major Bedinger was dressing it, and Stovall sitting partly behind him on a log handling his rifle upon his knees, the gun went off, and the ball barely missed Major Bedinger & would have passed directly through his body had he not, the moment before, suddenly changed his position. Suspecting, from Stovalls character, that it was not the result of mere accident, but still preferring not to charge him with an intention to take his life, he rather sharply reproved him for his carelessness. A foolish excuse was made to serve Stovall's purpose; that, wishing to kindle a fire by flashing some powder, and desirous to save the load in the gun, he had plugged the touch-hole; but the fire had in some way communicated to the load, and thus the accident happened. This was no good reason, Bedinger thought, why Stovall should not have pointed the muzzle of the gun some other way, and he pretty plainly told so.

With a small supply of buffalo meat, they resumed their journey in better spirit directing their course for the mouth of Big Barren. The Earth was now covered with 3 or 4 inches of snow. Stovall every now and then bore off to the left of their rout, and after a little fall in behind Major Bedinger, and follow

[p. 49]
along behind him as though he was endeavoring to steal a shot at his companion. Maj. Bedinger's vigilance prevented Stovall from getting any such

advantage. The next day or the day after, he again took off to the left; and Major Bedinger concluded he would let him go, ~~as he would rather be alone than run the risk of~~ and pushed on several miles, when he heard the distant report of Stovall's gun, & shortly after another. For some time Maj. Bedinger studied whether he had better answer, and first examining his powder & finding he had five charges, beside the load in the rifle, and that load from its age not reliable fired in reply. Further reflection induced him, as he was then out of Stovall's reach, to keep clear of him; & with this view, though another distant alarm shot he bore off considerably to the right, to break the course, as well as to take the south of a range of hills where there was little or no snow, & thus prevent Stovall following his trail. At the close of the ... third day he reached an elevation with a valley below; it was the valley country along Green River, some distance below Big Barren, though he did not convince himself of it until he reached the stream. As he descended the hill he saw fresh tracks, & concluded there must be Indians around, and struck a cane-break for the river to make further discoveries, and had proceeded scarcely a hundred yards in the cane when he suddenly met Stovall! So thick was the cane, that they had nearly come in contact before they discovered each other; and the meeting was as cold as it was unexpected. "Is this you, Stovall?" was the formal inquiry of the one; and the little monysyllable 'yes' was pronounced with equal indifference by the other. They emerged from the cane-break in a few moments; and near the river bank a fine white oak, with a covering of dry tough leaves, furnished a suitable spot for camping. The overhanging leaves had rendered the ground bare of snow beneath; and at a desirable distance from the tree was a log against which to build the camp-fire. Maj. Bedinger set his gun down against the tree, and went and cut an

[p. 50]
arm full of cane, upon which to lodge for the night; and while in the act of spreading it, with Stovall sitting upon the log, with his rifle in his lap, again the gun went off, and once again Major Bedinger narrowly escaped, the ball and ramrod would have passed through his abdomen (i.e. lower extremity of the body) had he not at that moment bent forward to arrange his bed of cane; as it was, the ball and ramrod missed their aim & struck the oak, shivering the rod in pieces. Incensed at this treacherous conduct, Maj. Bedinger instantly snatched up his rifle and levelled it at Stovall's forehead; when he set up a piteous begging that his life might be spared, confessed that he was the d--dest fool in the world for his carelessness, & if Bedinger would only spare him, he would go before him all the way, and would not even flash a gun in his presence. The appeal came so feelingly, that a naturally kind & magnanimous heart like Bedinger's relented from its determined purpose, and the perfidious wretch was suffered to escape a merited death. Their buffalo meat was now exhausted, & Bedinger lay down supperless upon the cane, with his head near the trunk of the tree & his feet to the fire, his blanket his only covering, & his hand upon his

knife. ~~It was a cold and cheerless night; the trees creaked mournfully enough around them, and while here and there the tops and branches, displaced by the rude wintry blasts, came tumbling to the ground.~~ and by and by, Stovall, weary, shivering and sleepy, laid himself carefully down at Bedinger's back, and there passed the night in silence.

Having passed Green River, Stovall took his position a short distance in front, agreeably to his own proposition. A large gaunt wolf crossing his path, he drew up, and with a single shot broke both his fore legs; and in this situation the disabled animal made out, partly by hopping upon its hind legs & partly by tumbling over, to reach a fallen tree a few rods off, the trunk of of which was a little elevated from the ground. Under this the wolf sought protection; the two came up, and Bedinger placing

[p. 51]
one end of a pole under his feet & the other upon the neck of the prostrate wolf, Stovall drew his knife and plunged it to the animal's heart; the wolf, for ... dying effort, extracted his head from its confinement and snapped savagely at Stovall's hand, and barely missed its grasp. It almost immediately expired. In a few moments they had each a fine quarter of wolf meat for Stovall insisted that it would save life; but it was a sorry hope, miserably poor, ... distant appearance of a particle of fat, & withal most unsavory to the smell. Along they trudged, stumpting across the country to & then up Caney Creek, thence over to Rough creek, the main stem of which Caney was

but a branch, then up Clifty and the tributary, ... a trail, ... year... passing over a ... flowed, frozen ... of cane country ... of these streams, frequently breaking through the ice... & water, always cold, raw, and disagreeable in the extreme. The second night after leaving Green river, so keen was their hunger that they could no longer resist a meal of their wolf meat. Stovall attempted a stew in the little camp kettle, & succeeded in eating a trifle, but Major Bedinger roasted his quarter all night before the fire, & even then its extreme poverty in everything save its peculiar doggish flavor, constrained him to spit out the only piece he contrived to put into his mouth. The experiment in wolf meat was set down by Maj. Bedinger as a total failure, and he never tried it after.

During the afternoon of the fourth day of their fasting, from Green River, as they were nearing Severn Valley, they discovered some scattering grains of corn along the trail, which had evidently dropped from the ruptured bag of some solitary passer-by on horseback. This little discovery was cheering to the spirits of the half starved travellers; every kernel was carefully picked up and husbanded until the pint cup was more than half filled. Night was now stealing rapidly upon them; while looking out for a suitable place for camping they found on the bank of Clifty a poor wounded dog, unable to walk, who seemed exceedingly rejoiced at the unexpected meeting. Here they camped for the night, & the first thought was, after striking up a good fire, to fill the kettle with water & put in the corn, & set it merrily boiling. The cravings of hunger would not

[p. 52]

allow them to wait long enough to make a few ashes for hulling the corn; half-cooked and unsalted, they devoured the little pittance. The silent yet eloquent appeal of the wistful look of the wounded dog drew from Major Bedinger a spoonful of the precious food. By this time there were indications of a stormy night before them; the single blanket served to cover them both as they were stretched before the fire. A cold, sleety, disagreeable night ensued. The weight of the snow & sleet upon the surrounding forest caused many a low branch and tree-top to fall on every side fearfully around them. The blanket was soon saturated with water but the animal heat beneath prevented its freezing, which would have been preferable. Sleep under such circumstances seemed entirely out of the question, nor was it particularly desirable on the part of Maj. Bedinger. He was well convinced if Stovall ever intended to make any further attempt upon his life he would do it that night, as they expected the ensuing day to reach the nearest settlement; he was therefore constantly on his guard, with his hand upon his knife, to be used at a moment's warning. But the resolute & determined conduct of Major Bedinger, when the degenerate wretch had a second time basely attempted to shoot him, had evidently subdued his bloodthirsty spirit for the time being, and craven-like he yielded.

Early the following day they resumed their journey regretting the necessity to leave the helpless dog behind. Towards mid-day they met a man on horse back, who had shortly before been out bear-hunting where his trusty dog, the one they had seen, had got severely wounded in a tussle with one of these animals; & the kind master was now on his way with a supply of meat to feed his lacerated dog; then, intending to mount him onto the horse before him, & return to the settlement. Such is the value wh. the backwoodsman set upon a good and faithful dog: their trusty companion in the chase by day and their vigilant sentinel by night. The stranger informed them that it was thirteen miles to Van Metre's in the Valley, & gave them a sufficiency of meat to strengthen & refresh them until they could reach the settlement. Maj. Bedinger rejoiced that his toilsome & painful journey was so near to completion. It was now early in January, the 108th day since he had seen a station or a cabin; & within that long & dreary space of time, how many were his dangers, how great his sufferings — and thanks to God, he had escaped them all!

[p. 53]
After they reached Van Meter's & Stovall had refreshed himself with food & rest, Maj. Bedinger reminded him of his meanness & treachery, & then sternly remarked: "Leave instantly, and never let me see your face but once more: and that once at the Falls of Ohio on such a day of next week, when I will pay you every cent according to agreement, though you have richly forfeited it by your dastardly conduct." At the appointed day, Stovall made his appearance, with some few remaining evidences that he was not yet totally lost to every feeling of guilt and shame; and having received his money, in the language

of the day 'he made himself scarce'. Pursuing his career of infamy, he was finally detected, convicted and executed several years after at St. Louis; and thus perished John Stovall, brazen, reckless, & blood-thirsty to the last, without possessing a single redeeming characteristic.

Death of Capt. Nation

Maj. Bedinger remained several weeks at the cabin copying his field notes, & making plots his surveys. While there, several Indians of different tribes came in to visit Gen. Clark on errands of peace; among these was a Captain Nation, and another Indian named 'Mud', both Delawares, who had come in consequence of the repeated messages delivered the Delawares. One Joe Blackford, who lived somewhere in the region of Chaplin's fork of Salt river, & who had lost some relative during the Indian troubles, hearing that there were Indians at the Falls of Ohio, made his appearance there with the avowed intention of taking life for life. He courted the acquaintance of Captain Nation, drank freely with him, & they soon arranged it between them that they should go out on a hunting trip together. Captain Nation was cautioned to beware of Blackford, for he intended to kill him; "Oh, no!" said Nation incredulously, "my brother won't hurt me." It was deemed politic at that time for the Indians visiting Gen. Clark to retire at night over the Ohio & camp & thus avoid any bad consequences that might result from nightly orgies & carousals with the reckless and abandoned. That night Blackford had promised to go ford had promised to go

[p. 54]
over the river and spend the night with the old chief. Towards night they set out together, Blackford with his double-barreld rifle; and they had proceeded but a short distance, while in the path leading down below the Falls to the ferry, and between the grave yard and the river, Blackford secretly shot at Nation, but it did no other harm than singing the hair on one side of his head. With Blackford it was an accident for which he was sorry, re-loaded, and again proceeded on very lovingly together, until near the ferry when Blackford managed to get another shot, which proved fatal. The cold-hearted murderer immediately left, and poor Mud, with one or two Piankishaw brothers, was left to weep over the dead body of his chieftain. Maj. Bedinger, who witnessed the affecting scene, endeavored to pacify the poor Delaware by telling him, that it was one of the bad men of the whites that had done the deed, and if caught, would be hung for it. "Oh," said Mud feelingly, "let me kill him! let me kill him!" Some few evenings after, while writing in his room, Maj. Bedinger had his door suddenly burst open, and in rushed Mud, saying a man had chased him with a long knife threatening to kill him. Bedinger begged him to be quiet, that he should not be hurt, that he might stay with him that night for safety. After partaking some refreshments furnished by the kindness of his friend and brother, he threw off his overshirt & breech-clout & leggings and then stretched himself <u>under the bed!</u>

The Piankeshaws

It was during this sojourn a Piankeshaw chief, accompanied by four warriors, came to make peace. He was a large, noble looking chief, who brought written evidence in writing from whites and traders in that region, up the Wabash, that he had suffered in consequence of refusing to join in warfare against the Americans. He made a feeling speech, addressed to Gen. Clark, after smoking then went on recounting his sufferings in behalf of the whites,

[p. 55]
then alluded to his desire to live in peace with his white brothers, that the day had now come when the Americans must prevail, & it was well that it shd. be so, spoke of his destitute condition, contrasting his own ragged & bare-footed appearance with that of Gen. Clark. ...those present — that tho' his color was darker, his clothes less good, he had a heart as fair as theirs. He wished it might be remembered, that he had taken up on the side of the whites in their weakness, and hoped they would not forget him in the day of their greatness and prosperity.

This speech was delivered with great force, & much feeling with graceful gestures. Clark appropriately replied, & made some appropriate presents.

Addenda, Green River Trip, Spring of 1785

Maj. Bedinger was employed by one Henry Rhoades to survey off a little town on Green river, then called Rhoadesville, but probably since Vienna. While here he one day killed a rattlesnake near the residence of Andrew Rowan, & exhibiting it, Mrs. Rowan in her Irish simplicity observed, that "if any one would swallow a rattlesnake's heart alive, he would never have fits." Her son standing by then a lad of perhaps 12, opened the snake, and taking it yet trembling swallowed in a twinkle! This son, it is thought this was the one, was subsequently a Senator in Congress — a judge on the Bench.

Lynn's Station, No-Linn, &c.

In the Severn Valley country, now Hardin County, Ky., Maj. Bedinger thinks there was a Station, and a hill known as No-Linn. Certainly there is a Nolin, or probably No-Linn creek, a tributary of Green river.

[p. 56]
Death of Walker Daniel

Daniel, and a man with him named Kirtley, a merchant at Danville, & both had business at the Falls of Ohio. It had been proposed that they & Bedinger should go along together, all going on the same way. They were not ready quite so soon as Bedinger, who said he would jog along & they could overtake him. He went on some 20 miles, & in passing Mann's Lick, on the road towards Lexington probably, his horse was very uneasy, as though Indians were around, but got along. Six miles ahead stopped over night. Very soon after the horses of Daniel and Kirtley came up bloody & without their riders. They had been waylaid & shot at Mann's Lick. Bedinger's escape was singularly fortunate.

Bear Incident, Spring of 1779

While Bedinger, John Holder, Maj. Thos. & his brother Benoni Swearingen, John Taylor, Col. Wm. Morgan & his son Ralph, & perhaps some others took a tour in the Spring exploring the country along South Elkhorn. Near the present city of Lexington they discovered a bear in a large wild cherry, with a large rust hole on one side some thirty feet from the ground. The bear retreated. Benoni Swearingen (six feet 5 inches!) clambered up, & with a long pole forked at the end to pull hair, endeavored to oust the bear but failed, & came down leaving the stick in the hole. After a little the bear came up, gave the pole a spiteful knock & sent it flying, peeped out to see what was going on, when she was shot & fell back into the hole. Cut down the tree; found the bear dead, & four cubs. They made good meat. But a a few miles from Lexington, seeing a beautiful elevation Maj. Swearingen called it Lydia's Mount, in honor of one of his daughters, which name it retains to this day.

[p. 57]
Events of 1787

After leaving Louisville, he went to Va., was taken sick soon after, as elsewhere stated, married in Dec., lost his wife next year.

Near the close of the Revolution James Ramsey, who had a sawmill on Sleepy creek; a tributary of the Potomac, in Berkley Co., but 5 or 6 miles from the celebrated Warm Springs, proposed to Maj. Bedinger to join him, advanced means, did so a year, lost by the operation.

Rumsey was a man of great ingenuity: designed making a planing & grooving machine. Finally went to England, fell dead in a fit of apoplexy.

Maj. Bedinger had also mills, saw & grist, on Sidling Hill Creek, on the Maryland shore of the Potomac, which he owned several years.

His wife died in October, 1787. The next year he came to Ky. to see to his lands; found his land papers all gone & destroyed, O'Bannon hearing that he had sickened & died in Va., had claimed the papers, as having aided in their location.

Defeat on Little Sandy

He made one or two trips to & from Va. In the autumn of the year, & probably in '88, Maj. Bedinger, James Marshall, Col. Marcus Calamees, John Elliott, and three others, together with two servants, started for Virginia, by the way of Big Sandy and the Greenbriar Trace. Charles Vancouver, who had lands on Big Sandy, was to proceed with them as far as that river. Well mounted they set out from Strode's Station, & proceeded on Morgan's Station above Little Mountain, then over Licking Lick Tripletts Creek several days without any material occurrance. They camped one night within a few miles of Little Sandy, hoppled their horses & turned them out, & early in the evening they heard the hooting of an owl on one side of them, and soon that of another in an opposite direction. Col. Calamees & Maj. Bedinger, both old Indian fighters, began to suspect that all was not right; concluded to get up their horses & have them in readiness for any emergency. Some ridiculed the idea of being scared by owls, but the wiser heads secured their nags and the others followed their example. The horses were fastened to saplings at hand, & again they camped. themselves on the ground. Occasionally the hootings of an owl or croaking of a raven were heard around them, and by and by they would every now and then hear a stir among the leaves. Now more convinced than ever that an Indian party had followed on their trail, & were now trying to surprise them in camp, they concluded though sometime before day to mount and be off. Though in all ten persons, there were not more than four or five guns & one or two pistols in the party; thus poorly armed, to receive the first fire under disadvantageous ciecumstances, would be tantamount to defeat. They were suffered to leave unmolested. Several miles were gained, when, having reached a favorable spot for baiting their horses, they dismounted & turned them to feed upon the rich wild pea-vines which grew there quite abundantly; after refreshing themselves & beasts, they resumed their journey, soon struck Little Sandy & bent their course up the stream on the western bank. While pursuing their course up the river they heard the croaking of a raven over the river; "there" said some, "is that hateful noise still following us." They all began to be very suspicious of an ambuscade, & had advanced scarcely a mile up the river when they entered a piece of low land, quite wet &

miry, through which they passed, & neared a bluff which left but a narrow defile between it and the river. Here their trail led them; and close on the river bank & near the entrance of the defile, lay a large fallen tree, from behind which issued a volley of rifle balls at the horsemen

[p. 59]
but a very few rods off. The horses snorted and jumped in every direction. Col. Calamees, who led the way, had just entered the narrow defile, and his horse dashed up a steep rocky bank, and escaped; it was an astonishing feat. Several of the party, by the sudden start of their horses, lost their hats or other articles; all wheeled, dashed off through the miry flat & escaped. Maj. Bedinger rode a young, fiery animal, & was in the rear when fired on; the report of the guns and the yells of the Indians caused him to jump suddenly to one side, well nigh throwing his rider, but he caught & recovered himself, & in the act of doing it he succeeded in saving his saddle-bags, which had nearly lost their balance. This was all the work of a moment, & while transpiring two Indians came running up beside him with uplifted tomahawks & blood-chilling yells; but seeing the Major partly unhorsed, & supposing him wounded completely within their power, they were evidently less intent than they would have been otherwise, and that moment Major Bedinger recovered his seat, put spurs to his horse and escaped. Again he found himself in the rear, and called out lustily to those before him "halt! halt! We'll return and whip the d___d sons of bitches"; but there was no disposition to obey; for all, save

Marshall, rushed on at the top of their speed. Bedinger and Marshall succeeded in getting a halt for a few moments about three fourths of a mile from the ambuscade. Neither man nor beast were found to be hurt, a miracle of an escape; they all agreed from the fire of the enemy & from what they saw, that the Indian party numbered about ten; and, fearing their retreat might be cut off, and poorly armed as they were, they thought

[p. 60]
it prudent to abandon the journey & return to the settlements. After passing Licking, and beyond the reach of the enemy, they were joking and laughing along about the incidents of the defeat. Marshall observed, half-seriously, half-sportingly, that he particularly noticed Vancouver was pale with fear. Vancouver was nettled at once, & told Marshall if he thought him a coward to dismount and he wd. give him a opportunity of trying his courage. Marshall was too proud to be stumped, and a foolish duel was on the tapis; at this juncture Col. Calamees rode up, and learning the drift of the controversy, manufactured a justifiable fib to meet the occasion, & remarked that Marshall was only joking for he had heard him say distinctly, that Vancouver in the attack was as brave as Julius Cesar. The proud Dutchman eagerly swallowed the extravagant compliment and dagger looks & angry words soon gave place to friendship.

Intended Trip to the Pacific

In 1790, Maj. Bedinger became acquainted with an old Indian trader of the name of Morehead who had been engaged in trading with them twenty years; & so scrupulously just was he in all his dealings with them, that they called him "the honest white man." Bedinger had conceived the plan of an exploring tour on foot to the Pacific, both to examine the country and the state and condition of the Indians. Morehead thought from his knowledge of the Indian character, that the project was not only feasible but desirable, and could rendered useful both to the government and frontier settlements. Simon Kenton, David Williams, and John McIntyre, all men of the woods and the equal of Indians in stratagem or the endurance of fatigue and hunger, were to join in the meditated enterprise; together with a son of the Indian trader Morehead, and three others. The patronage

[p. 61]
of Government was to be secured; but before the plan was fully matured, Bedinger unsolicited had been appointed by Pres. Washington to the command of a battalion of the Va. Levies, and his friends urged him to aid in bringing the Indian war first to a close, and then would be time enough to engage in so serious an undertaking. And thus fell through a noble conception, pronounced by some quixotic at the time, which might have been as successfully accomplished after the peace of Greenville as was the expedition of Lewis and Clark several years afterwards.

St. Clair's Campaign

At perhaps Indian Wheeling, opposite bank of Wheeling Creek he joined the army & took the command of his battalion. He was a rigid disciplinarian, and took pride in drilling his men several hours daily; no section of the army presented a more soldierly appearance than his battalion. Shortly anterior to the fatal battle of the 4th Nov '91, as he was suffering severely from the rheumatism he was detached on the dangerous and difficult service of returning to Ft. Jefferson with a party of invalids some among whom were a Capt. Lewis the Singer Johnson, of Rhea's battalion, and a Lieut. Vance and was not in the battle; his battalion was however, and fought valiantly that day, & out of 330 fully one third were killed & wounded in the action.

In re-organizing the army under Wayne, again Maj. Bedinger was placed at the head a Virginia battalion. He repaired to Pittsburg, and engaged at once in the arduous work of drilling the men to a quick and ready use of fire arms, the discipline of camp and the ... of battle. In the spring of '93, after the army had reached Fort Washington, having married a young lady in Ky., he resigned his commission and left the army. This was his last military service. While at Pittsburg they wd. frequently engage in sham fights. In conducting one of these one day, some officer came to Wayne informing him of an Indian attack on such a portion of the camp or army & desiring his further orders. Some ladies present, thinking it all a reality.

When Bedinger, by the advice of St. Clair, Gen. Butler, Col. Darke, & other officers returned to Ft. Jefn. they found not a particle of food of any kind, & were compelled to proceed on to Fort Washington. They left the army the 1st Nov. They proceeded slowly, for some were unable to make great exertions. Indians were scattered every where along the trace, & extreme caution was necessary. While in camp, a piece from the pond, Bedinger had ordered out sentinels. Dr. Johnson ridiculed the idea, he wasn't afraid of all the d---d cowardly rascals in the country. "Nor is my horse afraid" emphatically replied Bedinger. The next morning the report of a gun was heard not a great distance from camp & now a man came running in with the intelligence that a pack-horseman, with corn for Fort Jefferson had just been shot and scalped. Bedinger & Vance went to reconnoiter & ascertain the number of the Indian party, & found the number could not have exceeded three. While the Dr. was anxiously making inquiries of the man who brought in the intelligence, Lewis and Vance, who had a great contempt for the braggart Johnson, stepped a little outside in the & fired off their guns & gave the Indian whoop on purpose to test his courage as they expected he put spurs to his horse and came dashing by Bedinger who asked "Whats the matter?" Said Johnson Indians by God, Indians & never stopped until he reached Fort Washington who reported when he reached there that the whole party were fired upon & he believed all were killed. A couple of days after Bedinger & his band came in, & the next to broken man of the army. Jokes came so thickly upon Dr. Johnson that he found it convenient to leave shortly after.

Political offices held

Since the organization of Nicholas county (before the organization represented Bourbon & Mason Cos., living sometimes one side of Licking & sometimes the other & that was the line) was first judge of the Court of Quarter Sessions, until that court was abolished was county surveyor from the organization & resigned in 1803 when a candidate for Congress. Once an elector for Govr. for Mason County, under the first constitution. Was elected to Congress by a large majority in the district, and re-elected with great ease. He was a friend to Jefferson's administration. In 1807 declined running again, when there was no prospect of opposition, on the score of rotation. Except when sick, he never lost a vote in Congress. Brought forward & carried through a bill to prevent further importation of slaves into the country after the year 1808. He looked upon it as one of his happiest acts.

[p. 63]

In the early settlement of the country he sometimes made it his home at Boonesboro, Strode's Station, at Geo. Caldwell's near Danville, at Capt. Caplines Harrodsburg, at Gen. John Clarks, at Sullivan's Station, near Louisville.

Van Swearingen

Thos. Van, Andrew, Joseph & Benoni Swearingen raised near Shepardstown, Berkley county Va.

Capt. Sam Brady married Van Swearingen's eldest daughter. 'Indian Van' was at an early age an Indian trader; finally settled near Red Stone first near Shirtee Creek, above Wheeling & in Washington Co. Pa. While in the Kittaning battalion early in the Revolution captain on the Canada expedition was taken prisoner by the British. Some British officer ... one time: "Who the devel are you?" "I am a Virginia rifleman, a soldier, and a gentleman, Sir!" Such bold fearless conduct pleased his enememies.

During a short respite of peace a party of Delawares came to Washn. County & stole horses. Van S. raised a party & pursued; retook their horses with the death of over two or the Indians. With the Indian party was a squaw who lagged behind in the retreat; one of Swearingen's men leveled his gun to shoot the squaw, & Van seeing it reproached him, & saved the Indian woman. The Indians complained of an infringement of the treaty, and Van Swearingen went of his own accord to the Indians in the Muskingum country, and delivered himself up, & explained all the circumstances. While his fate was yet undecided, with the chances setting against him, & some even preparing splinters evidently for his torture, a squaw was seen busying herself in going from chief to chief and warrior to warrior in earnest conversation, & by & by she brought & set before him a basket of huckleberries. She was the squaw whose life he had saved; and now, in turn, she had been instrumental

[p. 64]
in saving his. His son Tom, a young man pretty well in his teens, desired to live with the Indians to learn the language & customs, in order perhaps to become a trader. He was a mischievous fellow

& would play off his tricks & pranks upon the Indians. His father consented with a promise on the part of the Indians that they wd. take kind care of him, & shd. he happen to die they wd. bring in his body to convince his father that no bullet hole was the cause of his death. They returned him safe. While out subsequently hunting over the Ohio in the Indian country, & collecting ~~ginseng~~ ginson root, was killed.

Indian Van survived the Indian wars many years; Maj. Bedinger saw him subsequent to 1803. He was a large dark-haired well made man, & brave.

His brother Andrew was no Indian fighter.

Kenton & the Indian Canoe

A party of Indians had come and stole horses on Hinkston, Bedinger & five or 6 others pursued them ~~on until near Cynthiana~~ pretty well down Hinkston, & gave up the pursuit. Kenton with a small band had got wind of the party, found their bark canoe sunk on the Ky. shore of the Ohio, there waylaid the party [vide Marshall's Ky. Vol. 1st p. 371.) This was in the spring of '91. If the Indian party, as Maj. B. thinks, was six in number, either 5 were killed & one escaped, or one was killed & five escaped; rather thinks the latter. It is possible the case alluded to in Marshall's history was another.

Orr's Campaign of Spring of 1791

After Hubbel's fight Col. Alexr. D. Orr. of Mason, raised between one & two hundred men; a Col. Horatio Hall was also along: Bedinger was adjutant, & Kenton was along. Marched from

Maysville (probably) & crossed Cabin Creek & down to the mouth of Salt Lick Creek, where Vanceburg subsequently rose into existence. Here was a squable between Orr & Hall for the chief command; one company, Thos. West's, sided with Hall, while the remainder of the troops, perhaps two or three companies, sided with Orr, & he prevailed. Went on

[p. 65]
to the mouth of Tygert's Creek where they found a fresh beaten path evidently where an Indian had stood sentry. Bedinger & Kenton finding a canoe were the first to cross. Found the deserted Indian camp a short distance above on the opposite shore of the Ohio; found feathers scattered around, the inside of several watches. Found one or two Indian bodies buried, killed probably in their attacks in May on Hubbel, and a skeleton a female still fastened to a sapling near the river which appeared that she had been burned or whipped as whips lay around. They followed on the Indian trail a few miles & then returned. Above Tygert's creek, & on the Ky. shore, found 21 bodies; they gave them interment. They were a party of soldiers from Ft. Washington on their way to Ft. Hamilton.

Edwards' abortive campaign of 1791, was often laughed about as "the blacberry campaign". Neared the Indian towns; filled themselves with blackberries & returned.

Extract of letter from Henry Bedinger
"Shepardstown, Feb. 27th 1792.
"You intimate to me yr. desire of undertaking

a business that I am convinced will receive no countenance by the executive of the U.S.; for we have already much greater territory than we can possess, & the Knowledge of the countries beyond the Mississippi, can be of no advantage to the present government. I advise therefore, that you give up all schemes of that romantick Kind; for we are now engaged in an arduous war with the savages, that inhabit within our own territory, & Congress would not thank anyone for <u>information</u> or <u>peace</u> with those who inhabit where they do not claim: This may possibly be a matter of some kind of inquiry 50 or 100 years hence, but not now; besides, the President has it at heart to humble the Indians who are at war with us."

Extract, signed "Henry Bedinger"

[p. 66]
Affidavit by George M. Bedinger, Nov. 28, 1787
<u>"Berkley County, Virginia, S.S.</u>

This day came Michael Bedinger, before me, one of the Justices of the Peace for the said county, and made oath, that Mr. James Rumsey informed him in, or before the month of March, 1784; that he was of opinion that a boat might be constructed to work by steam, and that he intended to give it a trial, and mentioned some of the machinery that would be necessary to reduce it to practice: and the said Michael further saith, that he set out for Kentucky, immediately after, in order to survey some lands, and resided there upwards of eighteen months, and that during the time of his stay there, he frequently mentioned Mr. Rumsey's boat scheme: He believes that he also mentioned, that it was to be wrought by steam.

The above was voluntarily sworn before me, by Capt. Bedinger, who is a gentleman of reputation.

Nov. 28th, 1787.   John Kearsley.

We whose names are hereunto subscribed, certify that the within mentioned Michael Bedinger is a gentleman of reputation and veracity.

Horatio Gates,   Charles Morrow,
Thomas White,   John Mark,
James Kerney   Philip Pendleton,
John Morrow,   Robert Stubbs.
Joseph Mitchell,

N. Y. Doc. History, Vol. 2d p. 1031,1032.

[p. 67]
Miscellaneous Scraps

Michael Rudulph. Raised from a poor boy, was of Swedish descent, resided in Maryland, served at the South in the Revolution, first a private, then a coronet, & then probably on up. Maj. of cavalry under Wayne. One of the best of horseman, & great success in training cavalry. Great ambition; used to say to Maj. Bedinger "Come let's go to France where we can reap laurels." Finally he went. it is uncertain whether he ever reched the shores of Europe. The supposition has gained credit that, when he reached Europe, under an assumed name he raised a band of Swiss, joined the French, & subsequently became the distinguished Marshal Ney. Well proportioned, middle sized: perhaps abt. 33, a man of powerful strength.

Maj. Zeigler a native of Germany, had served in the wars of Germany, came to this country: joined our army: was a heavy made, not tall spoke rather broken English: was a great disciplinarian, a great lover of neatness: When others gambled & spent their earnings, he would make presents to his soldiers, who loved him greatly. After the war, was a merchant in Cini. He & Wilkinson never could agree. Zeigler, when orders were given to charge bayonet, instead of exclaiming to his men in the customary way, "march, march!" would simply make a kind of whoop, after the old German style. This, Wilkinson considered undignified & it displeased him. They were for a long on unspeaking terms. One day after the war when Zeigler was merchandizing, he unexpectedly recd. an invitation from Wilkinson to dine with some friends. He went & in touching glasses with Wilkinson, the latter very adroitly observed, "This, Major, is not so good wine as I used to drink of yours; have you any of it left?" O, yes! said Zeigler. "Well, then", said Wilkinson, I hope you'll spare me a quarter cask to-morrow? Partaking as he was of Wilkinson's hospitality, & gentlemen around him, he could not well refuse, & replied affirmatively. The qr. cask went, &, as he anticipated, the pay was never forthcoming.

Col. John Logan was the first Treasurer of the State of Ky.

[p. 68]
Gen. St. Clair; Col. Wm. Darke

Gen. St. Clair raised his regt. at the breaking out of the Revolution at his own expense. Was a fine man & good officer. Many whom he made in the N.W. Territory, subsequently turned against him when misfortunes, old age & poverty overtook him. In his defeat an Indian rushed into his markee with uplifted tomahawk, when Col. Wm. Darke, rushed in & killed the Indian with his sword.

Darke, soon after the breaking out of the Revolution marched from Berkley county Va., of which he was a native, & of which his father was one of the early settlers. Went to the South the first campaign where he lost, by sickness nearly half his company. Promoted to Majr. & subsequently Lt. Colonel, & commanded a regt. at the siege of York. Was taken prisoner at Germantown, then a Major.

<u>Gen. Adam Stephens</u>: heavy formed, 5 ft.

Used to represent Berkley Co. in legislature, after the revolution. Was a native of Scotland; came to America at a very early day. A brother of his (Robt.) was a collector of quit rents for Lord Fairfax, himself a Scotchman. Was a regular bred physician, & a very skillful one. A singular instance is told of him. While on Braddock's campaign, was a surgeon in the army (& very like came to Ama. in that capacity.) One of the soldiers was badly wounded in the bowels, & one of the guts entirely severed; drew the separate parts over a candle, knitted the edges as nicely together as could be done, & by the time the candle had melted, the bowels had resumed their regular action, & the man recovered to the astonishment of all.

Comd. the right wing in the battle of Germantown. In the midst of the smoke near evening, at the close of the firing, two horsemen in American uniform came dashing up, exclaiming "For God's sake don't fire; you are killing your own men!" They were subsequently understood to be British in disguise. It had the intended effect: instantly Stephens ordered the right wing to fall back out of the smoke & fog & stand; did so. He was suspended from his comd.; but he didn't, it is thought, resume his command — unjust decision, Maj. Bedinger thinks. It may have been brought about, by those who his suspension would receive promotions; a long line would thus advance a grade.

Gen. S. laid out Martinsburg, in Berkley; just before the Revolution; it became the county town. Had five mills there: Left an only daughter, not a legitimate: her 2d husband was a Hunter, a connection of R. M. T. Hunter. A monument was proby. erected to his memory at Martinsburg: died after '86.

[p. 69]
Col. John Holder.
Had a captains' comd. from Va., & commanded at Boonesboro. Came from near Winchester, Fred'k. Co. Va. Came to Boonesboro; married Fanny (proby. Francis) Calloway, a daughter of Col. Calloway, who had several daughters. Fanny, said Maj. Bedinger, was the only daughter of Calloways taken prisoner; in this he is surely mistaken: She was a pretty, lively girl. Some of Holder's sons live near Boonesboro. Col. Holder settled, it is

believed, in Fayette county, near Boone. He was a large, 6 ft. man, not brilliant, yet useful, dark complexion.

The defenders & hunters of Boonesboro, 1779

Jno. Holder, Jas. & Sam. Estill (came into the country in summer of '79), Capt. David Gass, (Maj. Thos. & Benoni Swearingen, Col. Wm. & Ralph Morgan, John Taylor, Sam. Duree, John Strode, Jas. Duncan, John Constant,) Jesse Hodges, ~~Lawrence Thompson,~~ John Gass (now living) Wm. Cradlebaugh, Jacob Stearns, old Nichs. Proctor & his sons Joseph & Reuben, old John South, his sons Tom & Jack, & another John South, a distant relative, John Martin, John Calloway, James Bathe, James Berry, John Bankman, John Haweson, Chas. Edward Lockhart. Subsequently Aquila White, Joseph Doniphan. White came & his companion. Deducting from the above, the Estills & Bedingers gang, it would exhibit some 20 at Boonesboro when Bedinger reached there. Ralph Morgan says there were from 20 to 30 men in Boonesboro during 1779.

At an early day, perhaps the fall of '83, Maj. Bedinger went to Strode's Station went a few miles with the young folks, a dozen, to McGee's Station on Boones Creek & staid some to attend Ralph Morgan's wedding to a pretty young Irish widow, whose husband had been killed by the Indians. Old Parson McClure tied the knot, then passed around the watermelons — they were neither stinted in size nor number — & this was all. Pioneer simplicity.

Williamson's expedition to the Muskingum, 1781

Maj. Bedinger knew a very clever, respectable man, who was out under Williamson. When they reached the town, were kindly recd., & even welcomed; none offered to run away. Were all in the house & the work of death going on: Several, taking turns, would take the tomahawk & kill the poor the Indians, coming to an Elderly Indian, he said "It wd. be useless to die with a lie in his mouth, & he wd. honestly say that though formerly they had done the whites harm, but since they become Christians they had lived at peace". Having noticed that the executioners wd. frequently strike several blows with the head of the tomahawk before killing their victims, he requested that the blade might be used in his case; the next moment his scull was cleft. Some one more compassionate than

[p. 70]
his fellows, had taken under his protection a little Indian girl, intending to take her to his home in the settlement, & threatened he would kill any one who should venture to kill the little Indian girl. The unfeeling soldiers, on the return trip constantly annoyed & frightened her, when she would dodge behind and cling to her protector, but even his kindness & vigilance did not save her, for unseen by him, some monster clandestinely tomahawked the helpless & unoffending orphan.

Piomingo — St. Clair's Campaign

Had a good party of his warriors, about 40 with him, & went around the enemy, ~~took 5 scalps~~. They ... a wide distance apart, could not thus well be trailed, & they stood a better chance, thus spread out, to surprise their enemy; & when they wishd. to cook, 1st make a good fire, at a distance another, & then in some sly, unobserved ravine, make another where they would cook their hasty meal; the two former fires being intended for decoy while the other, least likely to be seen, would be the one for use. Wary & cautious! On their return they met some of the enemy, who taking Piomingo's party to have been some band from a distance, that reached too late to take part in the action, were recounting their success over St. Clair, saying they had tomahawked the whites until their arms wearied in the work of destruction. "Rascals," said Piomingo &c, & killd 5 & took their scalps to the army.

The Lower Blue Licks

Prior to April, 1780, were always spoken of as either the Lower Blue Licks or the two Salt Springs on Licking; they were not generally called the Blue Licks until after the battle fought there.

Andrew Hampton made a settlement there in 1779. He subsequently lived in Harrison County.

From written direction by H. Clay how to proceed, & what it was necessary should be proven, in a land case involving title to a portion of the Blue Lick estate

[p. 71]
From the N. Y. American, 1839:

"The Late James Rumsey.
"The House of Representatives recently adopted by unanimous vote, a resolution that the President present to the only surviving son of James Rumsey, "a suitable gold medal, commemorative of his father's services and high agency in giving to the world the benefits of the steamboat."

"When this resolution was before the House, Mr. Rumsey, of Kentucky, a nephew of the deceased James Rumsey, in an unpretending, but clear and touching speech, detailed the evidence which established — conclusively, as it seems to us — the fact, that as early as 1786, James Rumsey did succeed in propelling his boat against the current by steam alone, four or five miles an hour." The experiment took place on the Potomac, near Shepardstown, Va., in the presence of hundreds of spectators, & among the witnesses surviving, is Dr. Alexander, of Baltimore, a gentleman of the highest character, and who was on board Rumsey's boat.

"Finding, however, little encouragement in his own country, Rumsey went to England, and there with the perseverance of genius, confident in the results of its own clear apprehension, and not to be discouraged by the doubts, the coldness, or the sneers of the world, he labored to perfect his invention, and had all but finished his new boat of between one and two hundred tons, and named a day for the trial, when, in 1792, death arrested his hand.

"Hungry creditors seized upon his little property, and with him died, until revived and perfected by Fulton, the steamboat.

[p. 72]
"While thus vindicating the priority of Rumsey's claim, his honorable relative does full and ample justice to Fulton, from whose fame he seeks not to detract a single ray. To Rumsey, whom Fulton knew in England, and to Fulton conjointly, he justly ascribes the character of the highest benefactors of their species", and thus eloquently and forcibly depicts the immeasurable value to America, and to the West especially, of steam navigation:

"Sir, you have no arithmetick of powers vast enough, by which to estimate the benefits of the steamboat in a pecuniary point of view, alone. Their labors have rendered the whole Republick more prosperous in peace, more powerful and defensible in war. Their labors, too, have tended, in no small degree, to the preservation of human life. I am aware that the truth of this last assertion may not be universally admitted; but it will scarcely be questioned, at least by a Western or Southwestern man, who recollects the old mode of conducting our commerce. Small as that commerce was before the introduction of the steamboat, it drew off a larger portion of population than is now necessary to transact it, although so immensely extended. Even then, more died in the long and exposed and laborious voyages in keels and barges, or the exhausing return by land under a vertical sun, than now perish from steamboat explosions. But they dropped off one by one; they sank obscurely into the grave by the wayside; or, after reaching their homes, fell victims to disease incurred by a long sojourn and travel in Southern climes. The consumption of life, though known to be great in the aggregate, happening so much in detail, made no impression. But now, every steamboat accident creates a sensation, and is proclaimed in the universal press of the country. If the mighty commerce now in progress on the western waters had to be conducted in the old way, it would require the agency

[p. 73]
of so many individuals, that it would not be long before the sides of the public roads, from New Orleans to the upper states, and banks of that great river which pours into the Gulf the congregated waters of nearly half a continent, would be almost continued graveyards.

We have spoken of the clear apprehensions of results, which is one of the elements and powers of genius. The following extract from a letter by Brissot de Warville, Mr. Jefferson's friend and correspondent, presents an extraordinary instance in point. Rumsey anticipated in 1789, what, at the distance of half a century, the Great Western, in 1838, has proved. We quote from Mr. Rumsey's speech:

"In a work published by De Warville, in 1789, which will be found in your library, he states that, being in Philadelphia in September, 1788, he attended by invitation, and witnessed, Fitch's experiment. In a note written in the February following, in London, he says:

"I have just become acquainted with Mr. Rumsey, of Virginia, a gentleman of great ingenuity, who proposes building a vessel in which, without sails, and by steam alone, he will cross the Atlantick in fifteen days."

"This sublime conception, this bold undertaking of Rumsey, the accomplishment of which in the last year has created so vast a sensation, was not unknown to me and others of his family; but without the high authority of De Warville, I would not have ventured to have named it."

For additional information respecting Rumsey, see July No. of North American Review, '39 or '42, forgot wh. L.C.D.

The Harpes

"An act for the relief of Christiana Tully, approved Dec. 18, 1800. Her husband had been assassinated by the Harpes; in consideration of which this act gave her credit, without interest, for the State price of 200 acres of Green river land, until Dec. 1st 1810." — Littell's Laws of Ky.

[p. 74]

Wabash Expedition of 1786

Boats impressed; Capt. Rays company impressed a beef: Horses, flour & whiskey were impressed, & subsequently pd. for: Col. John Holder was ... & got a certificate for "about 30 pounds for services on that expedition." Holder died prior to 1812.

Logan's Expedition of 1786

Wm. Rout was a captain on Logans expedition agst. the Shawnees, in 1786 & recd. a wound wh. utterly disabled him from supporting himself. An act for his relief passed the Ky. Legislature, approved Dec. 2d 1801, granting him 18 pounds per annum.

Wm. Montgomery died about 1798, not after.

"The Georgia Settlement" was in Logan county.

A quantity of land, not exceeding 150,000 acres was granted to Gen. G. R. Clarke, the officers & soldiers of his regt. who marched with him when Kaskaskia & St. Vincennes were reduced, & to the officers and soldiers since incorporated in sd. regt.; to be laid off in one tract, north west of the Ohio, as a majority of the officers shd. choose, to be properly divided "according to the laws of Virginia."

In 1815, Col. Wm. Whitley was one of a commission to examine suitable location road from Danville to Tillico, some 2 months.

Hugh McGary, or Magary, in 1787, was living on Ky. River, near Harrod's Landing, at the new town of Warwick of wh. he was a trustee.

~~Col. D. Boone was in 86 & '7 living in Mason Co.; in 1st year a trustee copied Washington & latter year of Maysville, established in '87; in latter instance with Henry Lee, Jacob Boone & others~~

In May 1780, Wm. Fleming, Wm. Christian John Todd, Stephen Zingg, Benjn. Logan, John Floyd, John May Levi Todd, John Cowan, Geo. Meriwether, John Cobbs, George Thompson & Edmund Taylor were apd. trustees of the escheated lands of Rob. McKenzie, Henry Collins, & Alexr. McKee, formerly British subjects, 8000 acres, for the purpose of a public school or seminary of learning. [See more.

[p. 75]
Maj. G. M. Bedinger's writings.
Lower Blue Licks 30th May 1831

Dr. Sir   I receivd your 2 letters viz. the first of the 15th April, & next the 22 May. In answer to the first I immediately wrote a long letter, but finding I could not then comprise all the information I wished to afford, and which I thought my selfe in duty bound in justice, to the character of my <u>highly respected</u> and <u>Honoured</u> friend Colonel Wm. Oldhame) (who was out with Colonel Bowman expedition calld. Bowmans campaign agains the Shaw Indians in June 1779) and wish to do him and his friends the justice in my power his character and conduct meritted in contradiction to all the untrue statement made and published in the history of Kentucky, in the year 1824 (say 45 years after sd. campaign) but find I could not at that time, viz. about the 17 attend to the conclusion of my sd. letter, as I was calld. from home, to Bourbon county, to my sons, <u>sick family</u>. I declined writing for the present, but still intended to write fully as soon as I could (with convenience). Mr. Marshals history of Kentucky does not individually blame Colonl Oldhom, but unfeelingly unjustly and unresonably has deprived the vallunt and ... memory of that expedition. Generally, of the mout they were justly Intitled to; but of this I will at present say no more and it would have given me pain to have said so much if if his statements had ben correct, and I have still a hope that some of the many misrepresentations made in sd. history did not originate with the auther but with his informants.

But to attend to your letters, in answer to which I say I do not recollect where I first saw Col. Oldham but am confident he did not belong to our (Capt. Stephensons) company but that Conway Oldham his brother did belong to it, viz. Capt. Hugh Stephensons firs company of riflemen, Stephenson was I think the oldes or first Capt in the revolution Daniel Morgan near the same time marched a company from Frederick County to Cambridge near by Boston, from thence he went to quebeck I think he departed from near Cambrididu College about the first of July 1775. I remain'd in Stephensons company at Roxbury near Boston at the siege in sight of the enemy about nine months. Thence in the Spring 76 marched to New York Staten Island &c. I was intimately acquainted with Colonel Wm. Oldham on St. Clairs campaign but was not with him when he fell.

[p. 76]
That early in the month of March 1775 this affiant enlisted as a volunteer rifleman for one year under Captain Hugh Stephenson at Shepherdstown, then in Berkley, now Jeferson County Virginia and that he marched from thence as well as he recollects on the 10th or 11 day of the same month in Stephensons Company to the seige of Boston, pasing through Frederick Town Maryland passin through Little york Lanhaster & Bethlehem PA crossed the Delaware at Easton the Susquehannah at Wrights ferry, passd through Newjersey through Hartford Connecticut and re-

maind at Roxbury near Boston remaind there about eight months when early in March our company marchd from Roxbury & we took our station in the night on Dorchester point near Dorchester hights where we were not discoverd by the enemy until about day brake next morning, by which time we had by the hard labour and great exertion of a strong ... trenching party and by all means in our power requisite to screen our selves as much as we could against an ... attack of the enemy in the morning. This was so far effected that night, that it was not in the power of the eney to dislodge us from our position although they made great exertions to do so (to the best of my recollection, fierd on us ... our fortifications so sudenly erected (a brisk fire of cannon the first morning, from their <u>fleet, fortifications floating bateries</u> Blakhouses) more profusely than at any time (I recollect of, during the siege of Boston.

[p. 77]

That in the month of June 1775 this affiant entered as a volunteer rifleman under Captain Hugh Stephenson at Shepherdstown then Berkley now Jefferson county, Virginia and that he marched from thence as well as he recollects on the 10th or 11th of the same June to the siege of Boston, passing through Frederic Town Maryland passing Susquehannah at Wrights Ferry passing through Little York Lancaster & Bethlehem P.A. Crossed the Delaware at Easton, & passing through New Jersey & Hartfort Connecticut thence through part of Massachusetts to Roxberry near Boston. Remaind at Roxbury near eight months. In the Spring of 1776 early in March, he with sd. company were sent from Roxbury ...rchester Point ~~as we then called~~ it which was still nearer Boston & in front of the fortification on the hights, which had in one night been erected and so near the chanel through which I think two vessels attempted to pass that one of them at least ran a ground in shallow water to keep at a greater distance from the brisk fire from our fortification erected in one night. The British also kept up a hevy fire but did not anoy us much as our troops worked hard in the night to save ther lives in the morning. We had dug so deep that we were not in Great danger from their artilery. From Dorchester hights Capt. Stephensons company was sent to New York City where he this affiant states the company remain'd a few weeks from thence he with sd. company were sent to & stationd. on Staten Island where he remaind until he was discharged after having srvd out the full time for which he was Inlisted. Was in no General Engagement but in Skirmishes in one of which on Staten Island this afiant in company with 25 others took thirteen prissoners. His Lieutenants were Willim Henshaw, George Scott Samuel Finley, & Abaham Shepherd. The first named did not remain long with the company at Boston but came home. We were under Genl. George Washington from whom our captain I think generally received his instructions. Our captain was his intimate friend and companion at home in privet life in Berkly County Virginia ther attachment did not appear to diminish in times of war. We wer attached to no Regiment but

[p. 78]
Our captain I think Generally receivd his orders or directions from Genl. Washington himselfe Whos head quarters were then as I believe at or near Cambridge and it was near Combridge Collage that our company first saw him and presented their arms to him as he slowly rode by us looking attentively and affetionately at the solders of the oldest company & first in rank rank of Captains from his native State when he Shook hands with our captain ... it was said they both shed tears. We thence marchd to Roxbury. I ... within reach of British cannon ... from time to time and almost dayly the British feird ther cannon & morters at us. We or the privet solders with of M company with me were exposed to ther fire. had no Brst work to protect our house, we lay and slept with our heads towards the British cannon this being the safest position, as a cannon Ball would do less execution in this way than if we lay across their fire. Our captain in the Spring of 76 got as we were told appointed Colonel left us on Statten Island and returnd home to proceed to recruit and organise a regiment but he unfortunate got sick & died before he had the satisfaction of accomplishing this undertaking. His fate had a considerable bearing on my own as he had Signified to me that young as I was, then between 18 and 19 I had as well accept a corporals place, that his men should rise in relation

[p. 79]
on that account and to be relivd from standing sentry two hours at a time in the cold marshes

near Boston in the coldest of winter wether. I acted as Corporal, and in the following June was informd ... by Lieut. Wm. Kelly that I was appointed an Ensign that I was to belong to the same company with him ... in S. Stephenses Regiment.

After I had servd out the year that I had first Inlisted for I Continued with the army about 3 or 4 weeks as well as I can now recollect. Had to leave Statten Island by flight from the British army. They had pitched their tents near the watering place before Joseph Swearingen and my selfe left it we forced a negro boy into a ship with us in haste reachd the Jersy shore before the enemy Could overtake us but had to leave the most of clothing on the Island, they wer never recoverd by us. British troops were near us Scouring the Island and Serching for us, and from that time I think during kept possession of it to during the war.

New Jersey & Hartford Connecticut, and remain at Roxbury near Boston near eight months. When we march to New York City and from there went to Staten Island where I remained until he he was discharged having servd the full time for which he was Inlisted, was in no General ingagement this firstt year but was much exposed to the almost daily fire of the Brittish artilery, & all the time he was at

[p. 80]
Military Career of George M. Bedinger
[1833.]

An attemt made by G. M. Bedinger to state ... the time as near as he now can he servd in the army of the U.S. state troops or militia Indian spy and vollunteer at different times from the commencement of the war in the Spring 1775 to autumn of 1781. It will now be verry dificult nay impossible for me now to do with accuracy, as I am more in the 77th year of my age. (I was born in York County ... 1756. I had a severe spell of Sickness (in the year 1787) the nervous fever which I had about 8 months destroy'd my memory to so great a degree that I have never Since been able to recollect many of the important and familiar trans...ters ... my life previous to sd. fever. About the 25 of April 1775 I first took up my ... my rilfe with a rifle and marched towards Richmond in the Colony of ... having heard that ... had ...by orders to ... had taken possession of a quantity of powder which had been stored in the magazine at Williamsburg. A Lawyer George Root addressed a large meetting of ... (in Berkly County where I then lived) he concluded by saying that Every man that God had given arms to ought now to make use of them to save the powder thereby to Save his Country and his Liberty out of a large company (I think) two only turnd out at thet time, viz. George Morgan & my selfe. We immediately marched towards Williamsburg gathering ... strength in numbers as we marchd on. About the 3d or fourth days march we heard I think by Express or good authority (by Express or other ways that our aid at that time would not be necessary (amicable arrangement had previously taken place (our turn of source about

[p. 81]
Some time in June 1775 my Brother Henry Bed-

inger and myselfe enterd Captain Hugh Stephensons company of volunteer rifflemen of Berkly County Virginia, for one year we marchd in that company from Shepherdstown, through Frederictown in Maryland York town and York County in Pennsylvania Crossd the Delaware at Easttown, thence through (I think) Hartford, Connecticut, then to Cambridge College near Boston, thence was stationd at Roxberry at the Siege of Boston completed my term and was honorably discharged on Statten Island during the above mentiond years Service. I was in no battle the first year company (excepting the commissiond office) were constantly exposed to the dangers of the ennemy artilery as we lay in reach and had no brest work near us, except a short wort before the house occupied by our officers. We took possession of what we called Dorchester point or hights were thensce sent to New York in aprile thence to Statten Island, at which place viz. at the watering place about 24 of us too 13 of the Brittish Merines & boat casks &c cause a brittish vessel to cut cable, so that the wind being favourable drove them from shore where they had Suffred considerably from our rifles

[p. 82]
Affidavit of George M. Bedinger for pension application
State of Kentucky Nicholas County Set
    On this   day of   1834 personally appeared in open court, being the Circuit Court in this county in Nicholas now setting

State of Kentucky Nicholas County Set

On the ___ day of ___ 1834 personally appeared in open court before the Circuit Court of sd county & district in Nicholas county in the State of Kentucky being a court of record George Michael Bed- inger a risedent of said county aged about 77 years on the 10 day of december last pasd, who being first duly Sworn according to law, doth on his oath make the following declaration (in order to obtain the benefit of the provisions made by an act of Congress passed June 7th 1832). That his brother Henry Bedinger of Berkly county and State of virginia and himsefe the said George Michael Bedinger, both entered as volunteers for one year, early in the month of June 1775 in the company of vollunteer Rifle men then raising in Berkley County Virginia by Capt. Hugh Stephenson that they marchd in sd company and arrved at the Siege of Boston, and served out the full time for which they were engaged, after having also marchd to New York in sd company they were Stationd a short time on Statan Island where he sd George Michal Bedinger was discharged & which he thinks was about the 10 June 1776 (but has long since lost his discharge) he farther Saith that his memory or recollection is frail, he thinks that ... after he was discharged he remaind as a vollunteer with the army about 3 weeks longer as it was then expected a General enguagement or some Important transaction would soon take place, and it was certain our army then stood in nead of all the troops they could raisd to oppose the power full army and navy of the enemy under the British under Howe, viz. under Genl. How & Admiral Hows.

[p. 83]

In relation to the names of his officers in sd Rifle Company, they were Capt. Hugh Stephenson, Lieutenants Wm. Henshaw was he thinks 1st Lieutenent, who remaind but a short line in service at camp at Roxbury with sd Rifle Company George Scott Sam Finley & Abram Shepherd were also Lieutenents in sd Rifle Company he think to the end or near the ~~end~~ sd year of his service in sd Company

The same affiant farther states that Capt Stephenson paid up his company generally to the first of January 1776 and took their receipts on dated on that day that he now has in his possession a smal Book of receipts of the most of the company which Book he has this day presented to the sd Nicholas circuit court and of which a copy of sd receipt is here copied viz "Roxbury Camp January the 1s 1776

"Recied of Capt Hugh Stephenson four pounds thirteen shillings and one penny in full of all Wages due me for my Service as a Soldier in the United Colonies from the 26 of June 1775 unto this day — Sam Finley
"Recevd by me "   Michael Bedinger

This affiant here thinks it necessary to state that in the in the Early part of his life his parents generally call him Mike, or Michael, but they informd him he was calld and named after an uncle of his viz George Michael Bedinger and was at the time he was christened or babtized calld George Michael. So he subscribes his name the last 55 years although he had in the earlier part of his life been generally calld Michael and so he at first wrote his name. He this affant farther says he thinks he got home to Shepherds Town in Berkly Virginia about the 10 day of July 1776 that it was the opinion of his Brother Henry Majr Henry Bedinger on the 10 or 11 of June 1775 at a meeting of a number of persons at a spring calld Stensons or Stephensons Spring that 50 years prevous to that day or on that day 50 years had Elaps since Capt Stephensons Company had partook of a barbecu being in the ... the evning of the day we they left their native state and crosd the Potomac on their march & way to Boston

[p. 84]
but as to the exact time he cannot now positve say thinks it was about twenty days that he remaind a vollunteer after he was discharged and within that time was informd by Lieutenent Wm Kelly that it was the intention of Capt. Stephenson who was by that time appointed a Colonel in the U S army, and gown home to Berkley County Virginia preparing to have recruits inlisted for his future Command as Coloner of the Regiment to be raisd & that the sd George Michael Bedinger was to be an enseigne in sd Regiment under sd Kelly (all this is now

[p. 85]
State of Kentucky } Set
Nicholas County

On the   day of February 1835 personally appeared in open court before the county court for the county of Nicholas in the State of Kentucky being a court of record George Michael

Bedinger a resident of said county aged 78 years who being first duly Sworn according to Law doth on his oath make the following declaration in order to obtain a pension or the benefit of the provisions made by the act of Congress passed the 7h day of June 1832

That Early in the month of June 1775 this affiant inlisted enterd as a a volun Rifleman under Capt Hugh Stephenson at Shepherds Town then in Berkely now in Jefferson County Virginia and that he marched from thence as well as he can recollect on the 10th or 11 day of the same month to the Siege of Boston, passing through Frederick Town Maryland crossing the Susquehannah at Wrights ferry passing through Little York, Lancaster, & Bethlehem PA, Crossing the Delaware at Easton & passing through New Jersey & Hartford Connecticut and remaind at Roxbury near Boston about eight months when we marched to New York City & from thence went to Staten Island, where he remained until he was discharged having servd the full time for which he inlisted. Was in no General enguagment but was in frequent Skirmishes in one of which on Staten Island this affiant in company with 25 others of his company & 2 riflemen took thirteen prisoners — his lieutenents were William Henshaw, George Scott, Samuel Finley & Abraham Shepherd, Successively. We Riflemen were under Genl George Washington's Immediate personal command

[p. 86]
and from whom (while our sd company remaind at Roxbury & at Dorchester hights) Capt.

Stephenson Generally recivd his Orders, (as this afiant confidently believes, and has understood from seeing them viz his Capt & Genl Washington together and from hearing information of others whom he relied on. Said company was not attached to any particular Regiment, or Corps, but was kept in readynes on short Notice to act on Suden Emergencies, at no great distance from head quarters then at Cambridge until sent to New York City and Staten Island and was discharged he thinks about the 10 of June 1776 but thinks some allowence of time was made to the soldiers of sd Company to return home in but having long since lost his discharge and his memory now being very frail he cannot be certain as to the certain day the date of his discharge but perfectly remembers, that after he was discharged although he had great anxiety to see his Deer distress Mother who was a widdow poor and with a young & almost helpless family of children to suppot) he remained with the army as a volunteer about 3 or 4 weeks longer as it was then expected a General Engagement or some important transaction would soon take place, & it was certain our army then stood in nead of all the troops that could be raisd to to oppose the power full army and navy of the enemy under the British command of viz. Genl How & Admral How then laying in Sandy hook in sight of Statan Island & from which sd Island he this affant made his escape in a small boat in company with Joseph Sweringer his mesmate in sd Rifle company, who Sweringen was afterwards a Capt in the U S army. We landed on the Jersey shore, left our clooths Blankets &c as we had no time to spare to take them with us; in safty we made a hasty escape.

[p. 87]
The British he thinks from that time remaind in possession of sd. Island (& he never got his bagage). After his escape from Statan Island to the Jersey shore he went thence to New York and thence to Amboy where he was under the command of Capt Nicholas Billenger of Pa. during this Service

And again in January 1777 this afiant with a company of volunteer riflemen commanded by Captain Willam Morgan from Shephers Town Brkely County V.A. Edward Lucas ... Wiliam Lucas the ... later father of the ... gvner of Ohio & Himslfe Lieutenants by Philadelphia cross the Delaware at Trenton and joind the army under Genl Washington near Moristown and which company after wards Joind the Corps commanded by Colonel Charles M. Thruston of frederick county virginea proceeded to opose the Brittish army in Jersey at an action at a place he thinks cald Piscattaway near Brunswik about the first of March 77 as well as this afiant can now recollect the american troops amounting to about 400 were defeetied and dispersed by what was deems a Superiour force with light artilery cavelry and Infant but the fire from the enemies artillery particularly the grape or canister shot together with the limes that was shot of by ... falling from the trees and at the same time and at the some an outcry or rumor that the British were surrounding us induce our troops (who were Generally Melela young and inexperinced troops to retreat preciportately, with such spead, that in the shelter of the woods they soon got out of sight of those who had more experiance & fortitude but who alone could do no other with pridence than follow on and ...leave the field of batle to the enemy ...cape

[p. 88]
he this afiant thinks Capt Morgans Company returnd on the evening of this day of action to the place they marched from in the Morning previous to the action, as to the number of killd and wounded they were but few he is not certain whether Colonel Thruston was wounded or not; he recollects that Capt Wilson, of Berkly was shot in the arm; he thinks Wilson's arm was broke by a shot that musket ball; and he also remembers perfectly, that an ounse Ball went through a man in his compeany comnond of the was taken out one man in his plattoon of the name of Shields it had gown in on the other side the man lived and brought it with him to Kentucky. Captain Morgans company continued at this station until they had served the time for which they Enguaged which was at least three months, and would have been discharged at the end of the time they engaged for; but at the particular request of a messenger from General Washington that he wishd said company to remain I think 3 days longer they all agreed to stay at my this affiant's additional solicittation; 3 or four of the men who insisted on going when their time was out, set out accordingly; the others remaind as requested, got their discharges. This affiant remain'd to settle with some men on the 4th day was mostly spent at

camp: Thence with his friend Benoni Swearingen he determined to try to march home to Shepherd's Town to prevent those 3 or four who refused to stay sd 3 days from getting home first, they did so. Got home before those cowardly, or insensabel beings who had refused so small a favour. This company of Captain Morgan's was allowed a toore of militia duty and may at least be called 3 months & 3 or four days in actual service.

[p. 89]
State of Kentucky} Set
Nicholas County

On this   day of october 1835 personally appeared in open court before the County Court for the county of Nicholas in the State of Kentucky being a court of record George Michael Bedinger a resident of said county aged 78 years who being first duly Sworn according to law, doth on his oath make the following declaration in order to obtain a pension or the benefit of the provisions Made by the Act of Congress passed the 7th day of June 1832

That early in the month of June 1775 this affiant enterd as a volunteer Rifleman for one year, under Capt. Hugh Stephen at Shepherds town then Berkley County, now Jefferson County, Virginia, and that he marched from thence as well as he can recollect on the 10 or 11 day of the same Month to the Siege of Boston, in Captain Stephensons company of Riflemen, then raisd for one year, passing through Frederick Town Maryland, Little York Pa crossing the Susquehannah at Wrights ferry, through Lancaster, & Bethlehem,

Cross the Delaware at Easton & passing through New Jersey & Hartfort Connecticut, and arrvd at Roxbury, remaind at Roxbury near Boston about eight months when we marched to New York City & from thence went to Staten Island where I remaind until I was discharged having servd the full time for which I enlisted was in no general engagement but was in frequent Skirmishes in one of which on Staten Island this affiant in company with about 25 others took thirteen prissoners, his Lieutenants were William Henshew George Scott Samuel Finley, & Abahom Shephard Successively. We generally were under Genl. George Washingtons Immediate (and at some times) personal Command & from whom (while our company remain'd at Roxbury and at Dorchestor hights) Captain Stephenson Generally recvd his orders

[p. 90]
(as this affiant believes) as his capt (Stephenson) was ... the Rifle corps the oldest captain the intimate freind and, companion of Genl. Washington, long before the commencement of the Revolutionary war (he is confident) was an affectionate companion & friend of Capt Hugh Stephenson who was in rank the oldest Capt of the Rifle Corps whos company Generally near head quarters while near Boston and was not attached to any other corps or Regiment but was generally kept in readyness on short Notice to act on suden emmergencies, until sent to New York City in the Spring '76 & thence to Statten Island where he this affiant was discharged he thinks about the 10 day of June, 1776, he thinks, some allowance of

time was made to the soldiers of sd company to return home in; but having (long since) lost his discharge, cannot now to a certainty recollect the date of his discharge; thinks it was on or about the 10 of June, 1776. He perfectly remembers that after he was discharged, he felt great anxiety to see his Dear distressed Mother, who was a widdow, poor and with a young & almost helpless family of young children to support, her oldes sons being in the army he remaind with the army as a volunteer he thinks about 3 or 4 weeks longer; as it was then expected a General Engagement or some Important transaction would soon take place & it was certain that our army then stood in need of all the troops that could be raisd to oppose the powerful army and navy under the command of the Brittish Genl How & Admiral How (then laying in Sandy hook in sigh of us Riflemen on Staten Island, and from which Island this affiant finally made his escape in a small boat in company with Joseph Swearngeon his mesmate in sd rifle company & who was afterwards a captain the U S Army, we landed on the Jersey Shore, left our cloaths, Blankets &c as we had not time to take them with us after the near approach of the enemy who had already taken possesion of the Island, had pitchd some tents at or near the watering place & and were scouring the Island in serch of the (... as they calld us.

They slipt ... of the Island we last our bagage (cloaths &c)

[p. 91]
... never get them nor did I ever receive any pay for this extra service whch was of I think at least

17 or 21 days as a vollunteer Rifleman.

[p. 92]
That early in the month of June 1775 this affiant entered as a volunteer Rifleman under Captain Hugh Stephenson at Shepherds Town Then Berkley now Jefferson county Virginia, and that he marched from thence as well as he recollects on the 10th or 11th of the same month to the siege of Boston passing through Frederick Town Maryland crossing the Susquehannah at Wrights ferry passing through Little York Lancaster & Bethlehem Pa. Crossed the Delaware at Easton & passing through New Jersey & Hartford Connecticut and remained at Roxbury near Boston eight Months when we Marched to New York City & from thence went to Staten Island where I remained until I was discharged having served served the full time for which I enlisted, was in no general Engagement but was in frequent skirmishes in one of which on Staten Island this affiant in company with 25 others took thirteen prisoners, his Lieutenants were William Henshaw George Scott, Samuel Finley & Abram Shephard, successively. We were under Genl. George Washington & saw Genls. Putnam Ward & Lee

[p. 93]
after which I again immediately volunteered and remained at Staten Island until driven Thence by the British went over to Jersey thence to New York & thence to Amboy where I was under the command of Capt Nicholas Bittinger of Pa. during this service I was 13 months from Shepherdstown Va and again in January 1777 went with a

company of volunteer riflemen commanded by Captain William Morgan Edward Lucas William Lucas & myself Lieutenants, by Philadelphia crossed at Trnton and joind the army under Genl. Washington at or near Morristown N.J. fought the Battle of Piscatawa, served out our full term of three months, when at the request of Gen. Washington I remained some days longer for which the men who remained were allowed a full tour of duty.

And again afterwards having heard of the defeat of the Americans at Brandywine, Benoni Swearingen & myself left our homes at Shepherdstown Va. and went to the american army about 18 miles from Germantown & a short & and were permitted to take our stations in Captain Jos. Swearingingens company in the 12th Virginia Regiment Commanded by Col. James Wood, being in Genl. Scotts Brigade & in Genl. Adam Stevens division and remained in service for six weeks, when we were discharged having fought

[p. 94]
in the Battle of Germantown. In the spring of 1779 in company with ... home in he left old Virginia & came to Kentucky and arrived at Boonesborough April 7th where we found Captain Holder with about 15 or twenty men under his command and in great distress in consequence of a party of 10 or 12 men under a Mr. Stearns having left them a few days previous & who fell into the hand of the Indians & were with a single exception as he this affiant affirms was then infrnd killed or taken, only one man of the number re-

turning to Boonsboro the next day & so reported. The distresses of the inhabitants of the fort Induced me to join Captain Holder & I remained seven months in in service as commissary during part which time I was in continual service acting as an Indian Spy, and was Acting as commissary, scout, & taking my turn with the other men of the post as Hunter for the benefit of the inhabitants thereof. This was a kind of irregular service to which I was impelled by the feelings of Humanity & sympathy for defenceless women & children who were unable to leave the country & who must inevitably have fallen into the hands of the Indians had it not been for the timely arrival of our patry. It was a service too for which I never recievd any Compensation though I have ever considered this this service as the most dangerous difficult and at the same time most useful to my county ~~of my~~ life as we were almost continually surrounded by parties of Indians who were laying in wait for us, & we had to supply ourselves & the Inhabitants of the fort

[p. 95]
with provision mainly by the success of our Hunting excursions to effect which we had to slip out at night retire to some distance from the fort kill our game which were generally Buffleow and pack it in again in some the succeeding night and by our exertions the possession of Boonesborough was retained ~~in the hands of the United Colonies~~ and the lives of the Inhabitants preserved. Shortly after ~~my arrival at Boonesborough and during the next a number of~~ During this period the expedition against the Indian

Towns at Old Chilicothe then calld new Chilicothe under Colonel John Bowman was planned and Executed in which Expedition I acted as adjutant and Quartermaster, which service lasted about six weeks, when the men returned to their different forts, & resumed their former stations excepting a compony of those who lived near Red Stone & its ... & on the waters of the Monongohaly river they went up the Ohio. Again in May 1781 this afiant took command of a company of Malitia in Berkley County Virginia and was ordered to Join Colonel William Darke's regement which I did and marched to the siege of York in addition to his service as captain I had to act as adjutant to the regement, and occasionally to major & perform the duty of major and sometimes when specally calld B... This service lasted for a little more than five months. In addition to the aforementioned terms of service this affiant was frequently in service for short periods of Less than a month being an irregular service he does not think it necessary or proper to relate it.

[p. 96]
Memo. It may not be improper to state a few facts ... that ... at what was calld the Battle of Piscattaway near Brunswick ... March 1777 viz. about 400 of ... militia having marched near to the British Lines & near thir army ... conseald in the woods. When Colonel Wm. Morgan ... was ... in our Company with a few of my company with them advanced in sight of the Enemy to draw them out of their camp, to the place where we were wating in ... but as ... the small party were destroyed. ... from ... the place where we ...

should only meet with their Infantry & perhaps ... mistaken our ... known ... hoping ... where ... only two others we were ... last on and out of sight of ... of our party when we retreatd to ... a young man calld ... M. Morgan a half brother of my fathers being my grandfather's son by his third wife ... the last ... on in sight when I left the Battel Ground. In this action I do not recollect the number killd a remarkable occurrence however happened close to me as I was caling to the men to come on a man of the name of Shields was shot nearly through the middle of his body in at one-side and nearly out at the ... so near out that the skin only retaind the ball he lived and brought the ball with him to Kentucky.

Capt Wilson of Berkely County had his arm broke by a ball in sd action & I think Colonel C. Thruston was wounded of last, of the latter I am not certain as my memory is weak.

[p. 97]
From the foregoing it will appear that he has service as a private soldier about 11 months as a Lieutenant upwards of three months as adjutant and Quarter Master 6 weeks & as Captain and adjututant and occasionally Major 5 months.

Bomans Expedition

When in Bomans Expedition in the Evning before we got to this indian town called Chili-ecthy we stoped held a connsel of war divided our forces into 3 parts or companies containing on an average not far from 80 men in each company. One company was commanded by Capt. Benjamin Logan the 2d by Capt. James

Harrod the 3d company by Capt. John Holder. It was concluded we should all march on together until we got quite near the town, which was about 8 or 10 miles from, where we held our connsel (as well as I recollect). (I march with Holder's company, that company was to halt on this side of the town being I think on the S side or the sede we come from. Captains Harred & Logans Companies were to pass by the town the one leaving it to the right the other to the left and go so far round the far side of the town as to leave a space between the two companies for the indians to pass into at day break when Captain Holders Company in the morning were to rush on them on the contrary side. All were to remain quiet until morning when sd charge by holders Company was to be made. Accordingly Each Company that night marched to and took ther position as near as they Could that night a few hours after night. Captain Holders Company

    Sketch of a Declaration written by my Dear Son B. T. Jr. for G. M. B.

[p. 98]
got to within a short distance of some of the houses of the town where we laid down and expected to remain until about day break when we ware to make the attack according agreement or orders. I think we had not beene there long when an Indian come along on or near our trail stoped & mad some low nois with his voise I believ as if he wishd to know who we were when a man of the name of Ross shot him he hollowed a litle when Jacob Starns hit him on the head Selenced him with his tomehock & I think took

his sklp, this nois I think induced some of the Squas to whimper or crie a litle as some of our company said they heard them say Kentuck we then laid still a short time giving time for some of the Indians to come to see or know what causd the allarm about 6 or 7 of them came with ... arms come so near that they heard us cock our guns and were about to run back when some of fierd on them ... ran afore them, and got into some of their houses or huts and perhaps should have drove them out of their town, but some of the men in the companies beyond the town rais yell and hallowing. The Indians finding they were Surrounded their Brave Commander then spoke to them telling them they were men and warrers they must fight & be men! that we were Kentucky squaws they could whip us they all answerd in their way in the ... We could not move them from their town louje or strong houses. Our Company had had made had a man or two wounded and next morning a few more were killd. I was behind a log with two of the Souths laying near me. This log was low ... Thomas South raising his head to peep over the log he was killd his brother on my left askd me to strech him I could not

Maj. Bedinger said the food was deficient on Bowman's campaign, & not many of the men were mounted. L.C.D.

[p. 99]
State of Kentucky   Nicholas County
Set

On the 28th day of December 1835 personally appeared in open court before the county court for the county of Nicholas in the state of Kentucky, being a court of record now sitting, George M. Bedinger a resident of said county aged seventy nine years. Who being first duly sworn according to law doth on his oath make the following declaration in order to obtain a pension or the benefit of the provisions made by the act of Congress passd the 7th day of June 1832.

That he entered the service of the Colonies or United States under the following named officers and served as herein stated viz.

That early in the month of June 1775 this affiant entered as a vollunteer for one year & inlisted as a Rifleman under Captain Hugh Stephenson, at Shepherdstown, then in Berkly, now Jefferson County Virginia, and that he marched from thence as well as he recollects, on the 10th or 11th the same month, to the seige of Boston (in Capt. Stephensons Company of Riflemen) passing through Frederick Town Maryland, through Little Yorke Lancaster and Bethlehem P.A., crossing the Susquehannah at Wrights ferry and the Delaware at Easton, & passing through New jersey & Hartford in Connecticut and arrived at Roxbury near Boston, remaind there (at the siege of Boston) about eight months, when, about the first of March, our company marchd from Roxbury & we took their station (in the night) on Dorchester Point, (near Dorchester hights) where we were not discoverd by the enemy until next morning, by which time we had by the hard labour & great exertions of a strong in trenching party fortified our selves so strongly that it was deemd not in the power of the enemy to dislodges us from our position, all though they did all that was in their power without making to great & unresonable sacrifices of soldirs lives. We (Captain Stephensons Company) was sent from Dorchester hights (Soon after General Washington was convincd enemy could not retain in the in possession of Boston their fleet could not remain in safty in that harbor,

[p. 100]
he sent our Company from thence to New York City & from thence we went to Staten Island where I remained in sd company until I was discharged having Servd the full time for which I enlisted.

Was was in no general Engagement but in frequent Skirmishes in one of which on Staten Island this affiant in company with 25 others took thirteen prissoners. His Lieutenents were William Henshaw George Scott, Samuel Finley & Abraham Shepard successively. We were under General George Washingtons Immediate command perhaps more so than the captains of company Generally were.

While our Company remaind at Roxbury and at Dorchester hights, Capt. Stephenson I think Generally, receivd his orders directly from his old intimate friend and Companion Genl. Washington himselfe, whos head quarters were then at Cambridge & as at that time our sd Rifle Company was not attachd to any other regiment or corps, but was kept in readyness to act on sudden immergencies on short notice near head quarters until we were Sent to New York City and to Staten Island, and was discharged he thinks about the 10th of June, 1776.

He farther states, that he has long since lost his discharge and that, although he was discharged & had a very great desire to see his Dear afflicted & affectionate and almost helpless Widdow Mother with six children to support (in Virginia) these powerful attractions combined at that time did not induce him then to leave the army or the Island, as at that time it was Generally belivd that a general engagement between the two contending armies or some Important transaction would soon take place, as both the Genrl & admiral Howe with a British fleet and Army were then in sight, of Statan Iland wher I was stationed, these considerations induce me to continue ... at my station on Staten Island until part of the the Britis army had pitchd their tents on the Island at the watering heal and others ware scouring the Island in serch of the Rebbls as they

[p. 101]
they calld us. At this juncture I escaped from them in a small boat or skiff to the Jersey shore in Company with Joseph Swearingen, went to our army New York thence to amboy, where I remaind as a vollunteer with my uncle he recollects that a small vessel said to be one of the britis vessels which he says anchored in sight of Amboy and which vessel his uncle informd he thought could be taken by surprse and borded on a dark night; that he was taking down the the names of such as would be willing to under take to bord her & coptur the sd vessel. I think I told him I would be one of the company & I think he

took my name although the vessel soon departed, and perhaps fortunately for us. Capt Nicholas Bittinger company of Pennsylvania trops in all about 3 weeks as a volunteer, after I was discharged I was from Shepherdstown about 13 Months.

And again in January 1777 went with a company of volunteers riflemen commanded by Captain William Morgan Edward Lucas, William Lucas & myselfe Lieutenants by Philadelphia crossed at Trenton and joind the army under Genl. Washington at or near Morristown N.J. Joind the Corps comande by Col. Charles M. Thruston fought the Battle Servd out our full time of three months, when at the request of Genl. Washington we remaind Some days longer for which the Company who remaind were allowed pay & a ful tour of duty were afterwards honourably discharged.

And again, having heard of the defeat of the americans at Brandywine, Benoni Swearingen & and myselfe left our homes at Shepherdstown Va. and went to the American Army which was then about 18 or 19 miles from Germentown and were permitted to take our station in Captain Joseph Swearingens Company in the 12 Virginia Regiment Commanded by Col. James Wood being in General Scotts brigade and in Genl. Adam Stevens's division & remaind.

[p. 102]
and again afterwards this affint having heard of the defeat of Americans at Brandywine Bononi Swearingen and himselfe left their homes at Shepherdstown Virginia and wint to the

American army about 18 miles from Germentown he has forgeten the name of the place ... & perhaps Skippack and were permitied to take our Station in Capt. Joseph Swearingens Company In the 12th Virginia Regiment commanded by Colonel James Wood & in Maj. Genl. Stevens disivion & Genl. Scotts Brigade and remaind in Service about Six weeks. When we were discharged, having fought in the Batle of Germantown --Here this affiant thinks it ought in Jus to himselfe and his companion Bononi Swearingen to state some of the circumstances that took place at that time viz. on the day before said batle Genl. Washington rode along the lines of our army at our camp said to be about 18 or 19 miles from Germantown looking attentively at the at the solders, as he passd them they discharged their guns arms, over his head as fast as he rode from one end of the line to the other. We thence marched on in Good order Silently until after we got near the enemy, & then very slow frequently stopping & at times standing still an hour to pass the time away without laying down to sleep, least the Enemy Should in that case Surprise us, at day brake we had got to Chesnut Hill in Sight of part of the Brittis army; there the Adjutant Gen. address Swearingen and this affiant as well as he can recollect thus: Gentlemen vollunteers, You have now an opportunity to distinguish your Selves, you are not confined to any plattoon or part of the army", uppon this information we volunteers Immediately pushed forward towards the enemies camp prepared with our Rifles & swords to defend our selvs, a generan enguagement Soon commenced, and we vollunteers were between the

[p. 103]
fiers of the armies. The day being damp the air hevy & foggy litle could be seen but smoke. I need not say more on this subject, only that I think it but Just to say, that Majr. General Stephens (I am Confident) meant well when he orderd a retreat out of the as some of the enemies horse in desgise I believe deceiv'd him by saying we were firing on our own men; but there statement was found to be false, as soon as the right wing cleard the Smoke, the right then halted, faced the enemy, and maintaind their Ground, savd and pretected the wounded & baggage untill the left wing took over. But here I mus now stop finding it will be out of my power to take time to Eplain. So let it suffice to say that ... days the Batle was over. Gen. Wood; offered us Sub-loltrors appointments, but as our mothers were widdows & our Brothers in the army and prisoners we could not leave them our mothers long at a time but were M... and Melling and hoped to do our ful part in times of need. When we were ready to return home Gave us an Honourable discharge Stating that we had disstinguished our Selves in the most Brave and Extraordinary maner on the day of the action of the 4th of october (calld) at the Battle of Germantown. This affant for this service he never receivd any pay altho he went at consederable Expense ... for their horses from the time the left home until they returnd & got home

[p. 104]
& subsequently.

On the firs day of March 1779 he this affiant in company with nine others white men & 2 negros left his home in Brkely county Va & came to Kentucky, and arrived at Boonsborough April 7th when we found Captain Holder with about 15 or 20 Men under and in great distress in con Consequence of a party of 10 or twelve men under a Mr. Starns having left them not more than a day & a half before our arrival at Boonsborough. Sd Starnses party Intended to leave Kentucky & had left it and had gotten between 20 and 30 miles on the way towards the Setlement trace that we were on comeing from the Setlement, but fortunately & he hopes and believs providentially we missed the path but fell into it again within a Short distance, he think within about half a mile, when we saw the tracks or trail of as we thought perhaps 30 or 40 persons soon saw a broken bow and other indian sign we were now convincd that we had passd very near a Strong party of Indians our horses had snorted and appeard much allarmd a short distance before we got into the path but we saw no Indians we went on and at night it was proposd by some of the party to go off of the road and sleep without fier but one of the company said we would not die until our time come when Colonel Morgan made that observation we the younger party of the company did not insist on leaving the road as we did not then wish to be thought cowardly; and for once it so happend that it is believd that our extreemely careless conduct Induced an other party of Indions who pass without desturbing us, it was suppose the Indens took

... on the same path that night (a party that had ... two men (Spies) viz. Colonel Samuel Estil and another who went out of Boonsborough spying with him). The next morning we got into Boonsborough to the Great Joay of all persons in the fort. We had not been there two hours before one of Captains or Mr Starns party come in and informd us that Starns and his party fell into the hands of the Indians who he thought had killd and took

[p. 105]
the night before he got to the Fort at Boonsboro we afterwards heard that some others had escaped at the time the Indians killd Starns, only one man of the party that I know of returnd to the Fort. The distresses of the inhabitants by of the induced this afant to Join Capt Captain John Holder and remaind in service under his Controul or comand about 7 months In which time he acted a short time perhaps 2 months as commissary in alotting to divide or distribute some salt & provisions among the pent up inhabitants. He thence went under his sd Capt John Holder on all calls of in defending the Inhabitantes and the fort & about the first of June marchd under sd Capt John Holder on an Expedition against the Shawne Indians under the command of Colonel John Boman who was authorised by the State of Virginia to carry on sd Expedition and by whos authority he this affiant acted as Adjutant and Quarter Master for sd expedition he was specially calld on for that purpose, though then a stranger to the Colonel, his character as a man, acquainted with military disipline it is believd inducd sd. call and he

believes it was a fortunate circumstance that when sd detachment had faild in fuly suceeding agains the Indians at Chillecothe, had retreated in disorder and confusion that they had a man who under providence in whom all who knew him had ...in Such Extremities could form a hollow Square to prevent a a farther precipitate retreat, until great Exertions & night Should assist, and more confidence Should be restored. This affiant he this affiant is sensible of the old proverb that selfe prais is no recommendation would not have said so much if he had not thought it his duty to state these facts on his declaration on his oath he recollects that the Suksesful charge on the enemy at or near the dusk of the evening

[p. 106]
as well as he can recollect.

In the evening near dusk he went to Colonel Boman near dusk, stated to the Colonel that as the ... the surrounding ... and Strength and as we were Sinking with fatigue & hunger it was time a ... should be made (or words to that effect, his answer was (as well as I can recollect) do what you pleas, I do not now what to do... we ... with tomahook in hand they ... miss us, then with our loaded or ... fire we will force them to retreat. We did so! ... B. fish ... compelld them to disperse.

[p. 107]
Affidavit of George M. Bedinger for pension application
State of Kentucky}   Set
Nicholas County

On the 25 day of January, 1836 Personally appeared in open court before the Court of Nicholas County now sitting, being a court of Record George M. Bedinger a resedent of said County & State of Kentucky, aged 79 years the 10 day of december last. Who being first duly sworn according to law Doth on his oath make the following Declaration in order to obtain the benefit of the act of Congress passed June 7th 1832.

That in the month of June 1775 he enlised as a volunteer Rifleman that he Inlisted for one year under Capt. Hugh Stephenson at Shepherdstown then in Berkley, now Jefferson County Virginia, and that he marched from thence, as well as he can recollect, on the 10 or 11th of the same month in Capt. Hugh Stephensons Rifle Company to the Siege of Boston, passing through Frederick Town Maryland, through Little york, Lanchaster, & Bethlehen P.A. Crossed the Susquehannah at Wrights ferry the Delaware at Easton & passing through New Jersey & Hartfort Connecticut, thence to Roxbury, continued there (at the Seig of Boston) about eight months. Thene our company (early in March) left Roxbury & we took our Station in the night on Dorchester point near Dorchester hights, where we were not discoverd by the enemy until next morning, by which time it was not in the power of the enemy to dislodge us from our position, we had during the night by all means in our power, & by the aid of a strong working party, become so far secured that little doubt existed but that the Brittis Fleet and army would (not long be able to retain their station & possession of the harber & Town of Boston. Soon after this & a few days before Boston was evaquated, Capt. Stephensons Company was sent to New York City. I think we remaind there (perhaps) two or 3 weeks, from thence to Staten Island where we remained in said Stephenson Rifle Company until I had served out the full time for which I was Inlisted was honourably discharged

[p. 108]
discharged. Was in no general engagement but was in freduent Skirmishes in one of which on Staten Island this affiant in company with 25 others took thirteen prisoners. His Lieutenants names were William Henshaw, Samuel Finley, George Scott & Abraham Shepherd, successively. Lt. Henshaw remaind a short time with us at Boison then returnd home to his family in Virginia. We were Generally under George Washington's Immediate command, while we remaind at the Seige at Boston, were not attached to any regement nor corps but were Generly near head quarters prepared to act on short notice on sudden emmergencies. Our Capt was appointed Colonel came home to make preparations to recruit a Regement of Riflemen, but died soon after he got home. After I was discharged I immedeatly vollunteerd and remaind at Statten Island until driven thence by the Enemy. They had already pitched some of thier tents on Staten Island & were Scouring the Island in Serch of the "rebbels" as then calld us, when Joseph Swearengen and myselfe affected our escape from them in a small boat or skeft, Got safe to the Jersey Shore but lost some of our cloaths & beankets &c went thence to our army at New York where as well as I can

recollect Liut William Kelly, who had lately been appointed to Serve in the New Regiment to be raisd infornd me that Sd Colonel Stephenson told him he would appoint me an Ensign in his regiment to serv in the same Company with Kelly. The Brittish army and navy were then laying at Sandy hook Commanded by the two Hows viz. Genl. and admerel How. A Generale Engagement or some important ... action was almost daly expected would soon take place. Our army were weak comparetively when compared to the then powerful army & navy of the Brittis. We were in Great nead of all the troops that could be raisd; to think of leaving our army at

[p. 109]
Such a time occationd painful reflections, to <u>stay</u> much longer from a most affectonate Mother who was a widdow with an almost helpless family of young children <u>at home</u> to support, & who was anxiously looking for me, (as nearly all the rest of our Company had now Got home) this together with resonable fears that <u>accidents</u> or the <u>fate</u> of <u>war</u> might still deprive us both and all our family from the anticipated happy Happy Meeting. With such feeling as these I Continued with the army three weeks after I was discharged then left the army, got to Philadelphia Got there on the 4th of July 1776 Got home to Shepherdstown I think between the 10 & 15th of July.

And again subsequently, in the month of January 1777 the said George M. Bedinger Went with a company of volunteer riflemen Commanded by Captain William Morgan of berkly county Virginia. Edward Lucas, William Lucas

& himselfe were Lieutenant (all of Berkley county). That early in January they marched from Shepherds Town by Philadelphia crossed the Delawer at Trenton and join the army under George Washington near Morristown our company joind the Corps commanded by Colonel Charles M Thruston of Frederic County Virginia we were that winter Stationd at diferent places to guard against the incroachments and plundering parties of the Brittish army, by opposing them when ever called on early in March perhaps the first day of March we fought the Battle of piscataway, Served out our full time of three months, when at the request of Genl. Washington to Stay three days longer, the Company agred to Comply with his Sd request which which was communicated to me as our Captain Captain & Liuts wer not then present. I had the Company call to gether Stated to them the Necessity and propriety of ther Complying with sd request when the whole Company (with the exception 3 or 4) agree to stay &

[p. 110]
did stay and were Honourably discharged and were allowed a tour of Military duty (exept Sd 3 or 4). They inservice three months & three days.

This affiant farther States that afterwards having heard of the defeat of the americans at Brandywine, Bonony Swearingen & myselfe left our homes at Shepherdstown Virginia and went to the American Army about 18 miles from Germentown and were permitted to take our Station in Captain Joseph Swearengens Company in the 12 Virginia Regiment Commanded by Colonel James Wood, Beng in General Scotts Brigade & in Genl. Adam Stevenns's division, and remaind in Service Six weeks and were honourably discharged. Genl. Wood Stated in Sd discharge that we had distinguish our Selves in the most brave and extraordinary Manner on the day of the action of the 4th of october. From the time we Joind Said Regiment we messd and associated with the officers with Several of which we had been long and Intimately acquainted Most particularly with Capt Joseph Swearingen. Stevens from my infantry, in the Morning of the day of the Battle of Germentown as soon as we got in sight of the forepart of the Enemies encampment, next to us as we were going towards from chesnut hill the Adjutant Genl. addressd us thus "Gentlemen vollunteers you will now have an Opportunity, to distinguish your Selves, you are not confined to any particular plattoon or corps"; these wer his words to the best of my recollection, or words to that effect. When Benoni Swearingen Immediately advancd with such speed that we soon

[p. 111]
Soon left our advanceing army behind us prepared to defend our Selves with our rifles and swords we got between the fire of the contending armies but it being a foggy morning & smoky day I hope and through the mercies of God we were saved unhurt although we afterwards heard that it was believd we were both killd. Before we left the army to return home we were told we could have appointments as Subbalterns in the Regiment but us our Mothers were widdows & as

I had one brother who was then a prisener with the Brittes, and an other who had also been taken prisoner at Fort Washington & had just got home, and whose life was depared of I Returnd home with my worthy companion and well tried friend Benoni Swearengen to Shepherdstown for this Service we never askd nor recevd any pay, although our horses & traveling expenses were paid by ourselves, and were Sensibly felt by me as I was in low circumstances.

In the Spring of 1779 on the first day of March this affiant with nine others left his home in Berkely County Virginia and come to Kentucky and arrived at Boonsborough April 7th when we found Captain John Holder with about fifteen or twenty men under his command and the fort in great distress & imminent danger in con consequence of a party of about 10 or 12 men under a Mr Starns having left there not two days (a day or two) previous, and who had nearly all fell into the hands of the Indians, one of sd party who escaped Came into Boonsborough about two hours after our company arrived and informd us of the defeet of of Starns and his party. Our company had missd the road so fortunately that the Indians

[p. 112]
Indians who killd Capt Starns that night were then so close behind him, and his party, at that Juncture that they mus have discoverd us, if we had not been In a thick cainbrake, when we passd them to our night. We got into our path agane about half a mile from where we left it, but were surprised to see a large trail that had Just been

made, and from a broken bow, the Shape of the feet particularly the pigion great tow as Some call it, we were convinced a number of Indians had passd and that Providentially our lives were saved. We went on that evening in the path that led to Boonsburo about 7 or 8 miles got wethin 6 or 7 miles from Boonsbarro where we Stay all night made a fier and laid by it until day break without a cintinel or Spy to watch fo the approaches of the Indians, this incautious Conduct was occationd by Colonel Wm. Morgan. He was I think the oldes man in company exept one, had been in General Braddock's time an Indian warrior Scout and Spty (and who) when some of the young boys (as three of us were then calld, proposed going out from the path for greater safety, observd that we would not die until our time came; we remaind neare the path, and it is belived that this apparently impropper conduct, induced another party of indians, who were seen that evening & had chased two spies, viz. Collonel Estil and another man. The Indians come out on the path we were on and it was believd they saw our fier and horses &c. but that they expected the fiers were made to deceve them & draw them into an ambuscade. This they were the more ready to beleve as the people at Boonsboro had but a short time tied an old mair out in a canebreak by the heel, then laid in ambush but the Indians discoverd the deception cautiously avoid the trap laid for them; a prissoner who escaped from them reported that

[p. 113]
the Indians lauchd at the that the white people

should think they could be caught in a trap like a bever, this affiant for fear of not giving the General circumstances of his Service find he has here been too profuse and regrets that he has already been so tedious has trespasing on the patience of this court and of all who are requierd to attend to this sd declaration, he hopes that when it is considered that he is now in the eightieth year of his age, having past his 79 year his memory frail, his body & mind weak, he will try to omit useless explainations, that he will be excused for what passd viz. the degressions. When we arivd at Boonsboro The Distreses of the inhabitants of the fort Induced me to Join Captain Holder John Holder who then had the comand at that place and remaind about Seven months in service excepting a few day when I assisted in planting and raising ½ an acre of corn and some fue days looking for a place to locate and make a small improvement to intitle me to land all of which together did not amnount more than 3 weeks, and in which time I was Generally as much exposed to danger as I comonly was durin my Service in the fort. My service as a an Indian Spy hunter and skout always taking my turn with the other men of the fort as Hunter for the benefit of the inhabitants thereof this was a kind of irregular Service to which I was impelled by the feelings of humanity & Sympathy for distressed women and children who were unable to leave the country and and who must inevitably have fallen into the hands of the hands of the Indians had it not been for the timely arrival of our party; It was a service two for which I never receivd any Compensation though I have ever considerd this

Service as the most dangerous dificult and at the Same time more useful to my Country as we were almost Continually surrounded by parties of Indians who were laying in wait for us & we

[p. 114]
had to supply ourselves and the Inhabitants of the fort with mainly by the Success of our hunting excurtions to affect which we had to Slep out at night retire to some distance from from the fort killd our Game which was Generally Buffelo and pack it in agane in some succeeding Night and by our exertions the possession of Boonsborough was retained and the lives of the Inhabitants preserd.

During this period an expedition against the Indian Town then calld new Chiliecothe, now Old Chilicothe under Colonel John Bowman was planed and executed in which Expedition I was called on, and acted as Adjutant and Quarter Master which service las about four weeks. When the men returnd to their diferent fortes & resumed their Stations, except a company of those who lived near Redstone ft. and its vicinity, on the waters of the Monongahaly; they went up the Ohio.

And again in May, 1781, he this affiant took Command of a company of Militia in Berkly County, Virginia under the command of Colonel William Darke and marched with them through diferent parts of Virginia to the Siege of York. In addition to this service as a Captain he had also to act as adjutant to the regiment, and occationally performed the duty of major; he perfectly recollects marching with a detachment to within sight of Yorktown, and in Sight of the Brittish army and which he thinks was some days before any other Corps or detachment went so near the Enemy and after the detachment he marchd with & ... (was under the command of Colonel Darke) had finished thier observate, they returnd to their

[p. 115]
Letter from George M. Bedinger relative to pension application
Lower Blue Licks Nicholas Cty. Ky. Feb. 15th, 1836
Dear Sir

Although I have not had the pleasure of an intimate acquaintance with you pesonally yet my nearest & dearest connections in ... most particularly my brother Henry Bedinger now my only Surviving brother, & Dr. Daniel Bedinger (my worthy Nephew have both long since, & lately, informed me of your Generous proofs of attachment to our family thier Interest & honour. Hence I have taken the liberty to address you in the most familiar confidential & I hope Respetful assurance of mutual esteem. I have for some years passd had an intention to make application for a pension under the laws or acts of Congress passd for the benefit of the officers & solders of the Revolution but as I have for several years last past been much distress by Sickness & deaths, in my family have my selfe been reducd by severe and lasting spells of Sickness and other disappointments So that I never made the necessary Declaration required, until our last Nicholas County Court, which was on the 26 day of January last. This my sd declaration I (a few days thereafter) enelopd in a letter to my Brother Henry Bedinger requesting him to procure Such additionl vouchers as probably might still be had (say his own affidvt & Peter Fishers) and send the same on to the Honbl. John Chambers of Kentucky who is the Representative for the Congressional District I live in. I have since written to Mr. Chambers requesting him to inform you of my Sd. Decleration and application & that I had full confidence that you would willingly assist in procureing a pension for me. When a question or proposition was put to me in Court to state the names of persons to whom I was known in my present neighbourhood and who can testify to my character for veracity & good behavior services as a soldier of the revolution &c, I, you will will see in the answer in my declaration mentiond, referd to

[p. 116]
to Sundry persons here. And I also refered the pension department to the following Gentlemen in Washington City, to wit, Hon. H. Clay, Hon. John Chambers, Hon. R. M. Johnson, Hon. J. J. Critenden, Hon. Ed. Lucas, Col. Jas. Perkins who I mention could testify to my character & standing were it necessary. I had mentiond your name &c to Mr. Chambers before he left Kentucky express my hope that you would be willing to do or assist me in doing what you could properly & ... do for me under present circumsances. I wrote to Mr. Chambers last week repeated what I had mention to him in our conversation befor he left home. He will probably show you my letter & I hope you will also See My Declaration after it

Gets to the City. My Brother H. B. in 1834 Sent to me a Copy of his ... affidavits. I was then sick and unable to attend to get Sundry others here ... from persons who have since departed this life & as the Depositions of my Brother & Mr. Fisher had not been duly certified nor the county Seal annexd it was missing. I shall Send my declaration to him to have it done in due form and as he has allways been ready and willing (when his health permitted) to attend to my interest, I am Confident he will not neglect a due attention to my call at on this occasion. In my sd Declaration I stated

And again, In the month of January 1777 I volunteerd in a Company of volunteer Riflemen commanded by Captain William Morgan of Berkly county Va. Ed Lucas William Lucas and My Selfe were the Lieutenants. I think it is ... probable that you may recollect hearing your Grandfather Ed Lucas or your uncle William Lucas (the father of Robert Lucas now Governor of Ohio) or some of the old inhabitants of Berkely, saying something on the subject of that campaign ... you are too young to recollect many of the old inhabittants of Jefferson near Shepherdstown. I have so old weak and frail that I finde my recollection has faild Greatly within the last 3 years. I am in hopes my brother will write to you

Letter from George M. Bedinger relative to pension application
Lower Blue Licks Nicholas Cty. Ky. April 19th 1836
My Dear Sir

I Receivd you letter dated 21 March (Post mark 23) in due time, and I intended to have answerd it without delay, but was calld from home to our Circuit Court as a witness and other busines, which together with sickness in my family added to my own negligence (which I hope you will excuse) have prevented me from writing sooner.

I receivd sever... letters from my brother H. Bedinger Since I first wrote to you, in his first he stated he had sent on his own affidavit in relation to my military Service, and had also also requested our much respected friend Daniel Morgan to have the County Seal or a necessary seal which is requird & properly procured & by the first opportunity have it sent on to you also, I was in hopes that if this was done, and my Declaration (although made in haste) in our court would have been Sufficient to have Satiflead all concerned to to whom the Justice of my claims are submitted. I have now before me a copy of Regulations Department of war pension office June 27, 18... (which has been handed me by a friend) although as their may be later instructions this may not be Safely relied on. It states "Tradionary evidence of service is deemed very important in the absence of direct proof, except the declaration of the party and the court are requested to be very particular in the inquiry and whether the belief is general &c. To require from the applicant positive proof of service from a temporary Surrvor would, after the laps of so many years, be to deprive many of them of the benefit of this law. &c Please see the instructions & let me know what farther testimony may be requird. Theire are still (I think), living in Mason County at the farthest within 30 miles of this place two old soldiers, who were at the Siege of York with me (but not in my Company) whose testimony I could get, as they Could Say they heard me calld & ... I was a Capt and knew me to do duty as adjutant it might afford additional assurance the men I alude to are Daniel Bell & ___ Peck

[p. 118]
I think I will if my health will permitt try to have ther testomony taken next week & send it on without delay. I think it is quite probable that Mrs. Manning the only daughter of my old friend Colonel Wm. Dark and some others in Jefferson or Berkely County may recollect my Services as a Captain & adjutant. But as to my being Commission as a captain in the militia and rumaing at home as such I think I was not. I think I nevr wishd to holde a commishion in the Militia except for the time I was calld into actual Service and I don't think I had such commishion, and theer were but fue of the officers or Soldiers that wie out in the commencement of the Revolutionary war that wishd to hold offices in the militia unless of a higher Grade. I had well traind in the U.S. Army have often traind & helped to train the Militia at home in virgina and in Camp I Generally traind the companny of Riflemen Commanded by Capt Wm Morgan of which Company Edward Lucas Wm Lucas and myselfe were Leiutenentts as I have Stated in my declaration and as the sd late Governor of Ohio is well acquainted with me and as a line from you to him & his answer to you would probably throw additional

light & confidence in my favour I shall take it as a Special favour if you will write him a line on this subject. My old Freind Colonel Darke from the commencement of the Revolutionary war was always a warm friend of our Families. I think he was instrumental with others in procureing a commishion for my brother D. Bedinger at the age of 16 after he had been taken prisoner at Ft. Washington & sufered more than a comon death although he recover. Colonel Dark I feel confedent was at the batle of Germentown & I think was taken prisoner on the 4 Octo 77 in which battle as I stated in my Declaration I was a vollunter Rifleman without pay. He was my warm friend and whether he sent for me or not I cannot now recollect. I was priveged by him to act as Captain and agjutant and marchd with him to the Siege of York the the most of the Company I Commanded had been

[p. 119]
as I now think were formerly commanded by Capt Mcintire although of this I am not certain as my memory is bad. He lived I think about 3 miles from Shepherdstown and I cannot tell to a certainty what companies the men were chiefly from but think Capt Mcintire went with us Several days. I know that Colonel Dark gave me the Command he had urged me to accept it and go with him in that distresing time when the brittess Brittis army were overrunning & plundering the Southern parts of virginia & driven our armies before them in every direction, at that time I was urged by Mr. Stronge's attachment to help Save the country as our prospect ware Gloomy the men

of the Company as well as all the officers I think had confidence in me as an Eperencd and useful officer & I hope My particular friend Colonel Darke never lost confidence in me. If he not preferd Me to any other Major of the Levies in the U.S. Army I Expect I should not have been so srongly urged to accept of the command of the first Virginia Battallion of Levies at a time when there were many respectable officrs offering their Srvice. It is worthy of notice that I was the only field officer Chosen to command U.S. troops in the State of Kentucky, by my old & bst friend Gen. Washington himself. who was then Presidnd. I have in haste written this scrall.

[p. 120]
Dec. 13 1838
Part of an unfinished lettre G. M. B. intended to have written but has perhaps been neglected or forgoten by G. M. B.

[p. 121]
Letter from George M. Bedinger relative to pension application
Lower Blue Licks 13th June 1842
My Dear Friend

I Recv'd your letter of the 25 within due time. I regret that I had it not in my power to have answered I it immediately, and to have ... to you the Greateful feelings of my heart, for your favourable attentions to my interest and feelings in Striving to have justice done to me, in my Claims for a pension. My delay in not writing to you (immediately) on the reception of yours, was occationed by my not being able to write Intelagably, owing to my weakness in my hand and lame finger, I was in hopes My son D. P. B. would have been here, & have wrote for me, he came but was obluge to leave us on other Important business, at ... Paris court. I continue to be in about the same (weakly) State of health I was in when I saw you last. I seldom venture from home to do any business owing to my weakness & lameness in my legs.

My Wife is as low in health as I am, altho 19 years younger.

In my youth at 18 When I turnd out a privett soldier, I did it for the love of Liberty, I had no thoughts of ever asking for a pensieon from my country, for my Services, nor would all the riches of this world, have induced me to have Indured all the dangers and privations of war 13 months prior to the Declaration of Indepenance, I then wore on my left brest in large letters (our moto, viz <u>Liberty</u> or <u>Death</u> an honourable death, (at that time, fighting for our Liberty, and country, was prefrable to an Ignomineous to death to be hanged as as a Rebbel, and having once (and with the army first, and Oldes company, from Virginia) embarked in Fredoms Cause, we dared not flinch, we had taken hold of the plow, & would not look back, the more our dificulties increasd, the <u>greater</u> our zeal, to combat with them.

My Mother was a weddow, not welthy, with, 8 children In charge as Father died (I think) 5 or 6 years before the war. The oldes 3 sons, all enter, the U. S. Service early. The 2 oldest, viz. myselfe, & oldes Brother in 75 the 3 son, in 76 when he arrived at the age of 15. Both my sd brothers, ware taken prisoners, the surrender of Fort

Washington, where most of the privets that were taken to the prison ships, where more than ⅔ died within 2 months,

[p. 122]
They blongd then (when taken) to colonel Rolins's Regiment of Riflemen; I was not with them at that time, as my Brother, H. B. came home (as soon as he had served out the first year) to recrut & enlist fresh soldiers for the afore sd Regiment, consisting partly of Virginia and part Maryland Riflemen, he was Successful in Inlisting 9 of his quota, joind the army, and soon after was taken, at Ft. Washington. I stayd at Staten Island, after the expiration of my first year, some Short time, until the Brittis trops took possession of the Island, and esscaped from them with Joseph Swearingen, made a narrow esscape (from the Enemy). I was Some Short time with my Uncle Nicholas Bettinger as he was called and spelt his name differently from the way my father spelt his name, but as taught by his School master, but I find, I am going on too lengthealy, and confusedly, and will try to conclude these Imperfect scralls as fast as I can, (to gain time) but hope to be able within the cours of a week, to write you more fully, after trying, to hunt our what I can out of the quantity of old papers that are about my house; but I am confident that most (If not all) the papers I had at the conclusion of the war, relative to my Services, were left, in my chest, locked up, with Title papers, & obligations for land.

Letter from George M. Bedinger relative to pension application

Lower Blue Licks 18th June 1842

My Dear Friend

I receivd you letter of the 25th ulto. I am sorry, that I was not able to answer you Immediately, owing to the low and debilitated State of my body, more Especially, the lameness of my right hand, (the fingers of which are stiff and croocked). I made attempts to write to you, (almost daily) intending to give you a brief Statement (or history) of all my Military Services from 75 when I was a volunteer under Capt. Hugh Stephen who was (the Oldes in rank of Captain in the army (at that time) from Virginia) to the last of my Services (as a major under Generals St. Clair ... surely p. 284 & Wayne.

I had got on with my intended letter (to you) until I had filled nearly two pages, as large as this sheet, & at different attempts and times). But, on attempting to read it I found it, so difficult, and tedious ... that I Reluctently had to conclude that I, at this time and under such present Circunstances, aught not to tier your patiens to read what I had written & could not myselfe read. I have therefore this morning (as my hand has got better) began a new most greatfully do I feel, and with pleasure, acknowledge your favourable attention to my claims.

I think it is quite probabel, that Some of the papers I had sent on, relative to my claims, for a Pension, were Lost as I think Colonel John Chambers (... that that I cannot exactly recollect, what he said, but from that time I have, been fearful, that some of sd papers are missing. My Brother Henry Bedinger Sent on this depositon of Peter Fisher, who was then (I think) the last, of the Soldiers of My Company in Colonel Darks Regiment (that I now recollect. Daniel Bells, deposition was taken in mason County, at the Court hous in Washington and thier was a man of the name of John Peck, who knew me and was often in conversation mentioning this having Served In Colonel Darks Regiment, & I intend to have

[p. 124]
have his deposition taken on the same and in the Court house, when and where Bells was taken but, on that Same day, and within an hour or less Peck departed this life and which I think happend before I and Bell left the court house. Now if the testamony of his widdow, or any of his family or of the clerk Marshall ... would now be of Service they could be had.

Some time Since I departed from home on purpose to go to see John Chambers, of Mason County, on purpose to take his deposition to prove that he knewe at the Seig of York, I got as far on my way toward his home place at Mays Lick where I just heard of his death, (he livd about 4 miles from Mays Lick. I intended (about last March) to have made an attemp to go to see the widow Thornsburg, an old lady) the daughter of Major Thomas Swearingen. Said Sweringen knew me from the time I was five years old, I was intimately acquaind with all his children, he came with me to Kentucky the Spring 79 to Boonsburg his son on Van Swearingen was killd at St. Clair's defeat was a Captain in My Virginia Battallion.

his Thos Sweringens Nephew White ... Morgan a double Cousin, and brother in law also of my Battallion, was wound at the Same time (Since dead) all this and much more, I was confiden, I could have proved by her, but before I started to see her, I heard of her death. I think she was about 5 or so years younger than I am, and I am in my 86 year. I do not now recollect if any person living in Kentucky, that was in the army at Boston Seige, in 1775 except my selfe and it is now dificult for me (week and frail as I am) to hunt up proof from their families, although this could be done, to coroberate better and positive proof. I was verry unlucky In loosing all the most valluable papers I had, soon after the peace of 1783 early in the Spring 84, I got to Kentucky after leaving my home, (near the mouth of Sedeling hill Creek where I had valluable mills,

[p. 125]
Ressted Sd homeplace place previous to my departure to Kentucky, to Joseph Doniphen, the Father George Doniphen, who now livs in Augusta, when I left my sd place I left my books papers cloathing &c. In my chest (I think well lockd) and secured (as also my household furniture, & knoing Doniphen to to be an honest man, (previous to that time in 79 he came to Kentucky with me in 79. I remaind in Kentucky about two years, and most of that time In the wilderness, and in the frunter Settlements & Exploring the wilderness between Green & Cumberland Rivers, and also along the Tenenissee State line as far as was then allotted to the officers & Solders of the Virginia Continental Line to enter Locate and

Survey thier lands South of Green River. In doing this business I was exposed to great danger and privations and which on the first of April 1784 were so allarming that although Surveyors were appointed, both for the Virginia Continental and State Line, allso superintending officers, with full powers direct and controul all sd business and although there were getherd at that time about 30 of said officers who came to locate and survey their lands with many depeties yet on holding a council the times were thought too dangerous. Therefore by a large majority declined doing or attempt at that time to proceed in said business. I was not present at sd council but was on my way alone within I met Jacob Myers just west of Ky river on the trail from Lexington to Louisville also alone who first inform that the officers had declined surveying. I pushd on through the thick cane zig-zag along a narrow but still muddy trace at times, but path, when near a Station of I then I pass on when I get I got to Louisvile & found that no surveying could (soon) be done, I determind not to relinquish all hopes of accomplishing, as far as I could, what I had undertaken, determined to go (alone) and Spend my time in exploring the land between Green & Cumberland rivers in attempting to find valuable land to locate, I accordingly

[p. 126]
To Colonel   Surveyors
ly set out alone had come, Marshals, office stayd all night, saw Lewis Fields, (who was then a young lad with whom I was acquainted), (he was a warmhearted friend) he urged me not, to go

alone, ... that if a snake, should bite, me or an Indian kill me, no one would know my fate. We slept together that night, & next morning when I was ready to leave him, and finding he could not prevail on me to decline going, he said, if he had a Shirt more than he had on, he would go with. I told him I had a Shirt to spare, but I could not ask him to make a sacrifice so great and had it not in my power to make him compensation, for so grat a favur. He went with me, and suferd much, (But Dr Sir, I ask your pardon, for all my Tediouss Digressions from a Short, plain, Statement which I ought, and do wish to give but, I find my head is nearly as weak as the hand I write with is lame). You I trust, will pardon me in both, as they seem, unavoidable. But hope hence to be more concise. I went on trips on business, within 2 years, Suferd much, was only half of that time, In the uninhabitted wiilderness. The last time I went out to Survey, I was out 108 days & near 120 days, (without bread) went twice to the Delaware Indians, to make Peace, Sufferd much, from Rheumatism in 86, when home & to my great mortification on examining my chest Ifound it rifled, and all my most valuable papers, taken lost, or gown, among which, I think were dischares appoint & perhaps Setlements, and memorandum and among which I think was one Given by Colonel James Wood in Gen. Scoots Brigade and Major Genl Stevenses Division which States that, Benony Swearingen & (myselfe) (whether he calld me George M. Bedinger, or Michael Bedinger, I do not recollect, as although I whas crisend George Michael after my Uncle, & Godfather, George Michael, I was allways when young calld either Mike or Michael, & that we had Distingushed our Selves in the most brave and extraordinary manner on the day of the action or Battle of the Germentown

[p. 127]
as the end of the 4 page is blotted and Interlined I here mention again the Honorabe discharg Given to Benony Swearingen and myself and as I have began on on other Sheet. If you have time to spare, I will beg to give you as brif an account as I Can, of the reason why we BS & GMB were at the Battle of Germentown viz. We had but Just before we prepared our selves for that trip, heard of the Battle of Brandiwine, and that our army stood in great nead, of all the troops that could raisd, to keep up their spirrits, which were then supposed to be sinking fast, & as My own brother Henry, was then in prisson, and had been taken at Ft. Washinton, my brother Daniel who was also taken, at the same time, and placed & who had sufferd on bord of the Brittish Prisson Ships, until more than ⅔d perish before they were paroled, or exchand, for the army Burgan taken near Sarratoga by Genl. Gates. I had therefore, as My Mother was a Widdow, and without a son at home I could not constantly remain in the army, altho I had heard from good authority, that I had been appointed an Ensign in the army) but I was allways willing to turn out as a volunteer and do all I could. Benoni Swearingen was nearly in the Same Situation his Brother Joseph was a capt in the army In Colonel Toddes Regiment, his mother a widdow & as soon as we could prepar our Selves, we left Shepherdstown in Virginia, armed

with hevy Swords, and good Rifles, & Joind the army, were in the Battle of Germentown remaind with the army afterwards until their was no prospect of another Genl battle soon, then Got an Honerable Discharge as above sd and came home. You abjured to me in your letter that If I have any discharg Settlement or other papers I believe I have Not any now at this time. I have a small book ... of Receipts that has been lent to me by a Grandson of Captain Hugh Stephensons small Receipt Bok I this day counted Eighty one Receipts given to Stephenson by sd 81 of his including officers & Soldiers

[p. 128]
The Company were on the first day of January Paid up according to said book to the 1 of January 1776 after my brothers ware taken at Fort Washington and had been placed on his parole within certain prisson bound at a place calld Flatbus (as well as I can recollect), but there he had to pay (I think) $2 per week, or go into close confinement; and thet in Specie, which was then very Scarce, and hard to get but, I determine, if it took all all I was worth, and all I and his poor disstressd mother could get with which to ... him from close confinement I then as often as I could get money, I took it to camp, put it into the hands of a commissary of prissoners, and thence, it would generally get to him safe, but when I had no other means, I would borrow whiche I did and with all I could do, I at last had to sell the small Patrimony consisting of 110 acres of land which I sold on credit, for (as as wel remember) about 2 £ ponds curency per acre for continental money an

which acpreshiated before I was fully paid to about 40 for one, I was Indeed made very poor, and that Intirely occasiond by the confidence I had In the Continental paper money and in my ... to the army not only as a Soldier in 75 & ... & in 77 as a Liut. in Captain Wm. Morgans Company of Riflemen, but also often as a vollunteer, without pay, when I carried money to camp, for the use of my brother, and others, and when I also, took and ... both money cloaathing and nurishment especially some home-made blankets, most of which were sent to our Soldiers, and Officers when at the Vally Forge at that time they were Nearly naked and barefoot in the ded of winter. But I have agane forgotten to be concise, let it rememberd that although I was allways a Sober & Indestrious young mand. I became poorly and from my zeal and long,

[p. 129]
1779 Services, in the army & ...apendent conciquences on the 1st of March, 1779, I Started to come to Kentucky. But as to my service under captain Wm. Morgan, as a third Lieutenant This company although I have now no document or paper of any kind to prove sd service I hope their is some documentary evidence of the Services of Colonel Thruston, who was our Colonel, and with whom Captain Morgan Company and other ... (I think) about 400 men I think about on the 4th day of March 1777 at a place then calld Pascataway In N Jersey near where I think the eneny had a large portion of their army perhaps Burlington where Capt Morgand & Lieutinent Edward Lucas of our company with a fue men wen to Sho them-

selves to the Enemy to draw them out after them while our main force were to lay in ambushe, but the the enemy followed so fast with ther Infantry, cavalry and Light artillery, that, our sm soon gave way & precipitately retreated their was a I think a captain wilson, who lived when I was late in Berkly, had his arm broke (from a wound ... in sd action, who was well well acquaintid with me and my brother Henry has livd within 3 or 4 miles of him many years I think if he is still living would be a good witness to establish that short campain, and I thing if I could get the deposition Robert Lucas former Governor of Ohio and now I think governor of Iawa who is the Son of William Lucas the Second Lieutenent in the sam Rifle Company in which I was 3d Lieutenant and or Capt Wm Morgan. About 2 years since I saw, Capt Thomas Morgan a son of late Abiatham Morgan who and grand son of Colonel Wm. Morgan and a Nephew of mine he told me he had papers that would prove his grandfathers appointment and Service as I have above stated and I hope that his deposition can be had and it may be a clue if any records of it can be found It is quite probable my name and rank will be found with theirs. In looking over Some papers (a few days since) I noticed the depos or a copy of

[p. 130]
A Deposition of <u>Ralph Morgan</u>, taken about the year 1815, In a Suit in Chancery In Madison County In which I was Plant. and Wm. Martin & Joel Walker, Def. I had a cornrigt preemption warrent, enterd on an Improvement I made In company with 9 or ten others all of whech but

one comes with me to this State then Caintucky County. Joel Walker had a claim that interferd with my own, I had been Induced to think as I had a preemption and older older claim, altho he by Surveying, Earlyer than I did, and got an older Pattent than I had, that as I was in the army of the US at the time others were Surveying that curcumstance might help my claim which induced me to question him, on the subject and what he knew of my being in the army, he then in answer & Stated that he knew me from a small boy that I went to boston, at the commencement of the war, that I was also with his father: (having found a coppye of Ralph Morgan's Deposition, I will try to State his answer altho my hand is now quite stiff viz.

I was acquainted with G. M. Bedinger from a small boy, until this day which is upwards of fifty years, and in the year 1779 the sd Bedinger and my self and a number of the neigbours started for Kentucky on I believe arrivd at Boons Bourgh in the 4 April the same year, and about the first of May following collected a party of ten men, to go and Improve land, then he states the names of sd company, where we went, and what we did, covering a space of 30 lines about locating, &c &c) (then says) That sumer we went a camppapaign against the Shawney Indians, and the said Bedinger was one of that campagn, and after that the said Bedinger was Generally in the Service of his country during the old Revolutionary war and had been In the service of his country to Boston before that period and I also know, that he the said Bedinger never made or claimd any other Improvement but the one aluded to in the country and it is my belief that said Bedinger would have carried his into Grant

[p. 131]
Grant a great deal Sooner than he did only he was actually in the Service of ths Country at the time the major Part of of the Surveying was going on. As thier is nothin more In R Morgans Deposition relative to my services, and as as it is with dificulty that I can hold a pen I will only mention, that I thint I took Major Sauire Greys deposition who I think knew me well at the Siege of York. I took his deposition but whether on hearing that it would be of no use to me, in my land suit, I had any thing done with or not; I cannot find it now. It may have remaind in the Clerks office. Gregg has departed this life. Some of thes hiers I recollect have some time since written to me on the Subject of trying to ged a pension for him I had then forgotten but since have an Imperfect recollection but know I took his deposition. Thier has been a great number of letters directed to me, by the friend, and heirs, of the officers, and Soldiers, of the Revolutionary war, wishing to obtain my depositions relative to thir services in the revolutionary war. I have most generally declined giving them, not because I would be unwilling to do them all the Justice in my power but because my Memory (when I was I think in my 31 year of my age was ruined by a mos dredful Spell of the nervous fever I was about 7 months confined to my bed and it was generally belivd I could not Survive. I have never Since been able to recollect many things that happend Some years before or a fue years after that time. Indeed, my memory has

never been lood since, and of late years is failing fast as I am now in the 86 year of my age, have have often advised those who call on me to prove their Services to My Brother, Henry Bedinger whos memory is Still vastly better than my own, though I am more than three years younger. Dr Sir I am now In doubt whether to Send you this hastily written lines fearing you will not be able to read what I have written as my long hand the last fue days has got no better, but I think rather worse.

When I saw my Son B F B last, I askd him to write, to one or both of our Senators In Congress for me

[p. 132]
me in relation to my applecation & claims for a for a Pension. I think about two months have Elaps since, & I have not Seen him nor heard, whether he has written, or not. I fear that his present embarrasments have prevented him from writing, as I have heard he was quite low spirited on account of not being able to pay his debts at this time of almost General distress, and as I have now have niether time, nor strength of body or mind fully to do justice to my claims I think It may be as well to let my case lay over until you meet again In the next session of congress, unless you should think this delay may be injurious to my Interes. I am Confident that, my claims, or Statements, can, yet, (after a laps, of the Great length of time, & under (all contingences considerd) be placed, out of doubts, as not only partially but generally known by most of the most earlyest and most noted Disstinguished Settlers in

this State, and many of our later, Inhabitants, who have attended to the Histories of our Country, must have taken notice of some of them, as In H. Marsshals first book or history (which was published some years before his second History of Ky) (In two vollumns). In the the first of sd Books he mention my Serveses under Colonel boman more fully, than he did in the last History, but in the first vollumn of the last hisy. Page 91 I will only here Introduce a short Extract 7 line from bottom viz., "Volunteeors were now calld for, In the name of Colonel John Bowman, who was to have the command, and who appointed the Rendezvous, at Harrodsburg, his own residence. Their was no want of ardour in either officers or Soldiers. Bengamin Logan, John Halder James Harrod & John Bulgon, were Captains George M Bedinger, who had been in the war to the eastward, was chosen adjutant, and many of the best men in the country ware privates: of whom their ware near 200. The expediton moved in the month of July. Its destination well known, and its march well conducted." I will decline farther quotation from this vollumn and refer you to the deposition of Jesse Hodges taken at his own hous In Madison by Squir Bush and sent on among my papers

[p. 133]
papers in or with my application for a Pension I will only here remark that Marshall in this volume has not been as full as he was In his first Book. In that he mention the charge made on the Indians when their Great Captain & commander Captain Blackfish was killd, he in that case men-

tiond me with a fue more In particular, that had made charge at that time, but ... is omitted in this first vol of the second edition of his History. I now recollect that at the time the Honorable Danial Wabster first came to Maysville I was Introduced to him he invited me into the carriage in which he came from Maysville to to this place when a young Gentleman in his suit ... on hearing my name, read In a history of me or about me, but as their are several histories that have honourd me by noticing some of my services, I do not recollect who was the author of that book. If you happen to be in company with that Respectable and Disstinguished character I hope he can and will, If he thinks me worthy of his attention and perhaps remember my General character and probity, State his opinion of me to some of the members of both Houses of Congress. I have Several very old and distinguished friends and acquaintances In both Houses that if I had had the use of my hand and health and Strength to set up, to write and at the same full confidence In my head, I should long since have written. I now hope that altho I am getting older I may Shortly be Stronger and more able to write, and if that should fail that one of my sons will be to see me, and write for me. I have here at this time <u>John McClangs Skitches of Weston History</u>. I find In sd Book, pag 282 of the expect scetch of ... Gen Arther St Clair and on the 283 and 284 where our army were the position and ground taken near on the river (he calld) St Maries. In stating the position of St. Clair's army, page 184, line three from top says the Second line was composed of the Battallions of Major Major Gather & Bedinger under the command of Lieut Col Darke; but St Clair's official letter from Ft. Washington, Nov. 9, in sd sketches page 362 in giving an account of the the lines of battle mentions and the left wing consisting

[p. 134]
Letter from George M. Bedinger to a dear friend

Lower Blue Licks June 26 1842

My Dear Friend

I Receivd your letter of the 25 ulto. I am sorry, I was not able to answer you immediately, owig to the Low & weak state of my health & esspecially, the lameness of my right hand. I made (allmos) daily attempts to write to you, a brief Statement, or history of most of my military Services from 1775, when a soldier under Capt Hugh Stephenson then, the oldest Capt (in Rank from Virginia, to the last of my Services (as a Major) under Genls. St. Clair, & Wayne.

I had gotten on by (piece meals) as I was not able to set Stil long at a time, & in the cours of a fue days after I had written Several pages, of a large Sheet, I attempted to read, what I had written, I found it difficult for me to read what I had written, but concluded to wate a fue days Exspecting one of my sons either D. P. or B. F. B. to be here & write for me, they did not yet, come. After that my hand and health (I thought) was beter, I began a new letter, viz. on the 18 Inst. I continued again (by piece meal) until I had written 1 or 2 pages more, a great part of which I found it was difficult for me to read, and what was (perhaps) worse, as my memory is bad, I often (as the saying is) put the cart before the horse, not recollecting ...the time when said occurences happend, and as my handwriting had Improved but little and fearing that too

[p. 135]
too much of your time would be required to read such a lengthy & perplexing a letter, I gave that out also, (for the present, and as nether of my sons have yet arrivd I have this morning concluded to wate no longer for them, (or either of them) but state to you as well as I can, in answer to your letter, that Immediately after Peace 1783 a number of the Revolutionary officers applied to me go out to Kentucky and Ohio, to locate and Survey their Millitary Bounty lands for them, to which I ageed, and entered into written contract with, Colonel William Darke, Colonel Joseph Swearingen, Gen Samuel Finly, Capt Abraham Shepherd, By brother then Capt. Henry Bedinger & Lieut Daniel Bedinger. I accordingly soon after left my home near the mouth of Sidling hull Creek in the Edge of Maryland (where I had verry valluable mills, both Grist and Saw Mills). I rented sd mills to an old and well tried friend, who in 79 came with me to Kentuky & raisd corn with me in Kentucky. I left all my most valluable papers, I think well locked up, in his house & in his care. I also left my houshold furniture clothing there came to Kentucky, remaind here more than two years exploring the willderness, was full half of my time outside of the setlements I went out 4 long trails, and a few short ones. I was at one time 108 day out & nearly 100 day of sd time without bread sufferd much, (Excus this

digression) when when I got back to my home I found my chist had been

[p. 136]
broke open my papers books & clothes, I well as I can now recollect wer all (or near all) taken and I think with them all the the papers relative to my Serises prior to that time were I think then left to me and gown. I have lately borrowd a small receipt book, of Capt High Stephen (My Captain in 75 & 6) from his grand Son, which book I have now in my possession in which are still containd, the the names of 81 or his company whos recepts are still to be Seen and which I hope to Shew you when you return, and from which, I think their has bee a mistake made of about 11 days accoding to the meeting held at what was calld Stephensons Sprng in June near Sheperdstown Suposed 4 & 5 1825 fifty years after our departure from thence to Boston, in which time (I thin) of our meetin a mistake of 11 days may have been mad, by those then living. I mention this becaus if there is a mistake that it may be rectified, and it is not strange that in fifty years a mistake of 11 days was mad, with those who (long since) had no memorandom of sd time.

In sd Book I find the following Receipt:
Roxbury Camp Jany 1st 1776

Receivd of Capt Hugh Stephenson four pouns thirteen Shilings, & one penny, In full of all wages due me, for my Services of as a Soldier in the United Calonies from the 26 of June 1775 to this day

Test Sam Findly   Recd for me
Michael Bedinger

I was then allways calld Michael, or Mike altho when I was christend, My uncle and Godfather as those men who Stand for children (in old times were call, and as my uncle Stood for me they then gave me the name of George Michael, but altho this was the Case Major Thomas Swearingen Enterd my preemtion in Kentuck in the name of Michael Bedinger at the end of my first years Service or soon after I was informd by Lieut Kelly of our sd Company

[p. 137]
"that I was to hav, or had an appointment In his company In a Regiment of Riflemen to be composed of men raisd In Virginia and part Maryland and in which Regiment, I expected to Serve I Stayd some short time after my first year had Elapsd in the army, came home by Philadelphia, on the day of the declaration of Independance on the 4th July 76. My Brother H. B. who came home Some time before, and had, as a Lieut nearly recruited his quota of fresh Solders, and soon after when he Got his complement joind his (Colonel Rolins') Regiment, I having got home after them although I ment to join the Same Regiment remaind at home a Short time (with my Mother) who had but 3 Sons then old enough for Soldeirs, the youngest of the 3 was 15 years old when he Joind the army who also joind Rolis Regement, and Both my brothers were taken at the time fort Washington Surrenderd; the sd Rifle Regement sufferd greatly and Defended the Fort bravely kept the Enemy at bay, killd many of the Hessians fell but were at length compeld to retret into the Fort when it Surrenderd under Colonel May.

(Please excuse the above digression as it is natural to speak or write of them we lovd in old times.)

I was on my way to Join the army previous to the Surrendder of Ft. Washington, several times but could not get Places the Enemy being in the way. I was opposite the ferry house which was below Trenton, when the Enemy occupied sd hous, as a guard house, I Saw some persone from our Side, cross the delawer opposite to sd house saw Smoke rising from them as they ran, and after a fue guns had been shot (small arms) I Saw the house in flames, I then Came home and In November or december Joind a Company of Riflemen of which Colonel William Morgan was our Captain, Edward Lucas William Lucas & My Self were chosen Lieutenants by Sd Company

[p. 138]
A copy of Peters Fishers Deposition
Peter Fisher
State of Virginia
Jefferson County   to wit

Personally appeared before me the subscriber a Justice of the peace in and for the county and State aforesaid Peter Fisher of said county who being duly sworn deposeth and saith, that he is well acquainted with Majr. George M. Bedinger that the said Bedinger commanded a company of Militia in the year 1781 said company march from Shepherds Town Virginia to the Sieg of York, when Cornwallis was captured; he was Capt. of the company also acted as Adjutant whilst there, and for a Short time Major, that he said Fisher was a Soldier in his Company from the time they marched until their return. Thus were in Service about

[p. 139]
County) and which Company Joined the Corps commanded by Colo. Charles M. Thruston of Frederick County Virginia, proceeded to oppose the Brittish Army in Jersey. This deponent knows not how long said Corps remained in Service, but the men composing the company it were allowed a tour of Militia duty.

Also that Said George M. Bedinger volunteerd his Services and was in the Battle of German Town on the 4th of October 1777.

That the Said George M. Bedinger Joind a Corps of volunteers in Kentucky commanded by Colonel Bowman made an attack on an Indian Town north west west of Ohio in 1779 were unsucessful, Compelld to retreat with loss. Said Bedinger also for the Greates part of the ...

[p. 140]
Deposition of George M. Bedinger, at age 78
State of Kentucky}   To wit
Nicholas County

Personally appeared before me the subscriber a justice of the peace in and for the County and State afore said, George M. Bedinger, of the said county who being duly sworn deposeth and saith that he is 78 years old & that his reollection is weak, he has yet a recollection of Peter Fisher of Shepherdstown which place was formerly in Berkely County, but is now in Jefferson County Virginia who he is confident was a soldier in the Revolutionary war, and in May 1781 Marched in a company of Militia from Shepherdstown in Virginia to the Seig of York (where Cornwallis was Captured) and that he this deponant, was a Captain and commanded Said company of Militia in Colonel William Darkes Regiment, and was also adjutant in said Regiment & for a short time Major and Several diferent times when Specially calld on, did the duty of Brigade Major.

That from the best of his recollection and information he thinks the said Fisher was a soldier in said company from the time they marched until they returnd that they were in no General Battle but that said company were in two instances were Exposed to Extreme danger, and in one of which, of being cut of, or captured, near York; (but acts of bravery hear he thinks are it needless to mention) but that after his sd company had Served out their Milita tour they to the best of his recollection and beelef were honouraly discharged and allowed pay and ration to their homes. The time they were in service he thinks was about 5 Months that Sd fisher and this deponent were raisd in Sheperdstown and lived many years near to gether.

That this deponent from the time he was 4 years old to the commencement of the Revolutionary ware when he was past 18 lived in Sheperdstown & he then, sd Fisher lived there also most most of sd time, but that he Continued to make Shepherdstown his home only a few years after ...

Estimate of crop yields from farm

```
250                         17
    |         | 60           14
    | 150     |30 at 300
    | 120     |
_____
        270           6
    Corn — 30 acres at bl   300
    60 acres wheat at 5 bus  750

              1100
reeping or cralelong    60 |
Seed wheat   30 |
2 hands 2 month         40 |
                       130
```

July the 4th ... calcuelation for the farm for one year from March 1836 if life & health permitt

Part of copy of G. M. B. Depo for Peter Fisher

[p. 141]
Deposition of George M. Bedinger, at age 78
State of Kentucky
Nicholas County

    Personally appeared before me the subscriber a Justice of the peace in and for the county and State aforesaid George M. Bedinger of the said County, who being duly sworn deposeth and Saith: That altho he is 78 years old & his recollection weak (as he had a severe spell of sickness at the age of 31 years when a nervous fever of 7 months runed his memory, so far as to disable him from recollecting many of even the most import transactions that happened then, and for years previous to said sickness, he has yet a recollection of Peter Fisher of Shepherdstown which place was formerly, in Berkely County, but is now in Jefferson County, Virginia, who he is confident was a soldier in the Revolutionary War, and in 1781 Marched in a company of Militia from Shepherdstown in Virginia to the Siege of York Where Cornwallis was captured, and that he this deponent was a captain and commanded said company of Militia in Colonel William Darkes Regiment, and was also adjutant in said Regiment and for a short time Major, and at several diferent times when specially calld on did the duty of Brigade Major, and from the best of his recollection and information thinks the said Fisher was a soldier in said company from the time they marchd until they returnd. That they were in no generel Battles, but that said company were in two instances exposed to extreme danger, & in one of which, of being entirely cut off or captured. In this last mentioned case Colo. Darke with less than 1000 men, chiefly Militia, marched from our camp near Williamsburg to the subburbs of Yorktown (in sight of and within reach of the enemy's fire; their cavelry bing in motion, a solid column was immediately formd, and prepared with fixed bayonets to recive their charge; in this bold position we remained a short time then returnd to camp near Williams burg. It is belived the enemy then consider'd our manoeuvre was intended to draw them into an ambush, or that our army were near us*; the other case alluded to

*this, it is believed, sav'd us from a defeat.

[p. 142]
aluded to happened during the Siege, where common acts of bravery he thinks need no description; his sd company behaved with such conduct that he does not recollect of any complaint being made of any of them and after they had servd out their Militia tour they (to the best of his recollection were honourably discharged & allowed pay & rations to their homes, the time they Seved he thinks was about five months but is not certain. He has no papers nor documents now to enable him now to render a full and more correct statement that he knows of.

25 Saracters is 255 Stage ferriages at 37½ is
15 63¾   55
      31½   52   38   17
              11   4
       ¼   ───
             ───   ───   385
             .52   152   55
              52
                          ───
             ───   935
             572   152
                    572   acres P.
                          10.59 P
             ───
                    160   1659   3.15
                          13.74 thirteen
acres 74 γ   Then
comes the soing of the 10th
187½   /5   62½
200 is 150   75
 50   37 50   20 62½

189 37½ $95 62½
       4.16
      99.78½

[p. 143]
State of Kentucky   } To wit
Nicholas County   }

    Personally appeared before me the Subscriber a Justice of the peace in and for the County and State aforesaid George M. Beding of the said County who being duly Sworn deposeth and saith That altho he is 78 years old his recollection weak he has yet a recollection of Peter Fisher of Shepherds Town formerly in Berkely County, but now Jefferson County Virginia who he is confident was a Soldier in the Revolutionary war in 1781 and marched in a company of Militia from Shepherdstown in Virginia to the Siege of York where Cornwallis was captured, and that he this Said deponent was a Captain and commanded Said Company of Militia in Colonel William Darkes Regiment and was also adjutant in said Regiment and sometimes when call on as Major & Brigade Major that he believes the said Peter Fisher was a soldier in sd company from the time they Marchd until they returnd which he thinks was about five months and having servd out the time required were discharged and that the said deponant says that the said company in two instances at least were exposed to extreme danger, and in one of which cases, of being intirely, cut off or captured by the Enemy, as they were in Colonel Darks Re... and under his command when (when he withe a detachment of less than 1000 of the American troops chiefly Militia marched to the suburbs Yorktown in sght of the enemy 10 times the ... & number reach of their fire and again returnd to camp near the main army near Williamsburg. The eny could it is belvd could certainly have cut of this detachment

[p. 144]
if they had not belived the amercan army was comeing on near said dietachment, (which detachment from the Boldness of its position, the spead and quickness in forming a sollid collumn, flanks & rear facing outwards, nealing & with bayonets fixd & prepared to recive the ... charge of the enemies cavelry) they would It is blivd have attackd and defeeted said detachment as their was then no part of the american army suficiently near to have savd them from being defeated.

A ... of Genl Paags Declaration inducd a fue remarks here on the westorn concernes

At diferent times served In the Revolutionary war

		Months	Days
under Capt H Stevenson about	12	21	
under Capt Wm Morgan		3	3½
Both			
In the army under Gen. Sedly & Wood		1	19
in Kentucky	7		abut at
Little York	5	0	
if he recollects right about 7 days to ...			½
The power Williams Burg			7
of this time he has a faint recollection		21	20
an the velly forge volunteer			
as Adjutant Captain & Brigade Major			5
as a Captain about			
as Lieut more than		3	
as capt say	5		
as comissary	2		
as quarter master & adjutant 6 weeks			

Peter Fisher
April 1835}   of no use more
   G.M.B. left Shepherds Tn March 18 '79 was
exposed to great danger from the 15th of March
to the 1 of november as a augetint
as a privet solder 1 y 2 m

[p. 145]
Letter from George M. Bedinger
Sulavens Station   June 4th 85
Sir
As I cannot possibly attend at the first part of the genl. Court in Lincoln I think propper (though In the greatest haste) to give you a brief account of Circumstances relative to a Clame I have of 400 acres of Preemption on Muddy Creek. In the year 1779 I came to this Country Rais'd corn and continu'd at Boonsburg about 7 months. In defense of it went to Chillycaughphy under Colonel Bomman in order to do my Courtry all the service I Coud. as I hope by such Conduct to be Intitled to the advantages of an Early adventurer. However I made but one Improvement in the courtry which is the above mentioned made the 4 of may by Cutting all the small saplings and gribs and deadening all the trees on Near a half acre of ground on a West fork of muddy creek that Empties into the Middel fork a small distane below Benoni Swearingens Tract, I obtain'd a certificate for a Preemption of 400 acres. In Consiquane of sd improvement got a Preemtion warrent and had it located the 29 of April 1780 on sd Emprovement as you see inclosed. I sent Cash for the surveying sd land which Coud not be done as the Indian In that fruntier Part of the

Country ware troublesome untill the Beginning of last may when I attended and had it surveyed Square' with the Improvement in the center which the surveyor was so Particular as to chain to place it Exactly in the Center. It may not be Impropper to Enform you the my services in the Continentle army may likewis be mentioned as they In a great measure hinderd me from attending here Earlyer. I never until the first of may 84 knew that any Person pertended to Claim any Part of said land, but then heard it had been survyd for Jool walker uppon this Information I Enquierd and found it surveyed the whole but 20 ares is included. I Walkers surveys of settlement and 500 acre Preemption. Uppon Inquiry I was told that Sd walker lived in Carolina had Pay come to this country Early but had made no Emprovement though he had by some means got a certificate from the Commishioners (at any rat I know he has none where he has surveyed his settlement) that he had given one M Thos. Allen one half of the Chance of his settlement and Preemption to locate it for him which he did in the big bend of muddy creek about one mile from gateses land. But finding that Place belonged to older Preemptons he has moved it down adjoining what he then Calld gateses land and has returnd gateses land by another name

[p. 146]
name in order to make the Entry Bare a B. better face. My Entry is of an Earlyer date than his Preemption but as to his certificate from the commitioners it is Earlyer then my entry though I believe not Earlyer than my Certificate. I went to

this sd Allen last may and told him my right he said he wished to have it settled without going to law accordingly I wated and did Caviate him immediately as he told me he had wrote Walker and hoped to be Empowered from him to leave it to arbitration and by such means the time of Caviateing in this County Expired finding this to be the cas I sent to my brother in Berkely to have him cavated in Richmond; have not heard from him since but think he has Caviated for me. I have been detaind by unavoidable acksadents in the Reservd land for the Continental line and coud not by that means be ready with my Evedences for trial and am now fourced to this measure and think it a faviourable opportunity by Capt Shelven. I hope to see you in a fue days this is only to Put Back the tryal. My witneses to the Emprovement are Major Thos. Swearingen Capt John Holder Colonel Wm. Morgan Bennony Swearingen John Tailor Samuel Dure, Ralph Morgan, Capt John Constant and Joseph Donathen all Priasent and helped to make sd Emprovement. I think Samuel Estill Capt Gess Can Both Enform you that he is not in the Big Bend and the former that Allen one Intended to survey sd land whare he claims and was hinderd by him and others I have included a bit of Paper on which I have Plotted the land in the manner it lays. I con Clud in haste as the Barer is waiting

    Your Friend Geo M. Bedinger

[p. 147]
Land claims on Muddy Creek
James Gates by Samuel Henderson this day claimed a Settlement and Preemption to a tract of

Land in the District of Kentucky lying on Muddy Creek about two miles above the Log Lick including his Improvement by setling and raising a Crop of Corn in the Country in the year 1776.

Satisfactory proof being made to the Court they are of Opinion that the Said Gates has a right to Settlement of 400 Acres 400 aires of land to include his Improvment in the Preemption of 1000 acres adjoining and that a Certificate issue accordingly.
28th December 1779

Joel Walker by Samuel Henderson this day claimed a settlement and Preemption to a Tract of Land in the District of Kentucky ly on the big bent of Muddy Creek about one mile above Gates land by settleing and raising a Crop of Corn in the year 1775

Satisfactory proof being made to the Court they are of opinion that the said Walker has a right to a Settlement of 400 acres of Land to include the above Location and the preemption of 1000 acres adjoining and that a Certificate Issue accordingly.
28th Decemb. 1779

Michael Bedinger by Colo. Swearingen this day claimed a Preemption of 400 acres of Land at the State price in the District of Kentucky lying on Muddy Creek on a west branch of the same below Benoni Swearingens about ¾ of a mile from the main Creek to include his Improvment by settling in the Country in the month of April 1779

Satisfactory Proof being made to the Court

they are of

[p. 148]
opinion that the said Bedinger has a right to a Preemption of 400 acres of Land to include his Improvment and that a Certificate issue accordingly
 6th January 1780

 James Gates Enters 400 Acres by Virtue of a Certificate &c lying on Muddy Creek about two Miles above the Log Lick to include his improvment Entered Feby 3rd 1780

 Edward Russel Assee. of James Gates enters 1000 acres of Land upon a Preemption Warrant No. 675 lying on the waters of Muddy Creek to adjoin his Settlement as Assee. of sd. Gates to begin at the South East corner of the sd Settlement and to extend South & West for Quantity
 Entered the 15th of March 1783

 Joel Walker Enters 400 acres by virtue of a Certificate &c lying on the big bent of Muddy Creek about one mile above Gates's land
 Entered February the 3rd 1780
This Entry has the precedence of James Gates' Entry of the same date.

 Joel Walker enters a Preemption Warrant of 500 acres adjoining his Settlement on the upper side on Muddy Creek and to run up the Creek for quantity.
 Also 500 acres on the lower side of said Settlement and running down the Creek for quantity.

Entered May the 30th 1780

Joel Walker Offers the following amendment to his Location of 500 acres part of his Preemption Warrant No. 406 bearing date the 30th of May 1780 which adjoins his Settlement on the lower side on Muddy Creek (Viz Beginning at Edward Russels North West corner of his Preemption two sycamores standing on the south bank of Muddy Creek about ½ a mile above Banta's Cabbins running from thence the said Russels line South 30 poles to a hickory and Walnut thence West 100 poles to the sd Walkers Settlement corner thence with the said Settlement line N. 438 poles to the North East corner of said Settlement

[p. 149]
thence East 188⅔ poles thence South to said Russels line 408 poles thence with the said Russels line West 88⅔ poles to the Beginning.

Also amends his Entry of 500 acres the remainder of his Preemption No. 406 which adjoins his Settlement on the upper side on Muddy Creek, Viz, to begin where said Settlement line crosses muddy Creek on the North side thence up thence up the Creek as it Meanders so far as if reduced to a straight line at right angles with said Settlement line will amount to 182⅔ poles thence North so far that turning at right angles to intersect with the Course of the Settlement Will give the quantity

November the 29th 1783

Michael Bedinger enters 400 acres upon a

Preemption Warrant and locates the same on a west fork of Muddy Creek that empties into the middle fork a small distance below Benoni Swearingen's tract including his improvment.

Entered the 29th of April 1780
Copies Entries
Gates, Walker and Bedinger
Mechees
Shuley
Jan Eve... Clainy

[p. 150]

Depositions relative to land claim of George M. Bedinger

the deposition of Joseph Proctor taken agreeable to notice given by George M. Bedinger taken on the 8th day of June 1815 at the place Claimed by Bedinger as his improvement to be red as evidence in a suit in chanceroy now depending in the Madison Circuit in which suit said Bedinger is Plantiff and William Martin the Heirs of Joel Walker & others are defendants who being of Lawful age and first sworn deposeth and saith by way of Questions and Answers.

Quest. by Pft: Mr. Proctor do you remember a company of about ten or twelve men coming to Boonsborough through the wilderness about the seventh of April 1779 and if you do who ware the Persons as well as you can recollect at this time.
Answer: I do remember that in the spring 1779 their was a company of men the number of whom I do not at this time recollect amongs whom was Thomas Swearingen Benona Swearingen Samuel Duree Michael Bendinger.

Quest. by complainant or Oft: do you recollect that William Morgan Ralph Morgan John Strouse or any others ware along.
Answer: I recollect all you have mentioned and Joseph Donathan ware along.

Quest. by same: Did not Colo. William Morgan Ralph Morgan Thomas Swearingen, Benona Swearingen, & others raised Corn near Boonsborough that Summer.
Answer: I believe their was corn raised by that Company.

Quest. by same: did not the inhabitants of that Station live very Friendly that summer.
Answer: yes.

Quest. by same: was it not a common thing for them to tell one another of their improvements. and when a strong Party went out would they not Generally tell where they would go to and what they had been adoing especially in makeing improvements and from those & other Circumstances you will please to inform us and answer Sutch Questions concerning sutch circumstances as you will deem necessary relative to my claim at this place to bring to light things

[p. 151]
that hapned at earley and Daingerous times both before and after my Improvement was made.
Answer: it was a costamary thing amongs the Inhabitants of Boonsborough to tell one another of their Improvements & where they had made them. it was Generally to the Inhabitants of

Boonsborough when a company went out what they ware agoing after. it was a General thing for them to tell one another of their improvements & where they had made them. I remember that, that Company above mentioned some time in the spring or summer of the year of the year 1779 Started out into the Country in order to explore the Country, and to improve Land. When the company returned to Boonsborough they informed the inhabitants of that place that they had made some improvements, upon the waters of muddy creek, which improvements I discovered or Saw several of them in the year 1780, that was said to be made by that Company, upon the waters of muddy creek but the improvement that we are now at, I did not discover untill some years after and the reason why I did not discover it Sooner was because it stood in a thick cain break, but when I did discover it, the marked & Belted trees was Generally standing the tree on which I suppose the letters ware made was ded and the letters not Discoverable the Shugar that was belted had grown up & a ridge grown round them where they ware belted

Quest. by same: did you hear that I had an improvement on the waters of muddy creek.
Answer: I did.

Quest. by same: when you discovered this improvement, what was your impressions and who did you think it was made for.
Answer: when I discovered this improvement my impressions ware that this was Bedingers improvement my reasons for believing this to be

Bedingers improvement was that the branch was Calld bedingers branch at that time and the Land then inclosed by Survey.

Quest. by same: do you think that this Branch took its name from the improvement made hear by that Company.

[p. 152]
Answer: I Should suppose it did, and by the company it might have been calld Bedingers branch ever since it was made but I do not recollect at this time

Quest by same: was not muddy creek a place of notoriety with the inhabitants of Boonsborough in the Spring 1780.
Answer: with all the woods men & hunters it was

Quest by same: is their not a remarkable bend at the mouth of what is now Calld. woodses fork on muddy creek.
Answer: their is.

Quest. by same: is their a remarkable cedar Cleft and A riffel or a fording place Just below it, on the creek, nearley a south course from this place.
Answer: their is a cedar Cleft nearley opposit where Mr. Gilbert now lives. I think a little above the mouth of woodses fork. A Riffel and crossing place Just below it.

Quest. by same: do you suppose that a Person well acquainted with the place that we are at now, could have directed an enquiring Locator of com-

mon Abilities and reasonable exertion to have found it from boonsborough being a person that was acquainted with the creek at the time.
Answer: I Suppose that A person being personally acquainted with the creek and with the improvement might have direted and enquirer by reasonable exertions to have found the place.

Quest by William Martin one of the defendants: do you or do you not know the above mentioned company where they setled and lived for the next five or six years after 1779 and where they now live.
Answer: I think some of them returned back to Verginia or to where they came from, and I think some of them Staid in this Country Ralph Morgan staid in this Country & I think that Colo. Swearingen Staid in this Country about boonsborough some time. old Mr. Duree and his family moved back to this Country and Setled at Boonsborough

[p. 153]
And Setled at the white oak Spring, as far where they are now I cannot tell for they have left time. I Suppose that Thomas Swearingen died in the old Country and Mr. Duree died in the State of Kentucky. I moved from Boonsborough to Estills Station the first day of March 1780 after that I was not so well acquainted with the Places they setled, nor the length of time they lived at them.

Quest. by same: how far do you think it is from Boonsborough to this Place And was their any Leading trace from Boonsborough to this Place.

Answer: I think it is about 16 or 17 miles from this Place to Boonsborough. I do not recollect of any Leading trace from Boonsborough that led directly hear. their was a trace Calld. the old log lick trace, that led through this neighbourhood and through a piece of Land that was calld Things rich Land.

Quest. by same: how far is it to Estills Station from this place.
Answer: I suppose it is four or five miles.

Quest. by same: how far from this place to the log lick trace.
Answer: I suppose about one mile or a little better.

Quest. by same: how long did you live at Estills Station after you moved their.
Answer: I lived their several years but how many I do not now recollect.

Quest. by Same: did you or did you not frequently while living at Estills Station frequently hunt up and down muddy creek.
Answer: yes.

Quest. by Same: State if you can or as near as you can in what date you Became first acquainted with this Place.
Answer. I do not know.

Quest. by same: was you acquainted or did you ever See the improve-

[p. 154]
ment while living at Estills Station.
Answer: while I was Living at Estills Station I new new nothing of the improvement only from information untill I moved out hear upon the waters of muddy creek near where Elihue Greens now lives. I then Became acquainted with this improvement and believed it to be Bedingers improvement from information mentioned.

Quest. by same: State if you please how many improvements you was acquainted with on the waters of muddy from Estills Station to Boonsborough while Living at Estills Station.
Answer: their was one on the waters of muddy creek thats calld. Boleses improvement or Spring, their was another that was Calld. Crewes' improvement their was another they calld. Swearingens improvement, their was another between this and Swearingens and their was another down upon the creek below this that was made by the Bantas, their was another improvement made down not far from Woodses Mill, And Gateses improvement which was on the waters of muddy creek and their was another down by where Sqr. Lipscomb now lives and I do not recollect of any more at this Present.

Quest. by Compl: how large do you think that the improvement was that was made hear.
Answer: from the Sign I could discover from the time that I became acquainted with this Place I Should about one quarter of an Acre maybe a little more for I was not particular to examin.

Quest by Dft.: State if you please as near as you can in what date you became acquainted with the above mentioned improvement.
Answer: I Became acquainted with the most of them in the summer 1780.

[p. 155]
Quest. by complainant: do you know where Cpt. John Holder John Constant Joseph Donathan John Taylor lived & Died.
Answer: Cpt. Holder lived some time in Boonsborough he then Crossed Kentucky River setled a Station & lived and died their. John Constant to the best of my recollection setled at Strouds Station, and lived their some time and then moved out some distance from the Station and their Died. Joseph Donathan staid some time in Kentucky how long I do not remember, went back to the old Country and I understand that he is since ded.

Quest. by Same: do you Suppose that Ralph Morgan when Calld. on to testify the truth would Deviate from it wilfully when duly sober.
Answer: I have been acquainted with Ralph Morgan ever since the year 1779 he was a young man in them days and appeared to be a respectable young man but since has taken to drink and has I suppose nearley ruined himself by that Pratice, but I Suppose when calld. upon, when duly Sober to give his deposition he would Declare the truth. And further the deponant Saith not.
                                        Joseph Proctor

Also the Deposition of Thomas Warren taken at

the same time and place who being of Lawful age & first sworn deposeth & saith by way of Questions and Answers.

Question by the Plantiff: Mr. Warren, will you please inform us how you first became acquainted with this place as my improvement. tell us what you knew relative to it which you may deem necessary in this suit,
Answer: I came with Majr. Bedinger and we did not hit On the improvement we then turned back to the mouth

[p. 156]
of Woodses lower fork then Mr. Bedinger said after seting a few minutes, said he could find the improvement by discovering a Cedar Hill and a Clear spot on the other side of the creek from hear, that he obsered that he or some of the company had shot a Dear in we then turned back and took up this Branch untill we came to this improvement and he said it was his own.

Quest. by same: how long do you think it was from the time that we left Estills old Station untill I found my improvement.
Answer: I Suppose it was three or four hours.

Quest by same: did we come along any water Course or did we Come a long a path.
Answer: some part of the way we came along the path and some part of the way through the woods.

Quest. by same: could not a Person that was acquainted with this place who had ever been at

Estills Station and was acquainted their have found it in mutch Shorter time.
Answer: yes.

Quest. by same: did you ever hear of my ever being at Estills Station before the time that you came to Shew me the path to muddy creek.
Answer: no.

Quest. by same: how far do you suppose that we are from the Bent at Woodses fork in muddy creek.
Answer: A half A Mile or three Quarters

Quest. by same: would it not be an easy matter for a Person acquainted with that bent to have directed an enquiring locator to my improvements at this Place and is not this the first west branch below woodses fork and said bend.

[p. 157]
Answer. I believe it would not have been a hard matter if he had been acquainted to have direted him and I believe this is the first west branch below woodses fork and said bend.

Quest. by same: how many years do you suppose it was from the time the improvement was made untill we came to hunt it.

Answer: I do not know.

Quest. by same: do you know when this Branch was first calld. Bedingers branch.
Answer: I think to the best of my recollection in

1784 or in 1785, but it has been so long ago that I cannot recollect it.

Quest. by Defendants: State if you please when you became acquainted with muddy creek.
Answer: in February 1780.

Quest. by same: State if you please how many improvements you knew on the waters of muddy creek from your first acquaintance with it untill the years 1784 and 1785.
Answer: their is Thomas Swearingens their was two that was Calld. Benona Swearingens Boleses at the spring, Crewses & Webers, Gateses & Durees & Bridges and in that period of time Bedingers.

Quest. by same: State as near as you can how long you lived at Estills Station before you saw this improvement.
Answer: I suppose it was four years.

Quest. by same: the first three or four years that you lived at Estills old Station was you not frequently hunting in these woods.
Answer: yes.

Quest. by same: how long do you think Mr. Joseph Proctor lived at Estills station before he moved out.

[p. 158]
Answer: he came the first day of March 1780 and lived their one or two years and moved over to Magees Station lived their some part of a year

& then moved back and to the best of my recollection he raised eight crops at Estills Station.

Quest. by same: did you or did you not know any forks of muddy creek known by the name of the middle fork or the west fork in an earley date.
Answer: I did not.

Quest. by same: state if you Pleas what was the names of the Different forks if any in an earley Date.
Answer: their was Little muddy creek Woodses fork and the Viney fork.

Quest. by same: how far is it from Estills Station to this Place.
Answer: Some where about five miles.

Quest. by The Complainant: from the appearance dont you belive that Bendingers and Swearingens Improvement was made at the same time.
Answer: by the appearance of the Chops on the trees it appeared as if their was not mutch ~~difference Odds~~

Quest. by same: did it appear that their was any Difference in the age from the Chops on the trees and do you believe they ware made about the same time.
Answer: I did not notice particular but from the Chops on the trees it appeared their was not mutch difference.

Quest. by same: how far from the mouth of the Branch that we are now on Calld. Bedingers

branch is to down to the mouth of the viney fork.
Answer: About one half mile.

Quest. by same: Mr. Warren, do you believe their was any difference.
Answer: I do not know.

Quest. by same: when we went out the first time and missed the improvement how far did we go back.
Answer, I do not recollet... And further the Deponant saith not.   Thomas Warren

[p. 159]
Also the deposition of Evan Watson taken at the same time and Place to be red as evidence in the same suit who being of Lawful age and first sworn deposeth and Saith by way of Questions & Answers.

Quest. by the complainant: Mr. Watson will you Please inform us how long you have been acquainted with muddy creek and particularly with the branch we are now on Calld. Bedingers Branch.
Answer: as well as I remember twenty one or two years ago this last winter I was Showed it by one Mr. White he calld. it Bedingers branch and it has gone by that name ever since as far as I know which was as Soon as I was acquainted with muddy creek.

Quest. by same: have you generally heard it Calld. by that name ever Since.
Answer: yes and not by any other Name.

Quest. by same: did you not understand that I had a corn right Claim on this Branch and do you or do you not Believe that It took its name from my improvement.

Answer: ever since, I have been acquainted with muddy creek I always have understood that Majr. Bedinger had a corn right on this branch and it appears reasonable to me that the branch should have taken its name from the improvement.

Quest. by Dft.: do you know any thing of your own knowledge as respecting his Claim or his improvement.

Answer: I do not more than I am hear to day which is the first time I ever was hear. And, further the deponant saith Not,   Evan Watson

Also the deposition of William Briscoe taken at the same time & Place to be red as evidence in the same Suit who being of Lawful age & first sworn deposeth & saith by way of Questions and Answers.

Quest. by Complainant: Mr. Briscoe give sutch information respecting my Claim hear as you Can.

[p. 160]
Answer: I think it is about twenty two or three years ago Bedinger and Alen Came to my house and Staid all night and asked me whether I could Shew Bedingers improvement I told them that I had been showed an Improvement, that I believed Mr. David Lyntch shewed me, and said it was Bedingers improvement. we came and found the

Place then Bedinger and myself carried the Chain & Thomas Alen the Compass the County Clerk of Mercer, and we run to find Benona Swearingens Improvement but whether we found it or not I do not recollect.

Quest. by same: Mr. Briscoe do you believe that Thomas Alen was ether Agent or a part owner of Joel Walkers Settlement & Preemption.
Answer: I considered him to be interested in Some Case but I do not know how.

Quest. by Defendant: does this Place seem familiar to you to be the same Place that was shewed to you.
Answer: I think the Lying of the ground appears to be familiar but it appears to me that the improvement was the other side of the Branch. And further the deponant saith not.

his
William X Briscoe
mark

Nicholas Hocker
Adjourned untill ten O Clock to morrow at this Place

Agreeable to Adjournment we meet on the 9th day of this Inst. at the place adjourned to and Proceeded to take the several depositions (to wit) the deposition of David Lyntch taken at the same place and said time to be red as evidence in the same suit who being of Lawful age & first sworn deposeth and saith by way of Questions & Answers.
Present: George M. Bedinger Oft. and William Martin & John Evans Dfts.

Quest. by the Oft: Mr. Lyntch is the place that was Shewed to you John Crooke & others by Ralph Morgan last Spring as Bedingers improvement.

Answer: Yes it was Shewed me some time in May 1814, by Ralph Morgan.

Quest. by same: was it when you was Carrying the Chain for John Crooke the County Surveyor the day he was Surveying my four hundred acre Preemption founded on this improvement & on thes Branch or about that time.

Answer: it was the day we carried the Chain that is it was one of the days.

Quest. by same: Please to inform us how this Survey corresponded with this improvement & the natural Boundaries, to wit the Branches, laid down on the Plat.

Answer: Beginning at the Black oak Corner, and running the Course of the pattern. then Starting from the improvement and running a west Course untill the two lines intersects seem to correspond very near together.

Quest. by same: I suppose you mean that the improvement was found near the Center.

Answer: it was no Great distance from the Center.

Quest. by same: I wish you to inform us as near as you can recollect when you first saw this improvement and mention Sutch other circumstances as you may deem necessary in this Suit.

Answer. the first time that I ever saw this improvement it was in the summer 1780, and I have seen it often since 1780.

Quest. by same: do you remember, a marked tree standing near where we are now are in the improvement and also tell us about the Size of the improvement.

[p. 162]
Answer: their was a marked tree stood in the improvement and the improvement the first time that I saw it appeared as if their might have been near a half an Acre with the under groth cut out and the Brush heaped, and the trees Belted.

Quest. by same: do you remember how the tree was marked.
Answer: It was blazed or a block taken out, and letters made with red Led or red Chalk.

Quest by same: I think I just heard you say the tree was Choped in in two Places a block taken out and hewed a little.
Answer: my meaning by the block being taken out was choped in below and then above and the Piece taken out between the two chops.

Quest. by same: what kind of a tree was it.
Answer: It was a white oake.

Quest. by same: do you believe this to be the tree.
Answer: yes.

Quest. by same: did you see it when it was green and before it fell down.
Answer, yes.

Quest by same: tell us all the years in which you have since seen it, as near as you can recollect.
Answer: I have seen it so often that I cannot tell which years I have seen it the oftenest.

Quest. by same: do you think you have seen it in the years 1780 & 1781 & 1782 & 1783 and Generally since.
Answer: I saw it in 1780 and often since.

Quest. by same: have not you since your first acquaintance with it untill now, been Generally informed that is was Bedingers improvement.
Answer: when I first saw it I did not know whose it was. but it was in the year 1784 or 1785 that I heard it Calld. Bedingers improvement.

Quest. by same: how far do you think it is down this Branch to muddy creek.
Answer: about three quarters of A Mile.

[p. 163]
Quest. by same: did you ever know or hear of any other improvement Calld. Bedingers improvement or any other Branch calld. Bedingers Branch.
Answer: no.

Quest. by same: did you ever know of any improvements Calld. Majr. Thomas Swearingens or Benona Swearingens if you did say what you know about them.

Answer: their was an improvement up above this near muddy creek about three miles which was Calld. Thomas Swearingens improvement, Benona Swearingens was about one mile and a quarter or A mile & a half. the improvement was Just on the Bank of muddy creek.

Quest. by same: do you remember, on which side of muddy creek the improvement of Benona Swearingens was.

Answer: it was on the other side to where we are now.

Quest. by same: was not muddy creek a place of notoriety in them times.

Answer: yes.

Quest. by same: how earley did you become acquainted with muddy creek.

Answer: I got acquainted with muddy creek in February 1780 and with Thomas Swearingens and Benona Swearingens improvements in the summer, 1780 or at least with the improvements that was Calld. theirs.

Quest. by same: how many improvements did you know by the name of any of the Swearingens improvements or did you know any others but the two that you mentioned.

Answer: I knowd. none but the two that was Calld. Swearingens improvements.

Quest. by same: was not you as well acquainted with the woods & the different Branches of

muddy creek near this Place and Estills Station in year 1780 & 1781 & 1782 & 1783 as almost any other Person at the Station or that you are acquainted with.
Answer: I was tolerable well acquainted with the woods and Branches but their might bee some others as well acquainted with them as I was myself.

[p. 164]
Quest. by same: did you or did you not hunt a great deal upon these waters.
Answer: yes.

Quest. by same: did you take notice of a block taken out of a shugar tree in the Spring of the year 1814 in the Presence of Ralph Morgan John Crooke and others and do you recollect the number of groths from the appearent chops in said tree and was it taken out of this improvement.
Answer: I was present when they cut the block out, and from the grothes I could not tell anything about the grothes, for I could not see how to count them for I had not my Specks.

Quest. by same: when you first saw the improvement how did you or did you not think it was about the same age of Thomas Swearingers and Benona Swearingens.
Answer: from the appearance of the improvements, they appeared like they might have been all made in one year.

Question. by same: could you recollect whether or not their was any difference from the appear-

ance in the age of these improvements.
Answer: I dont know that I examined them in Particular as to see whether their was any difference or not but from the appearance they seemed like they might have been made Shortly one after the other. but of the difference between making of the improvements I cannot tell anything about it.

Quest. by William Martin the Dft.: State if you Please when you first became acquainted with muddy creek, if their was any forks that bear a name & what their names was and in what date they took their names.
Answer: I got acquainted with muddy creek in February 1780 little muddy creek in February 1780 and Woodses fork some time earley in the summer 1780 the viney fork some time earley in the summer 1780 and the Branch that they calld. Woodses lower fork, was Calld. the indian Branch in the Spring 1781, the Branch that was Calld. Kings Branch in the year 1781

Quest. by same: did you ever hear of any forks calld. by the name of the middle fork or the west fork of muddy ceek from February 1780 to the Present day.

[p. 165]
Answer: No,

Quest by same: State if you Please what sort of ground & what sort of Land & what was the situation of this Place when you first saw it.
Answer: it was Pretty heavy cain a little round

the improvement but just at the improvement their was but little.

Quest. by same: could you have directed any Person enquiring for Bendingers improvement of Common understanding so that he could have found it in the years 1780 & 1781 & 1782 & 1783 or untill 1784, from boonsborough or Estills Station and if you could state in what date you could have done it.
Answer: I could not have directed any body to Bedingers improvement untill I heard it Calld. his,

Quest. by same: was their any trace leading from boonsborough or Estills Station by this improvement in the years above mentioned.
Answer: no.

Quest. by same: was their any leading water course or any water Course known by any name leading from Estills Station or Boonsborough to this Place.
Answer: no.

Quest. by George M. Bedinger Compl.: could you or could you not have directed an enquiring Locator of Common Abilities and reasonable exertion to have found this Place calld. Bedingers improvement from the first year you became acquainted with it untill 1783 or 1784 from either boonsborough or Estills Station.
Answer: I could have directed any Person of Common understanding from either of the places so as they could have found this improvement but

I Should have told them that I did not know whose it was in 1780 or 1781 & 1782 and 1783.

Quest. by same: is not Estills Station upon the head waters of Auter creek and Does not that run into Kentucky river near Boonsborough.
Answer: the Spring that we made use of was the waters of Auter creek and runs into the Kentucky river about one mile above boonsborough.

Quest. by same: did you see the letters Plain on the large white oak,

[p. 166]
tree at this improvement that you described that was marked with the red Chalk.
Answer: the Letters was plain and inteligible when I first saw them for any body that could have red them might have known them and they Stood so for several years and further the deponant Saith not

his
David X Lyntch
mark

Also the deposition of William Cradelbough taken at the same time & Place to be red as evidence in the same suit who being of Lawful age and first sworn deposeth and Saith by way of Questions & Answers.

Quest. by George M. Bedinger: Mr. Cradelbaugh was you at Boonsborough in the Spring 1779 and do you recollect a company consisting of Thomas Swearingen Benona Swearingen John Constant

Joseph Donathan Wm. Morgan John Taylor George M. Bedinger Samuel Duree & Sunday others coming to Boonsborough in April 1779.

Answer: I remember them all very well, but John Taylor.

Quest. by same: you recollect the most of us raising corn at Bushes Settelment near boonsborough in the summer 1779.
Answer: I cannot recollect it for I was so mutch from home.

Quest. by same: was you well acquainted with muddy creek in the years 1779 & 1780 and 1781 And 1782.
Answer: not up this way at all.

Quest. by William Martin the Defendant: State if you Please in what date the Branch we are now on was Calld. Bedingers branch.
Answer: I cannot tell what date but I Suppose about twenty three or twenty four years ago since I became acquainted with this branch calld. Bedingers branch and I went into North Carolina in the year 1787 or 1788 and Staid their four or five years and returned back again

[p. 167]
to Kentucky and then Setled at warens Station and lived their about three years and then moved to where I now live.

Quest. by Complainant: from your first acquaintance with this Branch was it Calld. Bedingers

Branch.
Answer: yes.
And further the Deponant Saith not
        William Cradlebaugh

Also the deposition of Thomas Lamb taken at the same time & Place to be red as evidence in the Same Suit who being of Lawful age and first Sworn deposeth and Saith by way of Questions & Answers.

Quest. By the Compt.: Mr. Lamb how long have you been acquainted with this Branch calld. Bedingers branch.
Answer: the first time that I ever it, it was in the year 1803.

Quest. by same: was it then Calld. Bedingers' Branch.
Answer: Yes, Mr. Watson told me it was Calld. Bedingers branch and brought me through on this side of where Tyra Martin Lives now and told me that, that was Bedingers Land. and then we turned down through the lain between Cpt. Gilberts and Tyra Martins, and then I went Back to Virginia and made one Crop their in the year 1804 and that fall moved back to Kentucky and I have heard it calld. by the Peopel that was living hear bedingers branch ever since and I have not heard it Calld. by any other name since.

Quest. by Wm. Martin Dft.: was not the People Jenerally setled on muddy creek when you first became acquainted with it.
Answer: that Part of the creek that I was ac-

quainted with was Jenerally Setled. And further the deponent Saith not.

his
Thomas + Lamb
mark

Also the deposition of Samuel Gilbert taken at the same time and place to be red as evidence in the same Suit who being of lawful age and first deposeth & Saith by way of Questions & Answers.

[p. 168]
Quest. by Complainant: Mr. Gilbert how long have you been acquainted with this Branch that we now on hear.
Answer: I have been acquainted with it ever since the year 1796.

Quest. by same: when did you hear of my having a Claim hear on the said Branch.
Answer: in three or four years after I became acquainted with this branch I understood from the Neighbours upon this Branch. Some where their was an improvement belonging to Majr. Bedinger.

Quest. by same: has it not jenerally went by that name ever Since.
Answer: It has by the neighbours to this Place and by those far off. I dont know what it has been Calld.

And further the Deponant Saith not
<u>Samuel Gilbert</u>

Madison County Set. I do hereby certify that the foregoing depositions of Joseph Proctor Thomas Warren William Briscoe Evan Watson David Lyntch William Cradlebaugh Thomas Lamb and Samuel Gilbert was taken sworn and Subscribed to before me Nicholas Hocker, one of the Commonwealths Justices of the peace in & for said County at the place above Stated, on the 8th and 9th days of June 1815 given under my hand this 9th day of June 1815

        Nicholas Hocker. J. P. M C

Majt. Fee	$2.00
David Lyntch two days attendance	1.00
William Cradlebaugh same	1.00
Joseph Proctor one day	0.50
Thomas Lamb. Two days	1.00

The above Charges was paid by the Oft.

[p. 169]
6 Ken 8 & 9 of January 18,.
The deposition of Joseph Procter & others 1 to 6
8 & 9 Jan ...
Thomas Waren from 6 to 9
Evan Watson - 10
Wm Brisco from 10 to 11
Jan 9 1815 David Lynch from 11 to 17
Wm Cradlebaugh f" 17 to 18
Thomas Lamb 18
Samuel Gilbert from 18 to 19

[p. 170]
    The Deposition of Green Clay taken at the house of Robert Miller in the Town of Richmond Madison County on Saturday the 10th day of June 1815 to be red as evidence in a Suit in Chan-

cery depending in the Madison Circuit Court wherein George M. Bedinger is Complainant and William Martin and others are Defendants. This Deponant being first sworn deposeth and Saith:

Question by Defendant Martin: State when you first became acquainted with Estills Station and the neighbourhood.
Answer: I arrived at Estills Station about the 18th or 20th of October 1780 and made that my home until some time in the summer 1781. I became acquainted in the neighbourhood Shortly after I arrived there.

Question by same: did you or did you not make it your principle Business to make yourself acquainted with all the diferent claims of land in that neighbourhood.
Answer: that was my principle business.

Question by Same: did you learn of any improvement on the waters of Muddy Creek known by the name of Michael Bedingers improvement whilst you lived at Estills Station the first time you were in this Country.
Answer: I was well acquainted with an improvement called Tom Swarringens improvement and near Muddy Creek & have been often at it. I saw one or two other improvements on the east side of the Creek not fair below it. I understood that Benone Swarringen Claimed one of them. I have no distict recollection of having ever seen one called Bedingers Improvement.

Question by Same: State How many forks of

Muddy Creek had names at that time and what their names were.

Answer: I was acquainted with little Muddy Creek

[p. 171]
and Woods fork. There was the Indian branch that emptied into Woods fork, the Viney fork and I think the Hickory lick branch or fork, of Kings branch and the log lick branch and perhaps some others. There is a branch that empties into Muddy Creek a little above little Muddy Creek on which I was in company with James Estill, Colonel Boone and others at a time when he shewed what he called whortons improvement.

Question by Same: State how far you think it is from Estills Station to where Samuel Gilbert and Tyree Martin now lives or the branch now called bedingers branch.

Answer: I suppose it is about four miles to where Gilbert lives and I do not know bedingers branch by that name. I have been lately riding below Captain Gilberts and have heard a branch called by that name.

Question by the Complainant: General Clay do you recollect that before your Deposition was taken I proposed asking you if you were interested in the Claims of Thomas or Bennone Swaringins on Muddy Creek and that I was answered that I had not a right to continue asking questions as you was brought here by my opponents but was told I could answer my purposes in my time of asking questions.

Answer: I recollect conversation to that amount.

Question by Same: You State you arrived at Estills Station about the 18th or 20th of October 1780 in What time in the Summer of 1781 did you return to Virginia or did you return to Virginia between the 18th and 20 of October 1780 and the Summer following and came out again did you also in the Mean time go to Tennessee and other places and how long in that time did you Stay at Estills Station.

[p. 172]
Answer: I think that I returned for the first time to Virginia in July 1787 and between that time and the preseading October I went once to Cumberland and twice to the neighbourhood of the three forks of Kentucky. I was surveying in the present limits of Madison County and travling in the woods I considered Estills Station my home. I cannot say what part of the time was there.

Question by Do [ditto]: I wish you to State what you mean to convey by your answer to a former Question made by my opponent when you Stated the neighbourhood of Estills Station.
Answer: I had two Objects in view in answering the Question that if the Question related to the land laying about there I became acquainted with the land in that period. If it related to the Stations I became acquainted with all of them on the North side of Kentucky River and all on the South side from Danvill & Standford upwards.

Question by Same: do you not consider yourself

interested in the land on the Mouth of Woods fork claimed by Thomas & Bennona Swarringin and would not the establishment of their improvements clash with your interest.

Answer: I am interested with an entry that begins at the mouth of Woodses lower fork and Runs west and South I believe in a square for quantity in the name of Charles Lee for upwards of 5000 acres I believe I do not know exactly where Benone Swaringens claim is as to the boundary &c I am interested in a claim that covers part of Thomas Swaringins preemption of 400 acrs.

Question by Same: at the time Colonel Boone Shewed you and others where whortons improvement was, was not Colonel Thomas Swarringen also with you and did you not then and since frequently hear of the claims and improvements

[p. 173]
of Thomas Swaringin Benone Swaringin and Michael Bedinger, That Thos. Swaringin called for Muddy Creek That Benone Swaringen called for Thomas Swaringin, and that Michael Bedinger called for Benone Swaringen or a Small distance below Benones tract, that the above three corners Right preemptions were by Col. Swaringin Claimed and obtained for himself Benone Swearingen and Michael Bedinger and that as early as the sixth day of January 1780 and further that Entrys have Since been made for them all in their own names.

Answer: I believe Majr. Thomas Swearingen was in company with Colo. Boone &c. I do not recollect a long conversation at that time about them

but since have frequently heard of them. I have
no doubt but what I have seen the entries but do
not recollect what the Calls are. I Surveyed Thomas Swaringins preemption and have no dout but
I had the entry present with me. I fully expect
that I heard of the claims in those early day for
my Occupation was locating and Surveying lands.
                                        Green Clay
H Cy Paul
Will. Irvine cmcc
Green Clays first Deposition
taken June 10 1815

[p. 174]
    The deposition of Laurance Thompson taken
in the Suit of George M. Bedinger Compt. & Joel
Walkers Heirs defendants towit:

Question by Compl.: Capt. Thompson when did
you first come to Boonsborough.
Ans.: I came to Boonsborough the 24th day of
November 1780.

Question by Same: Was not Boonsborough the
Log lick The red Lick & Muddy Creek all places
of notariety at that time.
Ans.: They were places of general notariety and
is to this day.

[Question] by Same: Was you acquainted with
Cols. Thomas Swearingen Benone Sweringin
Ralph Morgan Saml. Duree Capt. John Constant
& Capt. John Holder & if so in what years &
where.
Answer: I was acquainted with John Holder

John Constant Thomas Sweringen Ralph Morgan Saml. Duree Benoney Sweringen In 1780 John Holder & Samuel Duree I knew at Boonsborough Thomas Sweringen Ralph Morgan and John Constant at Strouds Station in 1781 & 1782 and in the year 1783 or 1784 I became acquainted with Benoney Sweringen at Strouds Station.

[Question] by Same: Was you well acquainted with their general character

[p. 175]
I mean whether they were well and generally known in the Neighbourhood of Boonsborough Estills Station Strouds Station and other neighbouring Settlements & and whether they were respectable characters.
Answer: They were men of good characters and acquaintance at the aforesaid Stations.

[Question] by Same: Had Samuel Duree a son a son in law & daughter killed by the indians on or near the Log Lick trace which leads from Boonsborough to Muddy Creek and the Log Lick and where as near as you can recollect.
Answer: He had a son Peter Duree and Dina his daughter and his son in law John Bullock were killed in the Spring of the year 1781 and I with about 16 more burried the dead in a homely manner which men are all dead or out of the neighbourhood.

[Question] by Same: Have you ever been at the read lick and Estills Old Station and if so in what year.

Answer: I was at Estills Station and the Red lick In 1781 & 1782.

[Question] by Same: Did you become acquainted with any improvements on Muddy Creek and if so when were they.
Answer: In the Spring of the year 1781 in company with Capt. Nathaniel Hart on Muddy creek we passed some trees marked with red Chalk I inquired of him what improvements it was. He told

[p. 176]
me it was Sweringens and company which had been out improveing I think about a mile or a mile and a half from the red Lick or it might be three miles for what I know as I never expected to be called on to tell the distance.

[Question] By Same: If an enquireing Locater had called on you between the time you was with Capt. Hart on Muddy Creek above Mentioned and the 29th Nov 1783 and had shewn you the certificate and entry of Thomas Sweringen The entry of Benone Sweringen and the certificate & entry of Michael Bedinger for their corn right Preemptions do you not think you could shew when the impressions on your Mind were fresh have directed to have found them yourself but if you doubted would not have recommended them for information to Thomas Sweringen Samuel Duree or some other of said company for information where they might to a certainty have found them.
Answer: I suppose I could have directed a Lo-

cater so as to of found the Place, and I suppose he could have found the others by that.

Question by defendant: Capt Thompson how far is it to Strouds Station

[p. 177]
and what course from Boonsborough.
Answer: Nine or ten Miles about a northeast coarse.

[Question] By Same: How far is it from Boonsborough to where Bullock and Dina was killed and what course and how long did they live there before they was killed.
Answer: About 10 or 12 Miles from Boonsborough about a Southeastwardly course to the best of my recollection about 3 or 4 days they lived there.

[Question] By Same: How far from said cabbins to Estills Old Station and what course.
Answer: I suppose from 8 to 10 miles a Southwestwardly course.

[Question] By Same: State if you please if you ever knew of any fork by the Name of the Middle on the West fork of Bedingers branch of Muddy Creek as Places of notariety or Bedingers improvement as places of Notariety.
Answer: No I did not.

[Question] By Complanant: Capt Thompson as there are many large forks comeing in from both Sides of Muddy Creek which had no names when

Thomas Swerengen Made the three entries Viz. Thomas Swerengin Benoni Swerengen and Geo. Michael Bedinger was there any impropriety of calling the longest and in the middle fork.
Answer: No I see no improreity in caling the longest Branh the Midde

[p. 178]
fork furthermore the deponent sayeth not.
   Signed) Laurance Thompson

Commonwealth of Kentucky Madison County towit:
 I do hereby certify that the foregoing depositions were sworn to and Subscribed to before me Overton Harris One of the Justices of the peace for the County aforesaid On the 13th day of February 1816.
    Overton Harris J. P.
   A Copy Teste D. Irvine CkMCC
Bedenger
 copy
Cs Thompson
 deposition Laurance Thompsons
Walkers Heirs deposition
For Complainant
Taken the 13th of February 1816
Tax 50 Cents

[p. 179]
 Agreeable to notice given by the Oft. to the Dfts. in this suit, we meet at Samuel Garisons on saturday the 8th day of June 1816, to take the deposition of sundary witnesses, and Ajourned to the mouth of a branch on the East side of muddy

creek shown by the Plantiff for Benona swearingens improvement and proceeded to take the following depositions (to wit) the Deposition of Ralph Morgan taken at the time & Place above stated to be red as evidence in a suit in Chancery depending in the Madison Circuit Court wherein George M. Bedinger is Oft. and William Martin & others are defendants who being of Lawful age & first sworn deposeth and saith by way of Questions & Answers:

Question by George M. Bedinger Compt.: Mr. Ralph Morgan you will please to inform us what you know of Benona Swearingens improvement on muddy creek where it was made & whether you know of his having any other but the one improvement in this State.
Answer: I was along when Benona Swearingens improvement was made & this Place we are at now to the best of my knowledge is the place, the mouth of the branch seems very clear to me, as for his having any other improvement I never knowd. nor heard of any Claimed by him, and we were Generally together when he was in this Country I think we began to make one Between this & Thomas Swearingens improvement but was Calld. away and it was

[p. 180]
never set down nor Balleted for.

Quest. by Same: was the improvement you alluded to in your former deposition, made by the same Company that made my improvement on Bedingers branch.

Answer: it was and was made the 3rd or fourth of May 1779.

Quest. by Same: from what reason do you think that this Part of muddy creek was calld. the middle fork by the enteries of Thomas Swearingen George M. Bedinger & Perhaps others.
Answer: the reason I shall give is that their was forks coming in on each side for instance their is one that is now calld. Kings branch that comes in on the left hand side as we go Down the creek & heads with Bedingers branch, that this improvement is on Another fork on the right hand side comes in to the men creek about 200 Yards below the mouth of Bedingers branch now Calld. the viney fork & of Course the one between must be the middle fork & main fork which is the same thing.

Quest. by William Martin, one of the Dfts.: State if you Please how mutch work was done at the improvement you named that was begun and you was calld. away & it was not finished.
Answer: I do not recollect, but we began & done some, but I do not know how mutch.

Quest. by Same: was you acquainted as earley as the year 1780, 1781 1782 & 1783 on muddy creek farmillyar.
Answer: I was not.

[p. 181]
Question by Same: could you have directed an enquiring Locator to Benona Swearingens improvement from any other improvement on

muddy creek.
Answer. I expect I could from the improvements we made at that time, which was all I knew of at that time & in this way they might find it, it was the only one made at the mouth of a branch coming in Just above the improvement on the right hand side going down the creek.

Quest. by Same: how long did you stay at this improvement when you made it.
Answer: no longer I expect than we was making them.

Quest. by same: how long was it after you made the improvement untill you saw it again.
Answer: About six or seven & thirty years.

Quest. by same: Where did you live after you made this improvement the first three years.
Answer: at Boonsborough and Stroudes Station.

Quest. by Same: how far is it from this Place to boonsborough & Strouds Station.
Answer: I think it is 20 or twenty Od miles to Boonsborough and near 30 to Strouds Station.

Quest. by same: how far is it from this Place to Estills Station.
Answer: I dont know certainley but I would Guess five or six miles.

Quest. by same by the Dft.: What does George M. Bedinger give you for showing this improvement.

Answer: their never was a word past between us on the occasion.

Question by same: how long & in what dates did you live at Boonsborough.
Answer: in 1779 I lived at boonsborough & part of the year 1780.

Quest. by same: how long did Duree live on the waters of muddy creek.
Answer: I do not know.

Quest. by the Compt. Bedinger: Mr. Morgan do you beleive that this whiteoak was Choped round when we made this improvement, and that all these Saplins between it and the mouth of thes Branch has grown up since.
Answer: yes I believe it was and I think these saplins has grown up since.

Quest. by same: do you or do you not recollect many circumstances that hapned upwards of thirty years ago better than Some things that hapned only a few years ago.
Answer: yes.

Quest. by Same: did you ever go from this Place to Estills Station.
Answer: no. And further the Deponant Saith Not.   Ralph Morgan

Also the Deposition of David Lyntch taken at the same time & place to be red as evidence in the Same suit who being of Lawful age & first sworn deposeth & Saith by way of Questions & Answers.

Quest. by the Complainant: Mr. Lyntch will you please to inform us what you know or believe of Benone Swearingens improvement at this Place.

[p. 183]
Answer: I have known this improvement ever since the Spring of the year 1780 and was then told by James Estill that this was Benona Swearingens improvement and two or three years afterwards old David Guess told me it was Benona Swearingens improvement.

Quest. by Same: have you not frequently been hear since that time.
Answer: yes I have been at it often since.

Quest. by Same: will you describe what sort of an improvement it was when you first saw it.
Answer: the under growth was all cut down and the brush heaped, some trees Belted arand with a tomhawk or an ax, and their was a block or chip taken out of a tree, and some writing where the chip was taken out, which was done with red Chalk or Paint.

Quest. by Same: Mr. Lyntch do you recollect that Benona Swearingen ever came hear, and surveyed or began to survey round to include this improvement.
Answer: yes.

Quest. by same: do you recollect who was with

him at the time.
Answer: old David Guess and his son John Guess I think was with him. The others I do not recollect who they ware.

Quest. by Same: did they not leave their hatchet on the line, as they ware Surveying and request you to come for it, and how did they instruct you to find.
Answer: in one day or two after they ware hear surveying old Mr. David Guess asked me to come down to this improvement and to go out an east Course about two or three hundred yards and to look Stick-

[p. 184]
ing up in the side of a white oak for his hand hatchet & I went and found the hatchet from what he had told me.

Question by William Martin: State if you please how far you think it is from this Place to Estills old Station and in what date Estills Station was setled in & what time you went to the Station to live.
Answer: I Suppose it is about three miles from this Place to Estills old Station, Estills Station was setled in the last of January or first of February 1780 and I was their at the setling of it myself.

Quest. by same: in what date was it when Benona Swearingen came hear to make this Survey.
Answer: either 1783 or 1784,

Quest. by Same: State if Please why he did not finish this Survey when he came to make it.
Answer: I do not know.

Quest. by Same: State if you Pleas how many improvements was you acquainted with on muddy creek from where Bedingeor now claims up to Thomas Swearingens improvement from the Spring 1780 unto 1784.
Answer: I know of two improvements from Thomas Swearingens on the east Side of muddy creek to Bedingers improvement.

Quest. by same: State if you Please the size of the improvement that is on muddy creek between Thomas Swearingens & this Place now claimed for Benona Swearingens.
Answer: I suppose their was about one half Quarters or A Quarter of an Acre, that the under growth was cut,

[p. 185]
down & the Brush piled and a few trees belted round.

Quest. by Same: state if you Please the size of the improvement that we are now at.
Answer: I suppose their was about one quarter of an acre.

Quest. by Same: the improvement made between this Place & thomas swearingens, did it appear to be as old as the improvement made hear when you first became acquainted with it.
Answer: yes.

Quest. by the Oft.: Mr. Lyntch, did you ever know whose improvement it was above this and Below Majr. Swearingens improvement, and was it marked like the others, or was it marked at all.
Answer: I dont know of any Person claiming of it and I never saw any marked like the others marked with chalk or Paint.

Quest. by Oft.: Mr. Lyntch from the length of time which had Alapsd. since you was acquainted with the last mentioned improvement which was neither marked nor Claimed by any Person to your recollection had you not entirely forgotten it untill you was shown it again by Col. Estill & others.
Answer: yes I had forgotten it untill I was on the ground with Col. Estill & others, and further the Deponant Saith not.

     his
  David ^ Lyntch
     mark

[p. 186]
David Lyntch one day attendance as a witness
summonsd. by the Oft. $0.50
Ralph Morgan Same   0.50
Majl. fee   1.00

The Commonwealth of Kentucky Madison County Set. I do hereby certify that the foregoing Depositions was taken sworn and Subscribed to before me the subscriber a Justice of the Peace for Said County at the Place & time before Stated given under my hand this 8th day of June 1816.
    Nicholas Hocker
the above fees Paid by the Oft.

N. Hocker
A Coppy test N. Hocker J. P. MC
Coppy of
Ralph Morgans
& David Lyntchs
Deposition
June 8 1816
Morgan & Lynch

[p. 187]

The Deposition of Nicholas Proctor of full age &c taken at the house of Major John Grugell in the Town of Richmond Madison County, on the 14th day of June 1816 to be read as evidence in a suit in Chancery depending in the Madison Circuit Court wherein George M. Bedinger is Complainant and William Martin and the heirs of Joel Walker and others are defendants. The said Proctor bing duly sworn deposeth and saith:

Question by defendants When did you first come to Kentucky.
Answer: In the spring 1778.

Question by same: Where did you live after you first came to Kentucky.
Answer: at Boonsborrough.

Question by same: how long did live at Boonsborrough.
Answer: I lived at Boonsborrough untill sometime in the year 1780.

Question by same: when did you settle at Estills Station.

Answer: In the Spring 1781.

Question by Same: where have you lived since untill this time.
Answer: I have lived at and within five miles of Estills Station ever since.

Question by same: how long did you live at Estills Station.
Answer: I lived at Estills Station four or five years and in the Neighbourhood of the Station ever since.

Question by same: State what buisness you followed for the first one or two years after you came to Estills Station.
Answer: I have no particular occupation a part of my time I spied three months and ballance

[p. 188]
of my time I hunted and Traveled about through the Country.

Question by same: State if you please If ever you knew an Improvement on the waters of Muddy Creek known by the name of Bedingers improvement.
Answer: I dont recollect that I ever did.

Question by Same: did you or did you not see an improvement on muddy Creek Just above the mouth of little Muddy Creek and if you did state the sise of the improgement and what was the situation of it when you became acquainted with it.

Answer: I saw an improvement in the Bottom of Big Muddy Creek near the mouth of little muddy creek — it was a Small improvement the under Growth chopped down and piled the Trees girted this is as much as I recollect of the situation of the improvement.

Question by same: was this improvement above or below the mouth of little muddy creek.
Answer: I think it was above the mouth of little muddy Creek.

Question by same: Is there not some marks of an old improvement on a Honey locust walnut & mulberry stump at this time.
Answer: Yes there is.

Question by same: at what time did you become acquainted with that improvement and what appeared to be age of it.
Answer: I saw it in the year 1781 and it looked like it had been made about Twelve

[p. 189]
months or longer.

Question by Complainant: where you follow spying those three months you have said you were spying.
Answer: Wherever I was ordered to go different distances and different routs.

Question by Same: when you lived at Boonsborrough was you acquainted with Capt John Holder major Thomas Swearingin Colo William

Morgam Ralph Morgan Bennonia Swearingin John Constant John Taylor Joseph Donathas & Samuel Dure and myself.
Answer: I was.

Question by same: do you recollect that most or all of us came together except Captn. Holder to Boonsborrough in the spring 1779.
Answer: I do.

Question by same: were not the times very dangerous.
Answer: they were.

Question by same: have you any recollection of the above Company coming out about the first of may 1779 to make Improvements or have you heard of their having made Improvements about that time.
Answer: I dont recollect the time of the companys coming out But I heard afterwards of their making improvements.

Question by Same: Did or did not the Inhabitants of

[p. 190]
Boonesborrough live with the greatest affection friendship and harmony for each other to a greater degree than is commonly known except in case when our lives and support depended upon each other did or did we not consider ourselves as one large family in so much that when a load of meat was brought in it was frequently placed in the middle of the station for them all to come and

take freely.
Answer: The people in Boonsborough lived in friendship and harmony and what one had they nearly all had and what one knew they nearly all knew and in a word they were as a large family.

Question by same: were we not in the habit of telling one another where we were making our Improvements to pervent interferences.
Answer: They Generally told those that enquired.

Question by same: Was not James Estill & Captain David Gass two very well informed respectable and well established Characters for the truth and up wrightness and had they not as Good an opportunity to be acquainted on muddy Creek as any others.
Answer: They were.

Question by same: I think Mr. Proctor that you informed me that your recollection was not as as good as many others that you are

[p. 191]
acquainted with that unless you charged your mind Particularly about things you frequently forgot them that in your spying and hunting excursons you tooke notice of the object in view but paid little attention to any thing else.
Answer: People that I had been frequently acquainted with and many things that I have seen have sliped my memory at this time and I think it is a common thing with all men.

Question by same: Do you or do you not recol-

lect ever having been at the Mouth of a Branch near three quarters of mile above the ceder Cliff now near Capt. Gilberts on the east side of muddy Creek.
Answer: I do not at this time recollect that I ever was.

Question by same: Do you recollect ever Going from the mouth of the first Branch below Woods fork up along the branch about a mile on the west side.
Answer: I recollect Travelling on the Branches above the cane But I do not recollect being at the mouths of the branches at an early day.

Question by same: Do you recollect of ever hearing of a Branch on Muddy Creek called Bedingers branch.
Answer: I recollect hearing of some branch called

[p. 192]
Bedingers branch but I do not know how long it has been since I heard it called by that name.

Question by Same: Was not Boonesborough the nearest Station to ceder Cliff near the mouth of what is now called lower Woods's fork or was there any other Station near than Harrordsburgh in the first of May 1779.
Answer: Boonsborrough was the nearest Station to Muddy Creek and there was no other station nearer than Harrardsburg but Logans Station.

Question by Same: do you or do you not know when the diferent large Branches of Muddy Creek

Got their names or do you believed they had any in that early day, and distance from any Settlement.
Answer: I do not know when they Got their names and I dont think they had any established name in that early day.

Question by same: Did you or did you not when a spie go out some distance please to inform us of your rout or were you not Generally ordered out some distance.
Answer: We were some times ordered to go as far as the Kentucky River.

Question by same: might not there have been many Improvements in the neighbourhood

[p. 193]
that you knew nothing about.
Answer: There might have been Improvements that I did not see and if I had I have forgotten them.

Question by Defendants: did you ever know or hear of any forks on muddy creek know by the name of the west fork of Middle fork.
Answer: I have never heard of any fork on muddy creek that was established by the name of the west fork or muddy fork.

Question by Same: Was you acquainted with a Branch by the name of Bedingers branch as early as the 29th of April 1780.
Answer: I do not recollect that I did.

Question by same: did you know of an Improvement on Muddy Creek known by the name of Benonia Swearingins Improvement as early as the 29th of 1780.
Answer: I did not.

Question by same: when you hunted from Estills Station did you not hunt Generallly for five or six miles round on muddy Creek and its defferent Branches.
Answer: we hunted in different directions from Estill Station.

[p. 194]
Question by Compl.: Did you not generally go thirty or forty miles from Estills Station a hunting.
Answer: Generally when we made our hunts for Deer or Bear or Buffaloe we went ten fifteen or Twenty miles.

Question by same was not their not Great danger of Indians at or near Estills Station from the time it was first settled for three or four years.
Answer There was.

Question by Same: did not that danger prevent the Inhabitants from a General knowledge of improvements near at hand.
Answer: The danger of Indians near Station prevented people from exploring things near at hand.

Question by same: In cases when a number of men wished to make locations upon a creek where the forks and large Branches have no par-

ticular names would it not be natural for them to call them by names expressive of the course from whence they came and the maine branch being near the middle might it not with proprity be called the middle fork or main fork.
Answer: yes.

[p. 195]
Question by Compl.: do you not think that an Improvement so as made on muddy Creek for Bedinger by the Company herein alluded to on Bedingers Branch.
Answer: I believe Improvements were made on Muddy Creek for him and his Company. And further the deponant saith not.
 Madison County Court
  Nicholas Proctor
 The foregoing depositions was subscribed and sworn to before me a Justice of the Peasce for said County at the time and Place therein stated.
 Given under my hand this 14th of June 1816
  Will Miller J P
witness for defendants claimes his attendance for one day 50 cents
N Copy Atteste Will Irvine
Bedinger
cs Depo of
 N Proctor
c Martin & others
fee $1.25
Nicholas Proctor 14 June 1816

[p. 196]
 The Deposition Oswell Townsend taken this

15th of April 1817 at the house of Robert Miller in the Town of Richmond to be read as evidence in a suit in Chancery depending in the Madison Circuit in which George M. Bedinger in Complainant and Joel Walkers heirs are defendants deponant being first sworn deposeth and saith:

Question by defendants: State how early you Settled at Boonsborrough and how long you continued there and in its Neighbourhood and how early you became acquanted with muddy Creek and its waters and whether you have been acquanted with it ever since.
Answer: I came to Boonsborrough in the fall 1775 and Continued there untell the fall 1777 at which time I went into the old Settlements and returned in the fall 1779 — and have been acquanted with Muddy Creek and its waters from that time to this.

Question by same: was the branch of Muddy Creek now called Bedingers branch known at and before the 29th of April 1780 by the name of a west fork of Middle for of Muddy Creek.
Answer: I never knew it was called so.

[p. 197]
Question by same: was there any part of Muddy Creek on or before the 29th of April 1780 known by the name of the middle fork of Muddy Creek.
Answer: I knew of none Called by the middle fork of muddy Creek.

Question by Same: did you know any place on Muddy Creek known by the name of Bedingers

Improvement on or before the 29th of April 1780.
Answer: I did not.

[Question] By Complainant: where did you live from the fall of 1779 for the three following years.
Answer: at Boonsborrough and part of my time at Boons Station the north side of the Kentucky River about six miles north of Boonsborrough except the time I was in Tennessee in the Spring & Summer of 1780.

[Question] By same: did you know any of the west branches of muddy Creek by any particular name before the first May 1780.
Answer: now except Kings Branch that I recollect.

[Question] By same: after the fall of 1780 was you often on the waters of muddy creek.
Answer: there has not been a year since

[p. 198]
that time but I have been often on muddy creek.

[Question] By Same: Do you recollect that you was on that part of muddy creek where Bedinger Branch comes in in the years 1781, 2, & 3.
Answer: I do not recollect that I was as high up as there about that time.

[Question:] By: How far below Bedingers branch did the log lick trace run Boonsborrough cross muddy creek and the mulberry lick.

Answer: I think nearly four or five miles the log lick trace crost and the mulberry lick trace crosses a mile or more below the mouth of Bedingers branch.

[Question] By Same: were these traces of which you have spoken in your last answer well know to the people at Boonsborrough in the years 1780 & 81, 2.
Answer: I beleive they were by hunters and those that hunted above the mulberry Trace crossed muddy Creek at the mouth of what is now called the Hicory lick branch.

[Question] By same: was you acquainted with Colo. Thomas Swearingin.
Answer: I had no intimate acquantance with

[p. 199]
him I knew him when I saw, that was all & I think he represented this Country in the Virginia legislatur in the year 1781 or 82.

[Question] By Same: do you know when Woods upper fork the hickory lick, Viny fork and little muddy creek first received their names.

Answer: they all received their names from the people about Estills Station in the year of about 1781, 2, 3.

[Question] By same: what were the Characters of Capt. James Estill and David Guest.
[Answer:] they were men of respectable Characters I knew them both at Boonsborrough and after

they went to Estills Station.

[Question] By same: was you acquainted with David Lynch in the years 1781, 2 & 3 was he a man of Good Character and well acquainted with that part of the Country.
Answer: I believe he was a man of Good Character and will acquanted with muddy Creek.

[Question] By same: do you know when Estills Station was settled.
Answer: in the beginning of the year of 1781.

[Question] By same: Do you think you would at Boonsborrough have directed a person to pursu the loglick trace and then the mulberry lick trace so as to have found the branch now called Bedingers before the year 1780 & 81.
Answer: I dont know that could as I did not know

[p. 200]
the number of branches below.

[Question] By same: by means of these traces would not a person have been directed to the principal branches of muddy Creek in the years 1780 & 81.
Answer: they could have been directed to Muddy Creek as to the principal branches I dont know that they could as they had no particular names.

[Question] By same: how many improvements did you know on muddy creek above the mulberry lick trace prior to the first day of may 1780.

Answer: I dont know I know any one above the mulberry lick trace.

Question by defendants: State how early you first hunted on muddy creek in the neighbourhood of Bedingers branch and mill and whether you hunted above that place and in the neighbourhood frequently.
Answer: I did hunt in the neighbourhood as early as 1776 and 1777 frequently and above it since that I never hunted much so high up as that.

Question by same: were you acquanted with all the hunters of Boonsborrough about that time who hunted upon muddy Creek.
Answer: I was and further this deponant saith not.   Oswald Townsend

[p. 201]
Also the Deposition of William Berry taken at the Same time and place and to be read as evidence in the Same Suit.

Question by plantiff: was you acquainted with Capt. James Estill David Guest and Colo. Thomas Swearingin in the years 1780, 81, 82 and what were their Characters.

Answer: I knew them about that time they were each one of men of Good Characters and well Known in this part of the Country and considered respectable.

[Question:] was Thomas Swearingin in either of those years a representative from this Country

and was he considered very competent to do business and make land Entries.
Answer: he was a representative from this Country in 1781 and was well qualifyed for making land Entries as much so as any man in the Country that I was then acquainted with.

[Question] By same: do you believe that the Greater part of the Grown men who lived at Boonsborrough in the spring of 1779 are now dead.
Answer: from my own knowledge and other Good information I belive that more than one half are since dead.
        James Berry

The fore Going deposition of Oswell Townsend and James Berry was taken subscribed and

[p. 202]
sown to before me a Justice of the peace for Madison County the time and place before mentioned.
        R. Caldwell
          ... Test
          Will Irvine C.M.C.C

Bedinger
copy   15 April 1817
Townsend &   Oswald Townsend
Berrys   James Berry
Depos
Walkers heirs &c
fee $0.87½

[p. 203]

Agreeable to notice we met at Thomas Swearengens improvement on the waters of muddy creek in Madison County on the 24th day of April 1817 and by the consent of the Plantiff and the Defendant in this suit they adjourned to the Place now calld. Bedingers improvement.

The Deposition of Samuel Estill taken on the 24th day of April 1817 at the Place calld. by Some Bedingers improvement in Madison County to be red as evidence in a suit in chancery now Depending in the Madison Circuit Court wherein George Michael Bedinger is Plantiff and William Martin in the Behalf of himself and the Heirs of Joel Walker Decd. is Deft. who Being of Lawful age deposeth and Saith by way of Questions and Answers.

Question by George M. Bedinger Oft.: Mr. Estill I want you to inform us whether you are interested in any way in Thomas Swearengens improvement or Benona Swearengens improvement or George M. Bedingers improvement in Madison County or if they was established would it injour you in any way.
Answer: in Col. Thomas Swearengens I am not interested but if Benona Swearengens was established where they Say his improvement is I should be but in Major Bedingers I do not know his Lines but I think if I am

[p. 204]
interested in his claim it must be very Little.

Quest. by Same: State if you Please if you was

not one of the Purchasers who bought the Lower five hundred acre Preemption and settlement, on the waters of muddy creek in Madison County of Joel Walker Decd.

Answer: yes myself and William Martin was in Partnership in the Purchaise we made from Joel Walker and this Lower five hundred acre Preemption now in Contention Between George M. Bedinger and William Martin was A Part.

Quest. by Same: Mr. Estill when you sold this Land alluded to did you think yourself responsible for the Purchaise money with interest &c, if the Land should be Lost.

Answer: yes.

Quest. by Same: Mr. Estill tell us what you know about Thomas swearengens improvement on muddy creek in Said County.

Answer: all that I know about it is that I seed it in the year 1780, the Place that is now calld. Thomas Swearengens improvement and Some years afterwards he got me to have his survey made, with Directions how I should know the improvement when I saw it that it was marked with red Letters, No. 1 and to make that the center of the Land which I accordingly did by measurement as I found it agreeable to his

[p. 205]
Direction marked with red Letters No. 1.

Quest. by Same: state if you Please what size the improvement was and how it was made.

Answer: I think their was at Least one acre that

the trees was deadened and the under groth cut out and the Brush heaped.

Question by Same: has not that Place been notoriously known ever since by the Majority of the People in the neighbourhood for Thomas Swearengens improvement.
Answer: I think it was at Estills Station and it has always been calld. Thomas Swearengens improvement ever since the Survey was made and I never heard it calld. by any other name.

Quest. by William Martin the Defendant: Mr. Estill state if you Please if you and myself have not Divided the Lower five hundred acre Preemption you have alluded to and now in Despute Between myself and Mr. Bedinger and if we have state when and whether your Part that you have taken interfers with Bedingers claim.
Answer: yes we have divided the five hundred acres alluded to in October 1812, and if my Part Clashes with Major Bedengers it must be very Little but I do not know his lines Also each of us Defends our own Part of the Division.

Question by Same: State if you Please when you Became

[p. 206]
first acquainted with muddy creek and its waters.

Answer: in the year 1779, and in February or March of that year.

Question by Same: have you not been acquainted

with them ever since.
Answer: _yes_.

Quest by same: did you ever know any fork by the name of the middle fork or the name of the west fork.
Answer: I never knew any fork ... known by the name of the middle fork nor any fork calld. and known by the name of the west fork emptying into muddy creek.

Question: ... the branch calld. Bedingers branch take its name.
Answer: I do not know what time Bedingers branch took its name. the People had made their settlements in the neighbourhood of Bedingers branch before I knew it by that name.

Quest. by Same: state if you Please as near as you can in what Date it took its name or in what date you knew it by that name.
Answer: I do not know when it took its name but I think it is about 18 or 20 years ago since I heard it calld. Bedingers branch.

Question by same: did you ever know of any improvement on Bedingers branch as earley as April the 29th 1780.
Ans.: no not as I recollect.

[p. 207]
Quest. by the Oft.: Mr. Estill from my first Questions that I Put to you, and your answers to them, I understood from you, that you are interested now in favour of Walkers Claim which I contend

with and against the establishment of Bedingers and Benona Swearengens improvements or claims consequently I asked you no other Questions about them. But as my oponant William Martain has asked Questions relative to them, I will ask you is not Bedingers branch a west Branch of muddy creek.
Answer: it runs in on the west side of Muddy creek, but I do not think it runs a west Course.

Question by Same: did you ever know Bedingers Branch by any other name than that of Bedingers Branch.
Answer: no.

Quest. by Same: did not Thomas Swearengens entery which you Direted the surveying of, and which you allude to in this Deposition call for a middle fork of muddy creek, and is not my improvement on A Branch that runs in Below both the swearingens improvements.
Answer: I do not recollect the entery and do not know whether it calld. for the middle fork or not. But the branch calld. Bedingers Branch empties in a considerable Distance below

the Said improvements.

Quest. by Same: does not the fork now calld. the Viney fork run into Muddy creek below Bedingers branch on the east Side.
Answer: yes.

Quest. by Same: Does not Thomas Swearengens

Survey include some of the waters of the Viney fork, on the east side of muddy creek.
Answer: I Believe it takes in some of the Drears.

Quest. by same: does not Little muddy creek run in on the west side of Muddy creek.
Answer: yes.

Quest. by same: as the one was on the east and the other on the west side of muddy creek and both being Large forks, was not the one Between them the middle one.
Answer: the main creek lying Between them two, you allude to, is certainly the Middle fork but I never heard it calld. the middle fork untill Lately. and it was always calld. big muddy creek ever Since the year 1780,

Quest. by same: are you acquainted with all the Branches on muddy creek and is their not a great number of them coming in on both sides.
Answer: I have seen nearley all the Branches on both sides from the head to the mouth, and their is a great many coming

[p. 209]
in on Both sides.

Quest. by Wm. Martin the Dft.: state if you Please how many forks puts in on the west side of muddy creek From Thomas Swearengens improvement down to the branch now calld. Bedingers branch, and the names of the Diferent forks, and when they took their names as near as you can.

Answer: their was Little Muddy creek and Woodses upper fork had their names in May 1780, and Woodses lower fork had its name at the mouth in the winter 1781 but a branch of Woodses lower fork, that headed round by where Thomas Warren now lives was shown to me by my Brother, for a branch of Woodses uper fork and calld. by that name in the year 1780 about the month of June in Said year their is another Branch that runs in Below Thomas Swearengens improvement and above the mouth of Little muddy creek that I now no name for yet, and their is another little Branch that Puts in Just Below what is now calld. Benona Swearengens improvement that I knew no name for, on the west side.

Quest. by George M. Bedinger the Oft.:   Mr. Estill,

[p. 210]
do you not think it was improper after you Said you was interested, on oath, to ask you any Questions about Benona Swearengens improvement &c, or my own.
Answer: I was not willing to Become a witness in this case at all, knowing the claims Clash. and further the Deponant Saith not.
    Saml. Estill

  The Deposition of Thomas Warren taken the 25th April 1817 according to adjournment at the Place of George M. Bedingers improvement to be red as evidence in the suit in Chancery pending in the Madison Circuit wherein George M. Bedinger is complainant and William Martin in behalf of Joel Walker his are Defendants who Being first sworn deposeth and saith by way of interogatones:

Quest. by compl.: when did you first Come to Kentuky.
Answer: in February 1780.

Quest. By Same: where did you first settle in Kentucky.
Answer: at Estill Station.

Quest. by Same: when was Estill Station first setled.
Answer: in the spring 1780.

Quest. by Same: what time in the Spring.
Answer: in March.

[p. 211]
Quest. by same: what number of Familys do you think Setled at Estills Station before the first of May 1780.
Answer: Their was Nicholas Protors family, Joseph Proctor Sr. and Cpt. James Estills Family they all came from Boonsborough and Also Ruben Proctor John Colefoot John Mitchel and James Hamilton who ware youn men and their was Samuel Rice, who Just then came from Virginia and one Barnett, also William Hamilton Thomas Venus, Edward Walton Richard Price Robert Walton John Moore, and David Lyntch together with Henry Cox, who all came from Virginia and Setled at Estill Station, the Sd.

spring of 1780 that is all that I now recollect.

Quest. by Same: was not Capt. James Estill the owner of the Station an active man and a great Locator.
Answer: yes.

Quest. by same: When did you first become acquainted with muddy creek and its waters.
Answer: in the spring 1780, I Became acquainted with muddy from Gates improvement to the head and in that summer I Became acquainted with it from the log lick branch up to Gates's improvement.

Quest. by same: Did you become acquainted with there improvement on muddy creek and its waters marked with

[p. 212]
red chalk or what is some times called red keel if so, Please state when Became acquainted with them, and what you know which you think material relative to them, and whose they ware called, generally.
Answer: the first improvement we was at yesterday was called Thomas Swearengens and was Marked with red keel and I think their was an acre or a Little more that was improved and then their was another improvement below it where their was a good smart choping but to the best of my memory I saw no marks on trees, and below it, their was a nother improvement that was marked with red keel as the upper one was but not so large as the first one about the improvements I

Became acquainted with them in them in the spring 1780, that is in March and when I first saw this Place, their was a tree marked with red keel, in the same manner the others ware, and I think the improvements was about as large as the Lower one was, on the creek and I think it was about four or five years after that I Became acquainted with the uper one that I Became acquainted withis one and it appeared to me to be made about the same time, of the above, and the trees all appeared to be marked in the same form, with a chop cut out and write on with red keel on the Place where the chip came from.

Quest. by Same: when you came to the last mentioned improvement was I not with you.
Answer: yes and the middle improvement was marked with red keel, and was calld. Benona Swearengens improvement.

[p. 213]
Quest by Same: was not those improvements that was marked with red Chalk Generally calld. Thos. Swearengens that is the first one and the next one Benona Swearengens and the third one which we are now at Calld. George M. Bedingers improvement.
Answer: in March 1780 I Became acquainted with Thos. Swearengens and Benona Swearengens and in 4 or 5 years afterwards I Became acquainted with the improvement that we are now at, calld. Bedingers, and afterwards I Became acquainted with the Swearengens improvements, they were Generally known at Estills Station and after I Became acquainted with Bedingers

improvement I then let the People of the Station know where it was and it then Became a Place that chief of the Hunters knew where it was.

Quest by Same: was their not a roade trace or Path that Led through Benona Swearengens improvement Between the marked tree and the creek when you first Saw it.
Answer: their was a small Buffalow trace.

Quest. by Same: was their any trace from Estills Station to the Mulberry Lick.
Answer: their was none untill in the summer 1780.

Quest by same: how far was it from the said trace where it crossed muddy creek to Benona Swearengens

[p. 214]
improvement.
Answer: I think about a quarter and a half Quarter of a mile.

Quest by Same: how far is it from this Place to the nearest Part of the log lick trace that leads from Boonsborough to the log lick.
Answer: about one mile and a quarter.

Quest. by Same: when did Cpt. James Estill and the People from Boonsborough that you have already mentioned first settle at Estills Station.
Answer: The first and second weak in March 1780 they all moved their.

Question by Same: are their not many large Branches or forks coming into muddy creek on both side of it.

Answer: yes, their is the log lick branch the Hickery lick Branch and the Viney fork coming into muddy creek on the east side, and Little muddy creek on the west side. They all had their names when I first Became acquainted with them in the summer 1780, and also Kings Branch coming in on the west side and their is several more branches that I was not acquainted with their names at that time.

Quest. by Same: I suppose you mean the People of Estills Station only in the Summer 1780 knew these Branches by those names as you ware not acquainted with the People at Boonsborough so earley.

Answer: I mean the People at Estills Station.

[p. 215]
Quest by Same: is their not a remarkable bend in muddy creek at the mouth of Woodses lower fork where the creek formerley run round, but now runs through and was their not a cedar cleft nearley opposit to it, which made it a remarkable Place.

Answer: yes.

Quest.: is not Bedingers branch the first branch below the above said Remarkable place coming in on the west Side of muddy creek, that is below Woodses lower fork.

Answer: yes.

Quest by same: Would it not have been an easy matter for any Locator being a Person of common understanding and acquainted with the woods to have found Bedingers improvement on Bedingers branch from said Woodses fork.

Answer: I could have directed any man of Common understanding how to have found Beddinger improvement that knew where Woodses lower fork was after I was acquainted with Bedingers improvement.

Quest. by Same: do you think that Thomas Swearengens and Benona Swearengens improvements on muddy creek were so notoriously known before the first day of May 1780 that any Person of Common ability wishing to find them could easily have got directions at Estills station and by Directions could have found them.

Answer: I think they could.

[p. 216]
Quest by Same: do you think that a Person of common Abilities and acquainted with Thomas and Benona Swearengens improvement, and acquainted with the woods could from either of them with good instructions find the mouth of Woodses lower fork alluded to, and from thence to Bedingers improvement on Bedingers Branch.

Answer: They could have found the way to woodses fork but in that earley day I did not know where Bedinger improvement was.

Quest. by Same: But if you had had known where Bedingers improvement was, could have Directed how to have found it.

Answer: yes.

Quest. by same: was Bedinger improvement to be Plainly seen from the Branch calld. Bedingers branch.
Answer: yes, and any man could have found it by ~~following~~ this branch from its mouth up to the Improvement.

Quest. by Same: Have not the hads of nearley all the familys who moved from Boonsborough Died since they moved to Estills Station.
Answer: all except one: which is Josep Proctor.

Quest. by same: state if you Please the size of the improvement that you call Benona Swearengens upper improvement and if it Looked to be done as earley as earley as the other improvements when you first saw it.
Answer: I think their was about a half a quarter of an Acre. That the things was choped down and it appeared by thus choping their was not mutch adds in them.

[p. 217]
Quest. by same: how old are you.
Answer: I Believe I was seventy three years old last January.

Quest. by William Martin in behalf of Joel Walkers heirs: State if you Pleas if you ever heard of any forks calld by the name of the Middle fork or west fork of muddy creek from your first acquaintance with Said creek to the Present Day or ever head of any of the People living at Estills or

Boonsborough know or talk of any sutch forks before the 29th of April 1780 or for any short time afterwards.

Answer: from the log lick where I first stated to the head of muddy creek I never new of any Place calld. by a name of a fork but the Viney fork at that time.

Quest by Same: State if you Please how many forks Puts in on the west side of muddy creek from Thomas Swearengens improvement down to the Place now calld. Bedingers branch.

Answer: five.

[Question] By same: state if Please how far you think it is from Thos. Swearengens improvement down to Bedingers Branch.

Answer: I think it must be nearley two miles and some Little over.

Quest. by Same: at what time did you see the first improvement on muddy creek Below Thomas Swearengens and whose was it calld.

Answer: I Saw it in the Spring 1780 and I heard it calld. Benona Swearengens upper improvement.

Quest. by Same: could you have Direted any inquiring Person with Common understanding to have found a branch known by the name of Bedingers Branch or Bedingers Improvement as earley as the 29th day of April 1780 as in any short time afterwards so as they could have known them.

Ans.: no.

[p. 218]
Question by Complainant: Did you ever hear Benona Swearingens claim the first improvement Below Thos. Swearengens as his improvement I mean the one that was not marked with red keel.
Answer: no.

[Question] By Same: did you ever hear any Person say that Benona ever claimd it.
Answer: I cant say I ever did

[Question] By Same: did you ever see Benona Swearengen.
Answer: no I have seen Thos. Swearengen.

[Question] By Same: where and at what time did you you see Thos. Swearengen.
Answer: I have seen him at Boonsborough and at Estills station and I Believe it was in 1781 or two.

[Question] By same: was he not then a representative for the County of Kentucky.
Ans.: they said sow not as I know.

[Question] By same: Did not Col. Thomas Swearengen and Daniel Boon go From Estill station with a guard to escort them a small part of the way through the wilderness.
Answer: yes.

[Question] By Same: when did Capt. David Gass move from Boonsborough to Estills Station.
Answer: in 1781 I Believe.

Quest. by same: How long did he live at Estills

station and where and when did he die.

[p. 219]
Answer: I think he lived there at Estills station three years and then moved to where he died near old Milford about five miles from Estills station and his Death was about nine or ten years ago.

[Question] By Same: When was Cpt. James Estill killed and where did his family live at the time of his Death.
Answer: he was killed in March in 1782 at the place that is calld. Estills defeat, and further the deponant saith not.   Thomas Warren

J. Crook   This the deposition of John Crook ... the same time and place he being of Lawful age ... sworn sworn deposeth and saith:

Question by George M. Bedinger the Oft.: Mr. Crook how long have you lived in this neighbourhood or County and has not the improvements that we ware at yesterday that is calld. Benona Swearingens improvement and Thomas Swearingens improvement and the one we are now at that is calld. Bedingers improvement been Places Generally known ... since your First acquaintance hear and ware they not all marked with red chalk, and have you ever seen any other improvements in this neighbourhood that was made in an earley day that was marked with red Chalk.
Answer: I came to Madison County the 26th day of December 1789. I moved to Muddy creek about five miles above

[p. 220]
hear in October 1796 and Lived their nearley twenty years and live now about three miles from hear the Place shewed for Thos. Swearengens improvement I have known by hearsay to be Thos. Swearengens improvement for twenty years and it has known by that name ever since by every one knowing or cearing any thing about it, or wishing to know. Benona Swearengens, I was Shewed it I think by David Lyntch when I made Bononies Survey in the year 1797 or 98, as well as I recollect, and the improvement we are now at I never saw to my knowledge untill I was surveying in the suit Joel Walker heirs against Samuel Gilbert, but as for either ... improvements being marked with red chalk I never Said it nor Did I ever hear of these Being marked so untill the Commencement of this Suit.

Quest. by Same: was not Thos. Swearengens improvement a Place of great notoriety.
Answer: it has been to any inquirer to my knowledge for twenty years, ... I kept the surveyors Office for that space of time within two miles or so of it, and could have Directed any one wishing to see it how to have found it and further the Deponant Saith not.
    John Crooke

[p. 221]
  Also the Deposition of John Williams taken according to adjournment at the Same Place on the 26th day of April 1817 to be red as evidence in the above suit ... Deposeth and Saith:

Question by complainant: how long have you been acquainted with muddy creek and its waters.
Answer: my first acquaintance with some of its waters was in 1785 and I have been more and more acquainted with it ever Since.

Quest by Same: do you know anything of Bedingers improvement on a west Branch of muddy creek and have you ever seen it.
Answer: I saw this improvement we are now at in 1794 or 5.

Quest. by same: Did you not make application once to Purchase this Claim thinking it to be a good one.
Answer: I did.

Quest. by Same: have you not frequently Been at Bedingers improvement on Bedingers Branch.
Answer: yes.

Quest by Same: have you not always from your First acquaintance Generally calld. a good Claim.
Answer: I have.

Quest. by William Martin Dft. &c: How did you know this to be Bedingers improvement.
Answer: I have seen it as above Stated but to know that

[p. 222]
it was Bedingers improvement only from the rumur and report of the neighbours I did not, none ever Shew'd me the Place untill this Controversy took Place between the two Parties, and

further this Deponant Saith not.
  John Williams

   Also the Deposition of David Lyntch taken at the same time and Place deposeth and Saith,

Quest. by Complainant: is this improvement we are now at the improvement you mentioned that Ralph Morgan shewed you and many others as Bedingers, and the same that is refered to in your former Deposition.
Answer: yes.

Quest. by same: when did you first settle at Estills station.
Answer: in the last of January, or the first of February 1780.

Quest. by same: was you one of the first that setled their.
Answer: yes.

[Question:] How many men of you went their first.
Answer: Their was six men and myself came from Verginia we setled at Estills Station, which was then nothing but woods their was Thos. Walton, Robert Walton Samuel Rice, John Moore Richard Price and Henry Cox together, together with Thos. Warren who came and setled their in a day or two after wards. Their was George Robertson & one Barnett who also came from Verginia and setled

[p. 223]
their prior to the 29th day of April 1780.

Quest. by Same: when did the first of the inhabitants from boonsorough move to estills Station. and how many men from Boonsborough moved their prior to the 29th April 1780.

Answer: The first came some time in march James Estill moved with his family John Colefoot James Hamilton Peter Hackett setled their with him Joseph Proctor and his family setled in the same month.

[Question] By same: are the above all that you recollect who setled Before the 29th day of April 1780.
Answer: yes.

Quest. by Same: were there Persons that you have mentioned that came from boonsborough all men grown.
Answer: all except one that was Peter Hacket.

Quest. by Same: was Estills Station on or near some of the waters of muddy creek.
Answer: it is near the waters of Little muddy creek, some of the waters of Little muddy creek heads up in the Plantation of the old Station.

Quest. by same: How far do you think it is from Bedingers improvement to Estills Station.
Answer: about four miles or four and A half at a Guess.

Quest. by same: How far do you suppose it is from Estills Station to Thos. Swearengens improvement.
Answer: about three miles.

Quest. by Same: are their not many Branches or forks coming into muddy creek on both sides of it and will you mention their names, and when or how they got thare names, as near as you can recollect.
Answer: Their is many Branches coming into muddy creek on both sides. Their is Kings branch, Debans run Bedingers branch, Branch or creek that is calld. Woodses lower fork Woodses

[p. 224]
upper fork and little muddy Creek they all run into the creek on the west side, and there is the log lick branch, the hicory lick lick branch, and the viny fork that runs into the Said Creek on the East Side. Kings branch had its name first of my being acquainted on the Creek, and Debans run I dont know when it got its name, nor I dont know how it got its name, Bedingers branch I dont know when nor how it got its name, wods's lower fork took its name by that name in fall 1782 or in the Summer 1783 I dont know which, Woods's upper fork took its name Some time in May 1780 and little muddy Creek took its name sometime in the last of February or March 1781 the Log lick branch had its its name when I first got acquainted withit. The Hicory lick took its name in the latter part of the Summer 1780, and Mulberry fork took its name the last of April or the first of May 1780. The first time that I ever heard

wods's lower fork calld by that name, I gave it its name myself and it has went by that name ever Since. Woods's upper Fork was named by John Woods who had an entry made on it, and Little Muddy Creek was named by Robert and Edward Walton and myself. The viny fork got its name by James Estill and myself by reason of So many grape vines growing in the bottom, the Hickory Lick got its name by a hicory tree growing in the Lick at the head of a branch.

Queston by Same: When the branches or forks that you have just mentioned first took their names, did not a considerable time pass away before Many of the inhabitants Knew their names even at Estills Station where the men lived who gave them their names

[p. 225]
I allude to the two Wood's forks little muddy the viny Fork and the Hicory Lick.
Ansr.: The inhabitants of Estills Station I think all of them knowed Little muddy from the time it took its name, the men the men that hunted from Estills Station knew the Creeks Shortly after they were named by their names.

Question by same: Pleas State your reasons how little Muddy Creek became notorious Sooner than the rest.
Ansr.: because the Station was within four hundred yards or four hundred and fifty yards from the bank of the Creek we calld little muddy creek.

Question by Same: When was you first acquainted with Thomas Swearingens Improvement.

[Answer:] It was Some time the last of February or the first of March that I Saw it in the year 1780 there was about an acre or Such a matter of ground. The under Shift Choped out of it, the trunk heaped and the ... timber was ... round and there was a walnut tree standing with a large block or chip taken out of it and writing with read paint or chalk where the chip was taken out of it and it is the Same place that I Shewed the Surveyor on the 24th Instant for Thomas Swearingens Improvement.

Question by Same: State if you please when you was first informed Whose Improvemenet that was and by whom.
Answer: I belive the first time that I ever was at it was was with James Estill and he told me it was Thomas Swearingens Improvement and I belive it was the first time I ever was on Muddy Creek it is on the west Side of the creek and about 200 yards from the Creek.

Question by Same: Has not Thomas Swearingens improvement been notoriously known Ever Since by the people of Estills Station.
Answer: I belive it has by all that followed the woods.

[p. 226]
Question by Same: Would it not have been an easy matter for you and many others at Estills Station before the 29th of April 1780 to have directed any man of Common understanding I

mean a Locator to have found Said Improvement from Estills Station.

Answer: James Estill or myself could have directed any one So that they Could have found it and have known it from the time that I Stated in one of my other answers.

Quston by Same: Could you not also as easily have directed a locator of the Like abillaties to have found Benoni Swearingens Improvement and have known it.

Answer: I could have directed any Such person to the Improvement that James Estill told me was Benoni Swearingens Improvement So as they would have known it.

[Question by] Same: do you not think that Benoni Swearingens Improvement was fully as notorious or more So in the Spring of 1781 2 3 as Thomas Swearingens & as Easily found.

Answer: as to the notoriety of the two places I think they were about equal and I think as easily found.

Question by Same: was their not a bufflow road leading to both the above Said improvements from Estills Station before the 29 day of April 1780.

Answer: their was no Buffalo road from Estills Station till we got down to big muddy Creek their was a Buffalo road there that went up through the Edge of Thomas Swearingens Improvement and the other End went down the Creek by Benoni's Improvement.

[p. 227]
[Question] By Same: If a locator wishing to finde the three improvements I mean Thomas Swearingens Benoni Swearingens and Michael Bedingers and if he had found the first two Could he easily been instructed to have found the last one Bedengers Branch by a person who knew them well and was at the making of them.
Answer: Any person that was at the making of the three Improvements and acquainted with them might have directed any person with resonable Sence that they could have found either one or all three of them.

Question by Same: Is their not a remarkable bend in Muddy Creek at the mouth of woods Lower fork where the water formerly run round but now the Creek runs through the near way was their not a ceder cliff on the East Side of the creek near that place which made the ceder cliff Woods's fork & Short bend a remarkable place.
Answer: yes..

[Question] by Same: Is not Bedingers Branch the first branch below that place on the west Side.
Ans.: yes.

[Question] By Same: Was not Bedingers Improvement plain to be Seen on on Bedengirs branch when you first Saw it, and could it not have been Easily found by Comeing up the branch from the mouth.
Answer: Yes.

Quston by Same: have not the greates number of

the inhabitants of Estills Station who Settled there in the 1780 in the Spring died Since and most of those who are not dead removed out of the State rear to a great distance from this place So that their testimony can not easily be had.

Answer: Their is only Thomas Warren Joseph Proctor Peter hacket and myself remaining in this County or near it that Settled in Estills Station as above Stated.

[p. 228]

The Deposition of Aquilla White taken at the Place calld. Bedingers improvement on a branch call Bedingers branch in Madison County Ky. on the 19th of August 1817, to be red as evidence in a suit in chancery Depending in the Madison Circuit Court in which George M. Bedinger is Plantiff and William Martin in behalf of himself and the heirs of Joel Walker is Defendant who being of Lawful age and first sworn deposeth and Saith by way of Questions and answers:

Question by George M. Bedinger the Oft.: Mr. White will you please to inform us what you know of this improvement being bedingers improvement when did you first hear of it and Become acquainted with it and also sutch things as will go to establish Thomas and Benona Swearengens improvement on muddy creek and sutch other things as you may Deem important in this suit.

Answer: in the year 1779 I came to Boonsborough the 17th of April and there some Gentlemen were their and I Became acquainted with them and finding we ware on the same arrant we used to inform one another where we made improvements. They came out to Muddy creek told me they had made four there for themselves and one for Samuel Duree, three they marked with red chalk and one with Black, 1780 or in 1781 I was going through the woods with one Rheuben Proctor and came to one of the improvements and saw it, which I believe was the uper one, and the next summer following I was hired and Peter Massie both then living at Gubbs's Station, was hired by the inhabitants of Estills Station to spy. our rout being from Grubbs's station to the red lick,

[p. 229]
Down station camp, and down the river untill we got against our own Station, we went two routs, and both routs, we came by all these improvements, and found the letters and marks according to my first Directions.

Question by same: Mr. White, did you mean Thomas & Benona Swearengens and George M. Bedingers improvements.
Answer: yes I did.

Question by same: were they marked with red.
Answer: yes they ware.

Question By same: did not the greatest Harmoney And Friendship prevail between the inhabitants of boonsborough in 1779.
Answer: yes the Greatest I ever knew in in all my life among so many People.

Question by same: as we ware all on the same Business Locating of land, was it not our interest to inform one another where we had made our improvements, and was it not a common thing when a large Party would go out to make improvements to inform the rest of the People in the station where we had made our improvements, in order that we might not interfere with each other.
Answer: yes.

Question by same: Mr. White did you ever hear that Thomas Swearingen Benona Swearingen or George M. Bedinger had any other improvements but these three, we was at this day with David Lyntch and others.
Answer: no.

Question By same: Mr. White whether or not Could you have directed a Locator of common abilities in the years 1780, 1781, 1782, Or in 1783, to have found Thomas Swearengens Benona Swearengens and George M. Bedingers improvement on muddy creek.
Answer: I think I could.

Question By Same: was not the red lick and muddy creek Places of notoriety from the month of January in the year 1780 to the month

[p. 230]
of December 1783.
Answer: yes.

Question By William Martin the Defendant: state

if you Please when you first came to Boonsborough and how long you staid their.
Answer: I came the 17th of April 1779 and made it my home untill August the tenth, and went into Virginia for my family and Brought them out against Christmase, and lived in the bounds of thirty miles ever since.

Question by Same: how long did you live at Boonsborough after you moved your Family their and where did you at next after you left Boonsborough.
Answer: I lived at Boonsborough about two months & then moved to McGees Station.

Question by same: how long did you live at McGees Station.
Answer: about two years.

Question by same: where did you move to from McGees Station.
Answer: to Grubbs station.

Question by same: how far do you think it is from hear to McGees station.
Answer: I think it is about twenty miles.

Question By same: state if you Please the names of the principle men that hired you and Peter Massie to spy for Estills Station.
Answer: John Woods & Archibald Woods the two Principle men, and we was to fetch in their Horses in Particular if we saw them running away.

Question By same: how far from this Place do you think it is to Grubbs's Station.
Answer: about fifteen miles.

Question by same: did you ever know any fork of muddy creek by the name of the Middle fork or any fork known by the name of the west fork.
Answer: No.

Question by same: if any Locator had of enquired of you for the middle fork or the west fork, what would you have told him.

[p. 231]
Answer: I would have told him I knew nary one by that name.

Question by same: state if you please as near as you Possibly can in what season of the year in 1780, Or in 1781, you first saw these improvements.
Answer: I think it was June or July 1781.

Question by same: state if you please how many improvements, you was acquainted with, on the waters of muddy creek from your first acquaintance untill the year 1785.
Answer: I knew five, their was Bridges Samuel Durees and these three.

Question by George M. Bedinger the Oft.: Mr. White what is the General Course of muddy creek.
Answer. it runs nearley north.

Question by same: was it improper to call the branches Comeing in from the Left hand side or the west, west Branches before they ware Generally known by othe names, or those on the east side, East branches, before they ware Generally known by other names.
Answer: I know no other Language to distinguish them by.

Question by same: was not Thomas Swearengen a man of high standing & well Qualifyd. to do business as a locator.
Answer: yes.

Quest. By Same: as their is a number of folks coming in on Both sides of Muddy creek, to wit, the Viney fork and others on the east side and little muddy creek and others on the west side, which in 1779 had no names, was their any impropriety, in the conduct or Description of Col. Thomas Swearengen, who made the three Locations, in calling the one lying between the others the Middle fork.
Answer: none.

Question by same: Mr. White how far Below this is Bridges improvement.
Answer: I think about seven Miles.

[p. 232]
Question by same: Mr. White which of the two improvements on the waters of muddy creek is Thos. Swearengens marked with red chalk.
Answer: the uper one is Thos. Swearengens and the Lower one is Benona Swearengens improve-

ment, and further the Deponant saith not.
                                    Aquilla White

Also the the Deposition of Thomas Townsend taken at the same time and place and to be red as evidence in the Same suit who being of lawful age & first sworn deposeth and saith by way of Qus. & Answers:

Quest. by the Oft.: Mr. Townsend how long have you been acquainted with this Place that we are at calld. Bedingers improvement, and please to inform us of every thing you know relative to this suit.
Answer: I became acquainted with this improvement, in the fall of the year 1782. it was one Charles Miller that showed it to me and said it was Bedingers improvement.

Question by same: do you know that this branch was calld. Bedingers branch at that time or not.
Answer: I am not certain, that it was at that time.

Question by Same: you have lived hear a long time and did you ever know or hear of any other person but my self claiming this improvement.
Answer: no.

Question by same: was this improvement notoriously known from your first acquaintance with it untill the last of the year 1783. and could a Person well acquainted with it, and the woods, have Directed a Locator of Common Abilities to have found it from Estills Station.

[p. 233]
Answer: I think any thing of a wodsman could have been dircted from Estills Station, so as to have found it.

Question by same: from the time the Country became Generally setled about this Place, was my claim not considered a Good one by the neighbours Generally.
Answer: Yes, I think so, myself and Brother Joshua Townsend made an attempt to buy it, about twenty years ago. Joshua Townsend went Over to where you then lived, which was at or near the blue licks.

Question by William Martin the Defendant: Mr. Townsend State if you please, when you first came to Kentucky and where did you first live.
Answer: I came to Kentucky in the fall 1782. and lived at Estills Station with Archibald Woods.

Question By same: state if you Please as near as you can when you first saw the improvement on main Muddy creek. that you showed to me in Company with David Lyntch, Peter Hacket, and Samuel Estill.
Answer: I think some time in the spring and Perhaps in February or march 1783.

Question by Same: state if you Please if the work Done at that improvement appeared to be as olde as the work Done at this improvement when you first Saw it.
Answer: I think it did.

Question by same: was their not a trace Leading from Estills Station that run through or near that improvement.
Answer: yes.

[p. 234]
Question by same: state if you Please what was the size of that improvement.
Answer: I think their was between a Quarter and half Acre.

Question by the Plantiff: Did you ever learn from any person that the Place you saw a little above the mouth of Little muddy creek, on main muddy creek, was an improvement at all or whether it was an Indian camp. did you ever hear of an owner for it. was it marked or not.
Answer: I never heard any Body claim it, nor I do not think it was Indian camp, and I saw no marked trees but what was Done by choping.

Question by the Defendant: was their not the undergroth cut out, and the trees Belted like other improvements that was made in the Country & some brush heaps made.
Answer: their was some things cut Down and some belting round. Their was some Brush but whether it was heaped or not I dont know. And further the deponant saith not.
    Thomas Townsend

Aquilla White one day attendance as a witness
              $0.50
and Milage for thirty miles   1.66⅔
and for Feraige   0.25

Thomas Townsend one Day   0.50
David Lyntch same   0.50
Majl. fee   1.00

The above charges all Paid by the Plantiff

Madison County Set. I do hereby certify that the foregoing Depositions was taken sworn and Subscribed to Before me the subscriber a Justice of the Peace for Said County at the time and place above stated, Given under my hand this 19th of August 1817.

                     Nicholas Hocker

Coppies of
Aquila White &
Thomas Townsends
Depositions
August 19 1817

[p. 235]

Stephen Hancook livs about 2 miles from Mr. Gass a S E course Joseph Procter on the waters of otter S... Procter, James Berry livs on Tates Creek a good witness David Linch, Thomas Warren Co. Wm. Estil.

from what reason do you think you did not see the other corners at the time sd. Survey was made.

John Gass deposeth and saith that the sd. deponent did carry the chain for Capt. Christopher Irvin in making a Survey for Geo M Bedinger on Muddy creek in Mad... County, and the Corner which this deponant Shewed John Crook Surveyor of sd County was the North West Corner of Sd Survey and he further saith that he has no recollection of Seeing any of the other Corners made of the Sd Survey but this being the last Corner of Sd. Survey he well recollects it from our remaining at Sd. Corner while Irvine the Surveyor was plotting or doing some writing and when done made said corner & cut the letters C J uppon the black oak tree. This Deponant further States that he thinks that they did not run from there to the beginning but quit at that Corner.

Question by Complainant: From what reason do you think you did not See the other corners at the time Sd. Survey was made.
Asr: from this reason I always Carried the hind end of the chain and when in Cainy ground never went up but Stood at the end of the chain as it was troublesom in Getting the chain up through the Cane.

Notice must be sent on for taking this dpesitior.
Copy of John
Gass's deposition

[p. 236]
the two Waltons Price Moore and Cox moved back to Virginia. ned Walton is dead, and the others I dont know where they are and the last I heard of Saml. Rice he was Living Between Natches and Orleans. James Estill was killed By the indians.

Adjourned untill Monday the 28th day of this month at the House of John Evans.
Nicholas Hocker

Agreeable to an ajournment we met at the time & Place adjourned to, and Proceeded with the Deposition of David Lyntch, as follows (to wit):

Quest. by George M. Bedinger the Oft.: Mr. Lyntch was not Benona swearingens improvement near the mouth of a Small Branch or Dream and the tree standing on the Lower side of the Dream with the choped Part of the tree where the block was taken out and where the writing was Put or faceing towards the mouth of the Branch where the Buffalow roade went up and down the creek and could not A Person who was once acquainted with it easily know it again and Describe or direct others to it.
Answer: yes.

Quest. by Same: Mr. Lyntch do you know any other but Bedingers improvement on muddy creek Below Benona Swearengens improvement within a Mile or two.
Answer: I do not know of any only the one that Ralph Morgan shewed me for Bedingers improvement, but I had seen it often before

Morgan shewed it to me.

Question by Wm. Martin. the Defendant: Mr. Lyntch I think in your Former Questions you State you was showed Benona Swearengens improvement by James Estill. did you ever hear James Estill say that he was at the makeing of that improvement or that it was Showed to him by any Person that was at the makeing of it.
Answer: I do not recollect that I ever stated that

James Estill showed it to me but I think that James Estill told me that it was Benona Swearengens improvement and how he came by his knowledge I am not able to say at this time.

Quest. by Same: when you first setled at Estills Station in the winter

[p. 238]
1780 what was your occupation that spring and summer.
Answer: Some times I Laboured but mostly Hunting. Cpt. James Estill and myself and Samuel Rice took a trip A Hunting about 30 Or 35 miles up the Kentuky River from Estills Viewing the Country that was done about the first of March 1780.

Question by Same: state if you Please whether you was Frequently on muddy creek and its waters from the mouth of the Viney fork up to Estills Station in the Same Spring and Summer of the same Date.
Answer: I was tolerably well acquainted with the waters of muddy creek from the mouth of the Viney fork to the mouth of Little muddy creek, and from the Little Muddy I was Better acquainted with it.

Question by Same: could you have Directed any Person to the fork of muddy creek known by the Middle fork or the west fork or Bedingers branch at any time from your first acquaintance to the 29th of April 1780 or in any Short time after.
Answer: I do not recollect of hearing any talk of

a west Branch fork or a Middle fork in that Date or any talk of Bedingers branch in that Date.

[p. 239]
Quest. by same: was not the Viney fork the Largest branch of muddy creek on the east side And one of the Larges on the east side and one the Largest on the creek.
Answer: yes it is the Larges on the east side and among the Largest on the creek.

Quest. by Same: Mr. Lyntch do you think it the Largest above the Log Lick Branch.
Answer: yes.

Quest. by Same: how many Branches is their Between Benona Swearengens improvement and the mouth of the Viney fork on the east Side of the creek.
Answer: I Believe their is about one Branch and one what I call a small gut.

Question by Same: is not Bedingers improvement on the first west fork above the mouth of the Viney fork and could not A Person from the mouth of the Viney fork easily have Directed to Bedingers improvement from the Mouth of the viney fork as it is the Largest fork on the east side of muddy creek.
Answer: the improvement is on the first Branch on the west side of the creek and any Person that knew where the improvement was could have Directed any Person of reasonable Sense to the improvement.

Madison County
Land papers
Bedinger Vs Martin

[p. 240]
Question by Same: Could you have directed any enquiring Person or Locator of Common understanding to an improvement now calld. Bedingers improvement So that they Could have found it and known it to be the Same at any time from February 1780 to the 29 of April of the Same date or in any Short time after.
Answer: I could not have directed any person to Bedingers improvement untill I heard it calld Bedingers Improvement.

Question by G M B the Oft.: Mr. Lynch is not little Muddy Creek a larger fork of Muddy Creek Comeing in on the west Side of the Creek is not the Viny fork A larger fork Comeing on the east Side and is not what is now calld Muddy Creek Between the two forks.
Answer: yes.

Question by Wm. Martin the Dfd.: State in what year ralph morgan Shewed you Bedingers Improvement.
[Answer:] I think it was in the year 1814. And far-ther this deponant Saith not.

D Sir claim as about purchesing
procssioning
Surveying & if coming
So near ... most not how
Seen Sd I or hear next

The depositions of
Samuel Estill 24 April 1817
Thomas Warren 25 April 1817
John Crooke do
John Williams 26 of April 1817
David Lynch 26 of April 1817

[p. 241]
Jacob Miller of the thre forks of Kentucky, Estil County, Mguire is a Justice of the peace at the Spot.
Janiary 6 Date of Certificate
29 April 1780
questions Mr. Wicklif gave to Banta
1. Was not Geo M Bedingers & Benonie Swerenjns Improvement notoriously known known to hunters & others acquainted on Muddy Creek at & before the 29 of April 80.
2. Do you not believe that G M Bedingers Improve-ment & Benonie Swerenjens Improvements was no-torious by & Generally known by them names at and before the 29 of April up to the 6 of January 80.
3. Could an Enquirer easily have found the above Sd. Improvements by Enquiring for them by their names at Boons borough or Sstles Station at & before the 29 day of april 1780.
3. Do you not belive that a majority of those who were acquainted near Bedinger ... Bedingers Improvement & Benonie Swerengens Improvement knew them by their those names, at & bfore the 29 day of April 1780.
4. How far was Bedingers branch from Boons borough & Estles Station Did not the people from boorsborough Estles report about that part of

Muddy where Bedingers Improvement & Benony Swearingens Improvements wer about the 29 day of April 1780.
... Harris you Say you was acquainted with the different Branches ...

[p. 242]
Ask Mr. Warren when did you first Come to Keontucky.
Answer: in February 80.

[Question:] Where did you firs Settle in Kentucky.
Answer: at Esstils Station.

[Question:] When was Estills Station firs Settled.
[Answer:] in the Spring 80.

[Question:] What time in the Spring.
Answer: In March.

[Question:] was What number of famieles Settled at Estle do you think.
[Answer:] ther was Nicholas Procters family & J proctors family and Captain James Estles family from Boons borough thir was Rhuben procter John Colefut John Colefut John Michel & James hamilton; he went on to enumerate.

[Question:] was you acquainted with along muddy creek and sone of its branch.

[Question:] When did you becone acquainted with the muddy creek & its waters.
[Answer:] In the Spring ... I became acquainted

with the waters of mudd cre from Gass improvement to the head and that Summer I became acquanted with it from the Log lick up.

[Question:] Mr. Warren did you become acquainted with three Improvements on Mudy creeks & its waters marked with Read chalk or what is Some times call read Keele if So please State when you become acquantd with them Whos they were and what you know which you think material relative to them.

[Question:] When you first come to this Improvement was I not with you Bedingers.

[Question:] Was ther not a road or trace or road or path that lead hicorys Benoni Swearinjens Improvment between the markd tree and the Creek When you firs Saw it.

[p. 243]
Instructions of J. W.:

G M B Jr 3 Mar lay down T. S. Swearingens improvement Laid down & prove the notoriety of the Improvement you depend on Benoni S___n and your Improvement on a West branch of Muddy creek. B. S. depends on T. S.s. The calls of the M. T. would Seem on ol__l but if the Improvements were known at Bons__g to the majeruty of the Inhabitents there and that those who lived at that place wer dead previous to the Commencement of this it might Supply the defect of proof.[2] it is not Shewn in the depositions the time of Est 3 Station being first ~~Settled~~ Improved. it was proved that Shortly afterwards the

Improvements were Seen. is thier no leading trace, is thier no leading trace the log Lick must have been known about that time, also the mulbery Lick. I would be will to prove when the different Branches of m'y C took their Names.

for instance Wods forks viny fork Kings branch Little muddy this inquiry you had better make before you take your depositions.

    the Surveyors report amend

Capt James Estill	1
John Colefut	1
the 3 Johns Souths & Thomas South	4
M Procter	1
the two boughmans	2
Edward Nelson	1
Wilson dead or moved	
Capt Gass	1
Jaco & F A Starns	2
John Calaway	1
Wm Collins	1
Charles Wisherd Lockhart	1
John Bullock	1
Thomas Brooks	1

of the 10 in the Company of Locaters out between the 2d & 6 of May 1779 the dead ar 8

                Dead

Colonel Thos Swearingen	1	1
Colonel Wm. Morgan	1	2
Benoni Swearingen	1	3
Samuel Duree	1	4
Capt or Col John Holder	1	5
Capt John Constant	1	6
John Taylor	1	7
Esquire Joseph Doniphan	1	8

of Mason C
Persons who lived at Bonsborog in the Spring 1779 who have died

 Samuel Estill Interested in Esp. T. S. [1]Emprove[1], lay[2] it down & prove[3] its notoriety MB dp_s on Ben_s S.N & your[8] Imp[4] on a W/orkin Creek. B.S. depends on T.s, the Calls of M.T. woold Seom on. abt. But if the Improvements were Known at Boons Bh to the Majority of the inhabitants there and that those and that those who lived at that were dead previous the commencement of this it might Suply the deficientcy of proof they

 It is not Shewn in the deposition the time Estills Station was settled. it was proved that shortly afterwards the improvements was were Seen

 Is their no leading no leading trace the log lick must have been known about that time also the
Mullery lick
It would be well to prove when the different branches took their names for Set Wds. fks. K B ... muddy
The Surveyors report amind
ask Mr. W. when he firs come to Kentucky
 where he first settled
 when Estill Station was first Std
 was it not by Chiefly Setled by the Inhabitants
  of Bonb
 was it owned by Capt Estle who moved from
  boonsb
 was their not old M procter & two ... Some of
  the procters
 remember Capt Gass was

Enquire about the trails or roads
Enquire about dilons run & Bantas cabins if Mr Durees daughter Winey and her husband was not killed Living near this place

[p. 244]
were So notoriously known before the first of May eighty that any person of Common abilities wishing to finde them Could easily have got directions at Estils Station to have found them and by directions Could have found them.

Mr do you think a person of Common abilities acquainted with Thomas and Benoni Swearingens Improvements and acquainted with the woods, Could from either of them his Improvements with Good instruction find the mouth of Woods ower fork aluded to, and from thence to Bidengers Improvement on Bedingers Branch.

State if you please if you ever heard of Calld the West fork or Middle
Stu Lowr forks puts in
how far to bedingers from S W S
at what time inquiring and etc.
Did you ever see Benoni Swearingsn ashes I mean the one that was not marked with read keele. did you ever hear any person say that Benoni S I cant say I ever did.
Where & at what time did you see Thomas Swearinger.
do you recollect when Capt. David Gass moved with his family from Boons Borough to Estils Station.
how long did he live at Estills Station and where did he die.

Walker & Martin

[Question:] how how long have you been acquainted with Mudy creek & & its waters.

{Question:} Is not this Improvement we are now at the Improvement you mention Ralph Morgan Shewed you & others as Bedingers Improvement & the same that is refered to in your former deposition.

[Question:] was you one of the first that Settled there.
answer:

[Question:] how many of you wen there fus.
[Answer:] Thomas Walton Rober[2] Walton Samuel Rice[3] John Moore[4] D...k Wood[5] Henry Cox[6] Thomas ____ War them come in a day or two Joined us there; George Robison &c.

[Question:] was you acquainted with the that part of Muddy Creek will you mention names & when & how ... they as and from the the log Lick. The first ... upper fork, the viney fork.

[Question:] when the branches or forks which you have Just mention Stated which took their names was it not D not considerable time pass away before Many of the Inhabitants knew of their names Even at Estills Station where the men lived who gave them thier names; I mean alude to the two Woodes forks the viny fork little muddy & the Hicory Lick.

[Question:] Please State State your reasons how it became so notorious So Soon.
[Answer:] it became notorious Sooner than the rest because Estills ... almost no.

[Question:] Was their not a Buffillow road Leading to both the above Said Improvements, from Estils Station Before the 29 of Aprl 1780. Could not a person Comeing out if a locater wishing to have found the three Improvements I mean Thomas Swerngens B S & Bedingers and if had found the first two Could he not have Easily been Instructed to have found ... to B by a person who knew them well and was at the making of them.

[p. 246]
[Answer:] any person that was at the making of the Improvements and acquainted with them might have directed any person with reasonable Sense to So th that he could have found any either one or all thre as the In of them.

[Question:] was ther not a remarkable bend in muddy Creek at the mouth where the water formerly run but now the Creek runs through the near way and a ...

[Question:] is not Bedingers Branch the firs branch the firs branch below said rema place on the.

[Question:] Is was not bedingers Improvement plain to be Seen & Esply to be found and Could it not have been easily found by any person Comeing up the.

[Question:] Where far is it from this place to the log lick trace.

[Question:] have not the Greates number of the Inhabitants of Estils Station who firs settled Sd Station in the Sprng 80 died and most of them who are not dead removed out of the State or to a great distance from this place So that thier testimony Can not Easily be.
    Mudy Creek Madeson County Ky
    Depositions concerning M. Bedingers Land

[p. 247]
Letter from Edward Carrington to George M. Bedinger
Col. Edwd. Carrington:
Richmond Decr. 21 1789

I have the pleasure to enclose your paper which contains the publication of what was done in our Meeting.

As My surveys that are the most valuable lie contiguous to one of your Brothers on the lake near the mouth of Cumberland, and as also there is another tract adjoining or perhaps between the two, belonging to my Brother Joseph Carrington ... will be convenient for you to attend ...and get settlers or then. Should you have an opportunity of this sort I hereby authorise you to make such contract for me as you shall find it wise & proper to make for your Brother ... defend to Settler; and you may act in the same manner as to the tract belonging to my Brother Joseph who will confirm whatever you do. Wishing you every possible success in your business,

> I am ... with great regard yr. Most O Vm.
> Ed Carrington

Letter from J. Swan to George M. Bedinger

To Michael Bedinger Esqr.
Winchester, Va.
Favd. by Col. Zane
Sir

I hereby authorize You to make Settlements on my Lands agreeable to the terms mentiond by the meeting of the officers & others therewith Concernd at Richmond on 9 November 1789 and Conformable to the above Letter of Colo Carrington any information You can give me respecting the Situation of these Lands and thier quallity will be ... favor confered upon D...

Cap M. Bedenger
Your very obt. Servant
July 7th 1790
> J. Swan

Majr. Rudulph to Maj. Bedinger
<u>Copy</u>

Well, my friend, how goes it? Being here in the neighborhood of our savage acquaintance, we begin to acquire the habit of getting up soon & looking out. You, I suppose, are slumbering, and making your days and nights happy in the downy Cap of Love.

'Tis now half after four in the morning, and I will begin to give you a short sketch of our politics here:

I met with a very friendly and polite receptance from the General, and we have been lying, ever since we landed, on a handsome spot of ground, less than a mile below the village, which I Christained Park Abbey. The Riflemen continue under my command, but are now dispersing to the several posts. Our destination is to be Fort Hamilton. <u>So much for ourselves.</u> The Military force in this quarter has been very weak, and much neglected. Set it down for a certainty that Genl. Wilkinson has performed

[p. 250]

astonishingly to keep the posts supplied & to keep a communication with them as he has regularly done throughout the summer, when they have not had two reliefs for duty at Ft. Washington. This Majr. <u>Adair</u> of whose skirmish you have had, no doubt, a full account, has been of great utility — for, be assured, the word is here among the regular troops that they must be beat on all occasions; & under this impression, poor creatures, I wish them to keep garrison. The officers here swig cheerfully; but worse even than that, their practices here have been so infamous, that at least five or six are now on arrest for a variety of crimes, and some the most unpardonable. To make short of a reflection, I have no hope unless unless a new plan is adopted by Congress. We cannot stand on our present foundation. You must join me, and stay, as I shall do, in the army, until we hear from Congress. Should their measures not favor us, I certainly shall travel with you through the wilderness; and suppose 'tis in the Spring, 'twill be a happy

[p. 251]
season to visit the fountain of conjugal bliss.

I want to give the Indians one trial, which you may soon expect to hear of, if they Do not retire from where they now are about Ft. Hamilton. When this event happens, you may count on one of two things: that I give them a Damn'd flogging, or that you and I do not meet again until in the Elysian fields; for I do hold that a military life is not worth supporting under the wretched reflection of being of no use but to gratify savages as subjects for their cruelty and insolence. I will in one instance try small'y to retrieve the reduced character of the American people as warriors.

I wish to God you could get out two or three hundred fine fellows from Kentucke, & come on here. The General will allow me to do any thing. I do think we could give one party a proper banging; but I suppose you are now so much deluged with politics, that a Military Excursion could not have a moments consideration with you.

[p. 252]
Let me have a long letter from you soon, & believe me when I say that the smallest assurance wherein your own happiness is consulted, will give pleasure to your sincere & unalterable friend & servant
        M. Rudulph
        Novr. 18 '92, encampt
        Park Abbey

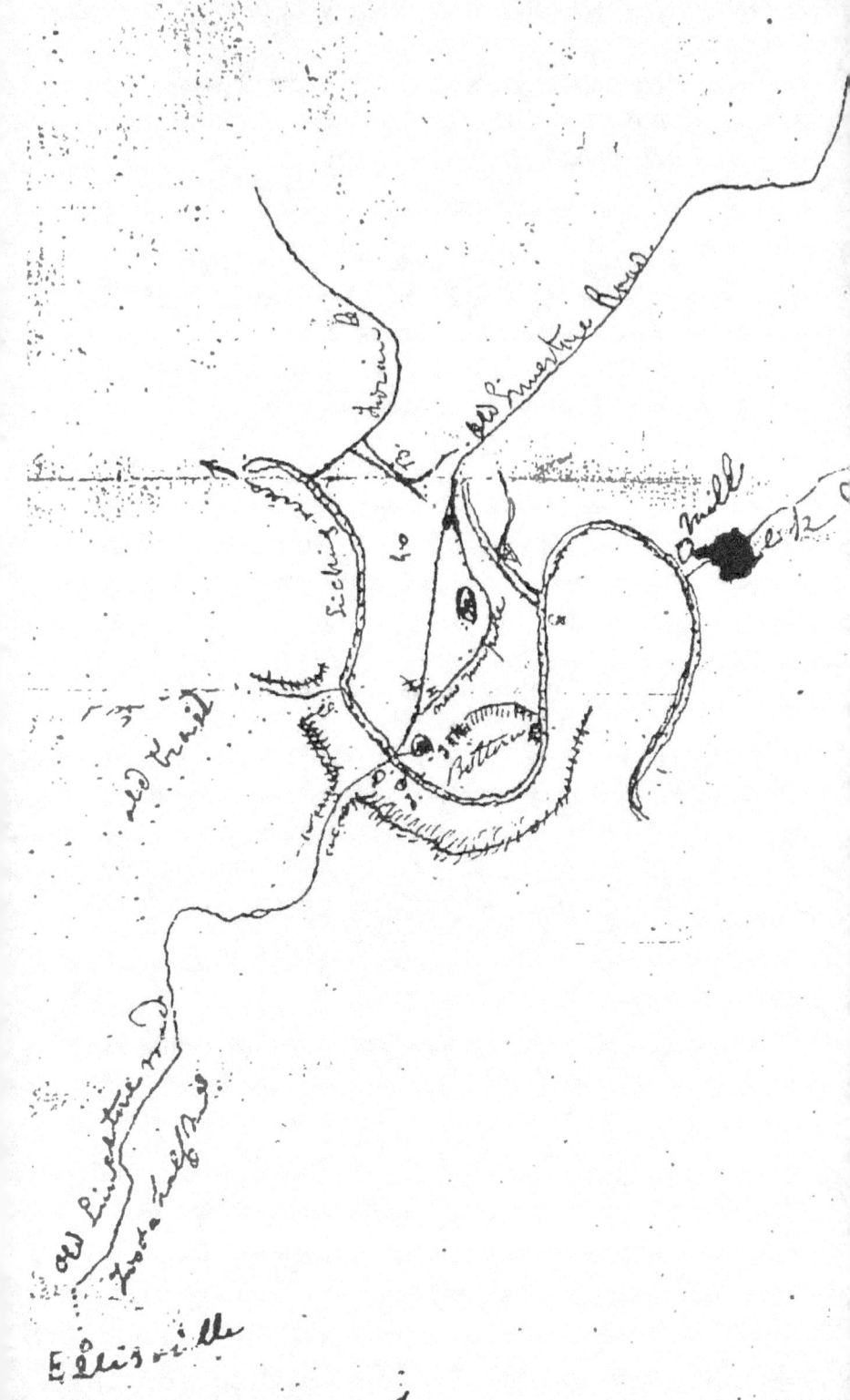

Majr. Bedingers

Endorsement by Maj. G. M. Bedinger: "M. Rudulph's Nov. '92

"The author went to sea, and was lost; if he did not take the character and name of Genl. Ney in the Revolution under Bonaparte, which last to me is most probable, from his strenuous solicitations that I would go with him to reap laurels, where they would be duly appreciated. May the God of all goodness and mercy on the soul of my brave friend is the fervent prayer of
G. M. B."

[p. 253]
Letter from M. Rudolph to George M. Bedinger

Copy.   Ft. Hamilton, Feb. 19th, '93

Well, Mister, where have you been, or where are you? In your last letter you told me you would soon be over, & 'tis the last I've heard of you, so that I take it for granted you are not coming, & therefore seriously prepare yourself for passing the wilderness in March. I shall be at Lexington about the 5th, & shall leave the Crab Orchard on the 10th.

You must meet me, or let me hear from you at Lexington, as I shall have no time to hunt you up. I will go with you to Shephard's Town, & from thence to the abode of my lovely family.

Have you heard from your intended wife? I hope all is well.

I am now at the old business C. M.* There is here not one word of news; no Indians out.

Yr. Friend & hble. St.
Maj. Bedinger.   M. Rudulph

[p. 253¹]
Superscription: "George M. Bedinger, Esquire Major, U. States Army, Kentucke"
  *The "C. M." on preceding page must be Cavalry Major, for he was Major of Cavalry, as the Dictionary of the Army shows.

The originals of these two Rudolph letters are placed among a separate collection of documents &c touching the Rudulph-Ney controversy.
            May, 1881.   L. C. D.

[p. 253²]
Notice
  Mr. Andrew S. Hughs: Take notice that on the twenty-fifth of August instant I shall attend at the court house in the town of Urbanna Champaign County Ohio For the porpose of taking the depositions of Philip C. Kenton as evidence in a certain action of Trespass brought in the Nicholas Circuit Court, but removed by change of Venue to Fleming Wherein William Whittamore is plantiff and I am defendant and also as evidence in a certain suit in Chancery now depending and undetermined in the Nicholas Circuit Court in which I am complainant & said Whittamore & others are defendants, and that on the twenty-ninth inst, I shall at the dwelling house of Thomas Davis of Ohio proceed to take the deposition of said Davis also as evidence in the above mentioned suits at which places you may attend if you please.
August 19, 1823   George M. Bedinger
Mr. Andrew S. Hughs

P. S. Thomas Davis resides twelve or fifteen miles beyond Augusta Kentucky near the road leading from that place to Urbanna, Ohio; from the best information that I can obtain.

G. M. B.

[p. 253³]
Nicholas County Set

Personally came before me the subscriber a Justice of the peace for Nicholas county Josiah McCabe Jr. and made oath that he did on this day deliver to Andrew S. Hughes a True Coppy of the within notice. Given under my hand this 20th day of Augt. 1823.

Hen. G. Parks

Notice for taking
Deposition by Jh. McCabe
20 August 1823 to
A Hughs Attorney
for Wm. Whittamore
Trespas & Chancery

[p. 254]
To the Voters of the Congressional District, composed of the counties of Bourbon, Nicholas, Mason and Bracken.

Fellow Citizens:

When after a retirement from public office of more than twenty years, a man of my advanced age is induced again to present himself before the people, and solicit their support for an office, to which at an earlier period of his life he voluntarily declined a re-election, when he had no competitor; a decent respect for the opinion of society renders it necessary that he should present the public with the reasons which have operated upon his mind in influencing him to pursue a course,

[p. 254] *(continued)*

which by some might be considered inconsistent with the general principles upon which he has always acted. As American citizen though born a subject of Great Britain, under the old colonial dominion, and deprived whilst yet a boy, of the protecting care of a father, and imbibing at an early age a devotion to the cause of liberty and equality, it is now fifty four years since declaring for liberty or death, leaving a kind and affectionate mother denounced as a rebel, I stepped forward with a few gallant spirits as a volunteer in the first company ever raised in Virginia to offer our feeble arms against Great Britain, one of the most formidable powers on earth; in which situation for more than a year, it being before independence was declared, the halter was viewed as the only alternative should we fail of success, then despaired of by many, and considered doubtful by all; never however despairing myself of the final success of that bold and fearless band who were contending for liberty; an attribute of divinity and the best privilege of man. Having served out my first year, I flew again and again, whenever an opportunity presented itself of rendering service to my country, and whenever duty to a mother, bereft for the time, by the ruthless hand of war, of two sons who were confined on board the British prison ships, suffering worse than death, would permit, until after the capture of the British army at Little York, at which place I performed the double duties of Captain and Adjutant. It is now fifty years since I visited Kentucky, then the haunt of wild beasts, and the theatre of the bloody deeds of the savage, uncultivated, and still more cruel man of the woods. The defence of Boonsborough, there being no white inhabitants at that time on the North side of the Kentucky river, detained me in this country from the 7th of April till late in the fall of the year 1779. After the capture of Cornwallis I frequently visited Kentucky, and finally, after many perilous adventures against the savages, made my home in this, then part of Virginia, where it is with gratitude I recollect the kind confidence reposed in me by my fellow citizens, by whom I was repeatedly selected to represent their wishes in both state and national legislatures, until influenced by the opinion that rotation in office was favorable to liberty, I declined a further acceptance of office. When in taking this retrospective view of

[p. 254] *(continued)*

my life, I compare the present condition of this nation with our situation when I first entered public service, I behold great and surprising changes to have been affected for the better. At that time we had no national government — as a nation we were not known at all — without an efficient organization either civil or military — without money — without credit — without arms — without clothing — without military supplies — without manufactories; and in fact, without every thing necessary to carry on a war, save a determined spirit of resistance to oppression, engrafted in the hearts of the people, and an united determination in all ranks, that they would be free at all hazards. But when we look at our present condition, we are the admiration of the civilized world! We have a well organized government, efficient for all the purposes of defence as well as for advancing the general welfare; a well organized army, not so great as to be burthensome to the country or dangerous to its liberty — our treasury overflowing — our credit good — arsenals and public stores of all the munitions of war disposed through every section of the Union. And instead of thirteen small colonies, bound together by present danger, we now see twenty-four powerful states united together by a grand constitution, or national compact — an extensive commerce carried on with all parts of the civilized world, and a navy full adequate to its protection. At home we see a large and increasing internal trade carried on between the citizens of the different states, facilitated by the invention of steam, the improvements of roads, and the erection of canals, strengthening our union by creating a greater unity of interest, and causing an intercourse to be maintained between portions of the republic remote from one another, well calculated to do away sectional prejudices whilst by our manufactories, protected by the arm of government, we are becoming daily more and more independent of foreign nations — giving an impulse to the agriculture of the country, by creating a domestic market

for the productions of our soil, and by giving a new direction to the industry and enterprize of our citizens, converting thousands of those who would otherwise only serve to increase the general glut of unsalable produce into consumers of our surplus.

[p. 254] *(continued)*

In addition to all these advantages, we as a nation, are enjoying peace with all the world; individually secured in our rights of person and of property, we may sit down under our own vine and our own fig tree, with no one to make us afraid.

Grateful as we should be to the omnipotent Ruler of the Universe for all these blessings, still all is not well with us. There exists among us too much party spirit; too much intolerance for one another. We have lately been divided in our sentiments with regard to men, and had begun to look upon each other as enemies. This, fellow citizens, in my view, is grossly wrong. The constitution, the charter of our rights, guarantees to each one the liberty of speech, and the right of suffrage. One of us has as good a right to his opinion as another. In the late contest for president we have seen father and son arrayed against each other; brother arrayed against brother, and old friends against old friends. Fathers and sons, brothers and friends, have now all spoken their sentiments and voted their wishes, they all had the right to do so. Let the minority now submit cheerfully to the majority; let the father and son still be father and son — let brothers be brothers, and let old friends be old friends still. To conciliate the public mind, to restore peace and harmony among men equally interested in the public welfare, is as I conceive the duty of every patriot, and should be the desire of all good men.

It was for this purpose and upon the principle of equal rights that, at the solicitations of some old friends, who had differed with me in the late contest, as well as some who agreed with me in that controversy, I became a Candidate for Congress. I submit with deference and respect to the decision of the late controversy for president, and with great magnanimity too, have many of those who differed with me in opinion, extended to me offers of their friendship, seeing that we agree in our views; as regards the future policy of the country; they have declared their intention of giving me their support. Coming out upon these principles I claim the support of no man from party considerations, although it has been ascertained at several successive elections that the party with whom I have voted are much the strongest in this district; but I present myself to the people, a plain old man

[p. 254] *(continued)*

whose advanced age with the infirmities incident thereto, would under other circumstances, have prevented him from soliciting such a trust, but feels now willing, and even solicitous of uniting his feeble exertions with those of his fellow citizens, who concur with him in support of that policy of the country requisite to advance the happiness and prosperity of the nation. And gratifying indeed, will it be to me, if through the kind confidence of those friends and fellow citizens, of whom I have never been used to solicit favors in vain, should I even now in the decline of life, be the happy instrument, in the hands of Providence, of uniting & reconciling a divided people.

Having said this much of the motives by which I have been led to declare myself a candidate to represent you in the next Congress, it is necessary that I should declare my views upon such political matters as may probably come before that body for their consideration. The policy of internal improvement, and the protection of domestic manufactures, are subjects which appear to threaten the next Congress with much controversy. That the General Government has power to make roads through the states, I cannot doubt for a moment, when I look at the Constitution which declares that Congress shall have power to establish post roads. To have the power to establish without the power of opening and rendering them passable, is in my view, a nullity, and would subject the transportation of the mail to the caprice of every state in the Union. I am therefore, separate and apart from all selfish considerations, decidedly in favor of extending the national roads, and I do sincerely believe it to be the interest of the United States that a branch of that road, uniting the great Western and Southern roads, should be immediately passed through the heart of this State and district. Such a road being free to all persons will be of much greater importance to the people of this state and district than any road which might be made by a company of private individuals who would be necessarily forced to exact high tolls, and would thereby in good weather, drive many of our citizens from the interior, down the fine and pleasant Dry Ridge road to Cincinnati, for their supplies of salt, &c. where too, there is generally a more extensive market for their surplus produce than there is at Maysville, which latter place, had we a road free from toll passing through it, Paris, and the intermediate towns, thence on to Nashville, would always be the most convenient port, not only to this district, but to the people of the upper end of the state generally. To procure the establishment of such a road, with the appropriation necessary to carry it into operation, would be with me a grand and important object, and I should consequently exert myself for its accomplishment. Upon the subject of the protection of domestic manufactures I will observe, that to deny to Congress this power, is to deny to the nation the power of protecting itself. When there is no foreign demand for any of our agricultural products, except cotton and tobacco, with which the foreign market is already glutted, and the tem-porary demand of our ... which the failure of the crops in Europe has accidentally produced, and upon the continuance of which, we cannot calculate with any certainty longer than the securing of the next harvest, it must be evident that the grain-growing interest of this nation of people cannot sustain itself by importing goods without exporting something to pay for them. To be always buying and never selling, will bring a nation, as well as an individual, to poverty. The foreign demand for our bread stuffs having ceased, we must necessarily, and in self defence, endeavor to create a market at home. This can only be done by giving employment to a portion of our citizens as manufacturers. Let them furnish us with those articles for which, until the adoption of the Tariff, we have depended upon foreign nations, and in exchange let us supply them with the necessaries of life, which foreign nations will not take from us. Other nations to encourage their agriculture, prohibit us by heavy duties, from supplying their manufactories; in our turn, we must prohibit their manufactories from supplying us. With no foreign demand for our beef, pork and breadstuffs, should our manufactories be put down, and our manufacturers become farmers, it appears to me, that inevitable ruin must necessarily follow to the whole farming and mechanic interest of the United States. In order, therefore, to protect ourselves, we must protect our manufactories. They are yet young and feeble, but they will soon become strong, and will not only protect us, but

[p. 254] *(continued)*

themselves also. The principle of slavery, as recognized by the constitution of the U. States, seems to me to be a subject portentous of much difficulty, and upon which the people are becoming very sensitive. A friend to freedom and equal natural rights, I was induced to liberate, some years, ago, several of my slaves. The result however, of that experiment, has convinced me that it is bad policy to have them free amongst us. Since that time a Colonization Society has been formed in the United States, and a flourishing Colony has been planted at Liberia, on the coast of Africa. Approving highly of the object of that society, I have thought that if the general government could be induced to lend its aid in furnishing some of the means for the transportation of such free people of color to that country, as might be willing to leave this, the public interest, as well as the cause of freedom and humanity, would be advanced. I view slavery as one of the evils entailed upon us by the British government, whilst we were in a state of Colonial dependence, though this evil was permitted to be extended by the prohibitory clause in the constitution of the United States, by which no law could be passed to prevent their importation, prior to the year 1808.

To meet this prohibition I exerted myself, when formerly honored as the representative of this district, and finally succeeded in getting a bill passed in the house of representatives, prohibiting their further importation, as soon as permitted by the constitution, which bill became a law. The right of property held in the persons of slaves, I never wish to see infringed: but if there be persons in our country who are willing to give up that right, and restore them to the enjoyment of their natural liberty, upon the condition of their being colonized, I believe that the interest of the whole United States would be promoted, should the matter be taken into consideration, and a portion of our immense revenue appropriated for that benevolent, and I may add patriotic purpose. Upon the subject of the amendment of the constitution of the United States, although I believe that we ought never to approach that sacred instrument, except with the utmost caution, yet I feel favorable to such an amendment as would give to the people themselves the entire election of President and Vice President of the United States without the

[p. 254] *(continued)*
intervention of electors or the interference of Congress, reserving to each state its rights as settled by the original compromise.

Having now fellow citizens, given you a brief outline of my sentiments upon such political topics as I have thought worthy of your attention, may I be permitted to express for each of my competitors the utmost good will and highest respect. Should either of them, however, urge his claims exclusively, to your support as possessing more influence in Congress, and with the President of the United States on the grounds of his having been friendly to his election, and his habits of public speaking, may I not be indulged in the hope, if the President and myself were fellow laborers in the cause of freedom in our youth, that even now I should be entitled to an equal share of his confidence, and not only his confidence, but also the confidence and support of all those members of Congress, the sons of those sires, who in that glorious struggle defended their freedom; and that the plain, unvarnished statements of a soldier of the revolution should have equal weight upon the floor of Congress. Fellow Citizens, it is the last time I ever expect to appear before you in the same attitude that I now do, & if I should be so fortunate as to meet the approbation of my countrymen at the ensuing election, it will be a source of pleasing gratification, and in the shades of retirement a consolitary reflection to me to know that I enjoy the confidence of those for whose happiness and prosperity I shall ever entertain the deepest solicitude.

GEORGE M. BEDINGER

July 25th, 1829.

[p. 255]
To the voters of the second Congressional District.

Fellow Citizens, I have been not a little amused with the excessive spleen, which some writer over the signature of Homo, has vented at two old men, who as far as I can learn, have not done him any injury? With Judge Beatty I confess, I am so little acquainted, either politically or personally, that I should not know him were I to see him; but as to Major Bed-

[p. 255] *(continued)*

inger's character, and conduct I am better informed, and therefore cannot but smile at the harmless malevolence of this disappointed splenetic, who is so indignant and clamorous at, he knows not what.. He has however wasted many words in endeavoring to make you belive that it is a great piece of presumption in Major Bedinger again to offer his services to his country, and for this act of effrontery, advises you to "spurn him from you with contempt, defeat and disgrace." What! spurn from us the soldier of the revolution who has been so grately instrumental in procuring for us and him the boasted name and privileges of free men? What reward with "contempt, defeat and disgrace" one who has sacrificed the flower of his life and the vigor of his manhood on the altar of liberty, and has hitherto whenever he has offered his services met the cordial approbation and support of our fathers? Does he calculate that it is in his power to Disgrace the friend of Washington, the Defender of freedom the Lover of his country by going to the polls and saying that though he has spent his youth in our service his old age is obstrusive and he must retire and make room for a younger aspirant.

Kentuckians! not thus has Virginia rewarded the services of her Madison. No! though many years older than the deserving object of my panegyrick they did not reproach him for his age, but complimented him on his experience: and animated by the grateful remembrance of his youthful services, they in the true spirit of generosity and politeness, solicited him to assist them, in the difficult task, of amending their constitution.

But different has been the conduct of Homo and a few (with pleasure & to the honor of my country I acknowledge a very few) others of this stamp. This gentleman after a long tirade in which he endeavors to prove that our OLD FRIEND in whom our fathers used so affectionately to confide has become in his old age a faithless hypocrite, a traitor to his country, and a bankrupt in printciple, asks "what has been his course in this canvass"? As the gentleman has in his statements discovered the grossest ignorance I, as well as any other person acquainted with the facts can inform him that Major Bedinger came out in March at Carlisle his county seat, on the same day that our first candidate did, and as he

[p. 255] *(continued)*

offered his services in the sincerity of his heart; as he had always been received by his countrymen with affection and confidence, so unbounded that after serving them in Congress four years so great was their esteem for him, so complete their satisfaction that, no competitor advanced to oppose him. But he like his high minded friend the generous Washington whom, "James Monitor" calls upon him to intimate declined a reelection from the principle that "rotation in office was favorable to liberty" and it was ungenerous for one man to appropriate to himself all the good things in the people's gift. If this be ambition then I know not the meaning of the word. If after a retirement of more than twenty years under the circum-

stances I have mentioned the moderate offer of his services to that beloved country whose happiness and prosperity his course through an active and eventful life has proved to be the first wish of his heart; if this be presumption I confess myself ignorant of my own native language. And now he finds that again the sovereign people are solicitous to honour him with their preference by the promise of their support, and after, having under those circumstances pledged himself to continue a candidate for their favor till the last moment of the election, would it not be casting a shade on his unblemished reputation, to falsify his word by declining?

But Mr. Monitor, Major Bedinger is our oldest candidate and with claims upon our confidence certainly as strong as those of any of the others, if a life of toil and danger spent in our service entitles any one to our regard. He now for the last time, asks our suffrages. This is the closing scene of his public life; but with Judge Beatty it is entirely different, this is almost the commencement of his political career, he may look forward to a long life of honors if he do not by his obstinacy disgust those whom it is his wish to conciliate and thereby defeat his own desires and bring on his own downfall. He must know that in Nicholas and Bourbon he cannot obtain a great support, and even Mason and Bracken, I believe will be nearly as strong for Bedinger as for himself. For my part I cannot but acknowledge that as I desire the prosperity of my country, I feel perfectly secure in trusting her liberties to the protection of one so greatly instrumental in procuring for us

[p. 255] (continued)
the sacred blessings which cost so dear. If he who purchased it by years of suffering knows not its value and how to guard it with watchful vigilance then it is safe with no man.

But fearing my countrymen, that I have already trespassed upon your patience I shall close this address by merely observing that I trust the friends of Liberty and La Fayette who heaped such honors on the illustrious foreigner will not disregard valor and worth for being of American growth. To the friends of the AMERICAN SYSTEM this appeal must be irresistable, and with those of General Jackson it will have its due weight. I may therefore reasonably hope that my countrymen casting aside party spirit will unite in support of a man who had "withstood the shock" for nearly two years before the arrival of our distinguished ally upon the American shore.

Yes, the volunteer of eighteen breasted the most impetuous fury of the storm for thirteen months prior to the Declaration of Independence when an ignominious death awaited him, and his noble compeers in case of a failure in the hazardous cause. But God prospered the brave and preserved the patriot. Then why should he fear to place himself before the children and grand children of his worthy associates in that glorious struggle? No! trusting that virtue is inherent, that the sons of the brave have imbibed the sentiments of their fathers, that the hallowed tone of freedom yet burns in the breast of every descendant of his brothers in arms he may confidently place himself before the American youth.

I myself am one of them and can answer for my country and with pride with pleasure, fearlessly declare, that notwithstanding all the arrows of malevolence that have been levelled at the aged oak, it is still the favorite of the forest, and every warm and generous spirit will delight to come and shelter itself under its venerable shade. In other words, my countrymen grateful for the arduous services of 20 years will not disregard the claims of the old soldier, one of the very, very few remaining heroes of the revolution, but will in the enthusiasm of freemen flock to the polls & there prove that the love of liberty did not perish with their ancestors, but that they have determined not to repay with "contempt, defeat and

[p. 255] *(continued)*
disgrace" the obligations they are under to one of freedom's real tried and firm supporters.
    A Citizen of Bourbon.

[p. 256]
Letter from Henry Bedinger to George M. Bedinger
Dear Brother   Protumna Sep. 1832

  Your letter of the 5 Inst. arrived here in 8 days quick travelling. As I stated on my letter, I would make out Such State... of your Revolutionary Services, as my memory contained, make affidaved thereto that in Case of my death, so much should be left on paper as I recollected of those Services, which affidaved, might possibly be of Service to you. I did so, and left the Statement with Isaac S. Lauch Esqr. of Martinsburg a Majistrate, a son of your Companion, Peter Lauck, now of Winchester once an apprentice to Philip Wolwind (the potter), where it may be had if necessary. I stated in that paper that you and myself had entered Captain Hugh Stephensons Company of Volunteer Riflemen of Berkely County Virga. Sometime in June 1775 for One year, that we Marched in said Company to the Siege of Boston and Completely Served the term for which we engaged, that you had Served as a Volunteer in Captain William Morgans Company to oppose the Brittish Army in Jersey in 1777 & believed all the Company were allowed a tour of militia duty, for those Services. I had forgotten your tour in 12th Virga. Regt. Commanded by Colo. James Wood, of Gen. A. Stephens's division Scotts

Brigade Colo. Joseph Swearingens Company, and that you was in the Battle of German Town but Stated your expedation in 1779 under Colo. Bowman against the Shawnees North West of the Ohio river, also that in 1781 you Commanded a Company of Berkeley Militia & anexed to the Regiment Commanded by Colo. William Dark also acted as adjutant to said Regiment proceeded with the Company & Regiment to the Siege of Yorktown assisted in the Capture of the Brittish forces Commanded by Lord Cornwallis which Surrendered on the 19th October 1781 that said Regt. were allowed pay & Rations untill they arrived at their homes in Berkeley that the Company of Militia you Commanded was drafted Sometime in the month of May 1781 and discharged Sometime in the Month of November, same year. It was of Course impossible for me to State with precision the dates of the Commencement and ending, of the different tours of Services you performed but Supposed you had Served in the Capture of Cornwallis six months in the expedition under Captain Morgan (a tour Militia duty) at least three Months, & under Bowman say One Month & at Boston one year that would make one year and ten Months. The German Town expedition one Month and your Boonsburg Services about 6 Months or perhaps more. This will bring your Services to more than 2 years — I have not seen the instructions and Necessary forms, Vouchers required &^{en} &^{cas}&^{en} by the Secretary of the Treasury to establish the Claim under this late act, but am told, the applicant must State his Services in a Court of Justice make oath thereto, & also that the

Evidence as far as can be obtained

[p. 257]
be also taken in Open Court & Certified by the Clerk of the said Court with County seat anexed; all this may be learnt & known in due time. You Complain of want of Memory. I have to lament the like deficiency, and shall have to refer to the history of the revolution for dates for instance, the battle of German Town, the expedition under Captn. William Morgan, &c. I wish you would, as far as you can recollect and asscertain, and at as early a period as is Convenient State to me your Services in the rotation in which they were performed it will assist my recollections, as well as your own, and may be of Service in Judgeing of the time expended in each expedition.

The Government or the Secretary of the Treasury does not expect that possitive Eye witness proof can be brought to substantiate the testim... of Applicants in all and every Case but expects such proof as will enable him to judge of the probable truth of the facts Sworn to and for which reason all and the best evidence yet in existance ought to be Obtained & presented. I am very anxious for your success because I know of no man now living who risqued his person life property health &c. in Serving your Country in the perilous times of the revolution than yourself & that has obtained less Value or Satisfaction in a pecuniary way for those risques & services.

The Cholera has Surrounded us, there has been a case at Martinsburg, one at Parrotts Town one at Newkirk Mill on the Potomac, a number at Harpers ferry, Shepherds Town Charles Town and many cases, & deaths along the river among the thousands of Irish who are working along the Canal from below Harpers ferry to the mouth of Opukan. Sharpsburg is also afflicted by this fatal disorder. The lower order, that is the intemperate either in eating or drinking are Most liable to the disease & he knows that a drunkard always falls by it.

Brother Jacob Continues much as when you Saw him, he is now Very anxious to get to law in Town as much exposed and perstered with the Vagabonds employed on the opposite side of the river in the Canal. Mildred, too is now willing to leave "Mount Misery"; I hope he will see and ... Maning's house in Town. Olivia Morgan, sometime since in speaking of some transactions and affairs respecting Jo Morgans Estate, said ...thing about a suit being brought against your son Henry ...

[p. 258]
Executor but expressed herself thus, "This must not be done" or words to that effect. I had therefore no Idea that Coercive measures were about to be enforced against him.

I will when opportunity serves make some inquiry into the salt air. All our acquaintances & Dela were here as well. My wife is daily ailing more or less, yet moves about the house as when you last saw her. I do the same tho every day admonishes us both that we are old, ... & must soon depart, we hope to another and better world. My family are all well. hope you enjoy good health, that you have a ... that your good Lady Betsy Bedford & Henriette and all the family and

Conections are in the full enjoyment of health and prosperity.

Every day Convinces me that tis absolutely necessary Old persons should not expose themselves to Cold, heat, of the sun, or wet, and avoid fatigue.

We often forget our true Situation, and attempt improper exertions, beyond what is prudent and injure ourselves thereby. My frame has become so feeble tho that I am instantly on my Guard against bodily exertion & yet sometimes forget myself and feel the effects. hope you are also becoming Cautious in those respects. your Constitution and frame has been Severely tried, has stood firm among the thousands of our acquaintance who have faintd in the same time. tis therefore proper, that you guard an Nurse it now that you may enjoy a Serenity and good feelings in future during your stay here. You see by this, how easy it is to Philosophize on these subjects, and give advice to others when at the same time we neglect to practise upon the advice & reasons given.

You will observe I have written this letter without Method or order but I hate apologies. Shall therefore conclude with expressing my ardent wish, that I may be instrumental in obtaining the Object, in View and remain my dear Brother
    Yours with affection
    Henry Bedinger
Major George M. Bedinger

[p. 259]
Both of B... the 11 of September
of Germentown 4th octoberber 1777

Fort Washington taken Novemb 18 1776
Darksville   September 18 - 1839
Va Sept 17th
                Single
                Maj. George M. Bedinger
                Lower Blue Licks
                Kentucky
Via
Carlisle post office Ky

PS It appears a little doubtful who will be our next President, both the Jackson & Clay parties appear Sanguine of Success. The Veto on the U.S. Bank bill has had some effect against Jackson. A Measure that I think deserves the applause of the whole people. on the other hand Mr. Adams's attempt to browbeat Congress on the debate of Stanberry's card, and the insult offered by Clay, to the Venerable Genl. Saml. Smith, and his quarrels with Sagwell Benton &c. have arroused and fixed their enemies to a More than ordinary Opposition to them. I suppose you have read Mr. Latham Gaithers statement of bank Measures and Conduct, if not, tis worth reading.

[p. 260]
Statement by Henry Bedinger, July 1834

As there is little or no Chance to obtain many here, my advice is that you Set yourself at work most earnestly and diligently to make out a Statement of your revolutionary services both here and in Kentucky including those under Generals St. Clair and Wayne. That of St. Clair & Wayne will not Just now be of much account, but it will probably come in hereafter as efforts will be persevered in by the Kentucky delegation in Congress to Obtain lands for those services & may probably suceed in a few sessions more.

Copy. — Henry Bedinger of the County of Berkely & State of Virginia declares that his Brother George M. Bedinger now a resident in Nicholas County, Kentucky, and himself entered as Volunteers, for one year, early in the month of June 1775, in the Company of Volunteer Riflemen then raising in Berkeley County, by Captain Hugh Stephenson, that they Marched in said Company and arrived at the siege of Boston, and served the full term for which they Was engaged, that subsequently the said G M Bedinger entered as a Volunteer in a Company Commanded by Captain William Morgan of Berkeley and which company joined the Corps Commanded by Colo. Charles M. Thruston of Frederick County Virginia, proceeded to Oppose the Brittish Army in Jersey, this deponant knows not how long said Corps remained in service, but the men Composing it were allowed a tour of militia duty — also th... M. Bedinger Volunteered his Services and was in the Battle of Ger... on the 4th of October, 1777. That said G M. Bedinger Joined a Com... Volunteers in Kentucky Commanded by Colo. Bowman, made an at... an Indian town north west of Ohio in 1779, were unsuccessful, Compelled .. with loss. Said Bedinger also for the Greater part of the season ... assisted as a Scout or Spy, at Boonsburg, & acted as Commissary in the ... and distributing to the pent up inhabitants of provisions; but ... deponant knows not the length of time said G M Bedinger ... separate expeditions, but believes these several Expeditions as well ... of service as a scout Spy and Commissary must together have amounted ... month ... This deponant knows said G M Bedinger Commanded a Company ... Militia raised in May 1781 was ordered to Join the Regt. Com... Colo. William Darke, to which Regt. he then also acted as adjut... assisted at the seige of York Town, not at the Capture of Lord Cornwallis on the 19. Oct 1781 ... as they seek & Race home in a wagon were allowed pay & rations to their homes, in Berkeley, probably served something more than five Months.

The above is a hasty sketch of your services as far as I could recollect at the time when made out. This with Peter Fishers, and any others Corroborating, or in any way pertinent, can assist you in making out a full Statement of your Services so as to thus

[p. 261]
you was in actual, and active service, at least two years, of the Revolutionary War. I believe you will have to make affidavit to it, with the County Seal anexed. I wish much that it was Complete & sent on. I do not suppose there will be an absolute Necessity of fully proving by Separate Testimony all the times and places you served, tho, the more Corroborating evidence, the better; send it in with such vouchers as you Can procure, in regular form as Soon as may be; traditionary evidence I find is also sometimes of Service; remember you and I are old, my deposition is Essential. Peter Fishers is secured; Jacob Haynes's and George Shaners, would have acted traditionary. The first is nearly dying if not dead the latter died, a week or two since. John Miller

lives & might Corroborate traditionary.

Majr Henry Bedingers letter of the first of July 1834 relative to gathering Testimony for a pension.

July 4th Majr. George M. Bedinger
Deposition of   Lower Blue Licks
for Pension Kentuckey
M Majr. HB
& Peter Fiser

Enclosed is Peter Fishers Statement or Deposition also my Dear & only remaining brothers Copy of his Deposition relative to some my services in the Revolutinary War.

                           G. M. B.

Received the 14th July 1834

I have thus spun out my letter to great length; without giving you much Satisfaction. We have Commenced harvest. Congress I suppose disperses to day, the Senate have rejected A. Stephenson the late Speaker as Envoy to Brittain. This together with its General Conduct of late is Causing a Revulsion. Hampshire and Conecticut have forbiden a Recharter or return of deposites &^{en} &$^{en.}$ Affectionate respects to your family, your Brother

                      Henry Bedinger
Majr. Geo M Bedinger

[p. 262]
Letter from Henry Bedinger to George M. Bedinger
My Dear Brother   Protumna June 25th, 1835

The boy which Carried my letter directed to you date 23rd May brought me yours of the 17th of the Same Month, having nothing of importance to Communicate I postponed writing. Yesterday I recd. yours of the 7th Inst.; this will therefore be a reply to both.

Our Niece Olivia Morgan and Our Cousin Maria Winrot the Granddaughter of Our much respected departed uncle Colo. Henry Slagle happened to be here yesterday, when your last Came to hand. Mrs. Ransom had Visited us a few days before. They Seemed to regret that Richd. Henry had Cancelled the bargain with Mr. Allen, as Richd. Henry had informed them that Estate would now bring a Much higher price than he was to pay. My Opinion is Still the Same, & I must Still believe the purchase was too large for his funds, tho Olivia thinks Otherwise. How Dick Henry will do in the Mercantile line is Very uncertain, he is inexperienced in that line & you already know my Opinion of Mercantile pursuits generally.

I am extremely Sorry your Son D. Continues in a delicate State of Health. I should advise a trip to the South possibly a Southern tour might restore him. Persons afflicted with Complaints of the lungs seldom receive any benefit from Mineral waters. By invitation I attended at a Barbacue at Our departed Sisters Spring on the 60th Aniversary of our March to Boston. Our Nephew Jacob Morgan has embelished and Ornamented that Spring where you and myself partook of a barbacue on the 50th Aniversary. That place has become almost Consecrated ground. Not one human being of all who knew those Springs in 1775 remained or could attend there, but myself, and there were probably 800 men at this last meeting, besides women children and Servants the general Estimate as to numbers was by some supposed to be nearly 1500. Tho I ... the number about 1000. It was a dinner given to Colo. Edward Lucas and as a festive meeting, & a rejoicing, at the Victory obtained in the Re-election to Congress of Colo. Lucas, against the Federal Candidate John R. Cooke; and purposely fixed on the Aniversary, to perpetuate, the pledge we had given on the 10th of June 1775. Many persons who know you & attended, then regretted greatly, that you was not, nor Could not make one

[p. 263]
of the party, as you and myself are believed to be the Only Survivors of Captain Hugh Stephens Company. Colo. Lucas gave us a Very neat Speech on the Occasion of the meeting, & in which he detailed the patriotic services & sufferings, of us (their Brothers) in the revolution &^{ca} &^{a}. Gentlemen were invited and attended from every County in this Congressional district, and I never saw so decent so orderly a meeting at a festive board; we had the Harpers ferry, the Martinsburg and the Shepherds Town band Combined, which greatly enhanced the pleasures of the meeting. All was Carried out and ended with the most Complete and unprecedented order. The table was more than 80 yards in length it Contained 240 plates, knives & forks, & More than 100 glass tumblers, and Other Necessary implements, all in the best style, most abundantly furnished. I remained at Jacob Morgans who resides in his Elegant New house, built about 50 yards on the height west of where the log barn of

our Sisters Stood. I visited the Scene of festivity next morning and was assured by the purveyors that such was the extraordinary Orderly Conduct of all Classes, not a single article of any description was Missing or broken, except one tumbler and One plate! This is but a Short description. I am sorry you Could not be with us to partake of, and mingle in the pleasing throng.

Our worthy Nephew D. Morgan requested me to say, he had sold the Bank Stock at par; that he Could by a Short notee, from you, raise five or six hundred Dollars for you, that he had paid the other Legatees, their Share of the avails of the bank stock, & that moneys could be had from the storekeepers, who had moneys loand to them by our departed Brother, on any reasonable or short notice that nothing has yet been done with the Maryland land nor has the damages been paid tho Mr. Lee informed me some time since he had secured the amount, in the hands of One of the Striders, which he thought fortunate as the Canal Company were Bankrupt. That Company as many others is frequently bankrupt, or nearly so; ... will never be bankrupt in fact, because whenever their resources ... exhausted, some means are devised to obtain, or Create additional Supplys, & the work goes on.

My Daughter Sally and Granddaughter, Ellen Augusta Miller have Just returned from Philadelphia, where they had went, on a Visit to Colo. Miller, remained there Only about three weeks, the Colo. has not enjoyed good health since the attacks on him by the Cholera, is however somewhat recovering his former activity. 'Tis astonishing to me to find with what facility the trip to Philadelphia is now made. My children breakfasted at Colo. Millers passed on to Baltimore the same day, Set out next morning arrived at Harpers ferry by 2 O Clock and at Colo. Davenports by four, thus making the trip in less than two days, & all in Open day light. The Carrs run from Harpers ferry on the railroad, the greater part of the way to Baltimore by Steam, and at the rate of One mile in three minutes.

You State that you had sometime since written to Thos. Morgan to induce him to take your farm on some terms. I had supposed that he was in a situation more independent than to rent, or undertake the Management of any lands other than his own, is he also brought low by the unfortunate Concition of his brother Abel? I had hitherto supposed that Thomas Still held his division, of the land where his Father first Resided after removing down to the Vicinity of Russelsville.

I find you still entertain some Idea of making us a Visit & Mention that you would probably bring with you some horses. This would be a troublesome Job unless you could bring an active young man with you. The Chance of Sale too has become quite precarious, but few horses are now wanting for any use; waggoning is broke up, everything is transporting by Canal ... road, no horses are wanted except for a few for riding & plowing, and Oxen ...tituting for the common plantation drawing. Still, ... well gaited horses will bring large prices about the largest ... but Common horses are and will Continue Cheap.

Our Nephew Doctor Daniel Bedinger had as

you have long since probably been informed, Caught the Smallpox, on a trip of experiment to Baltimore to assist make himself acquainted with the best means of Curing the Cholera he had the Smallpox quite Severe, is a good deal pitted in the face, and on recovery it was believed he had also recovered from the disease of his lungs appeared untill Very lately quite fleshy and in high health, but alas his disease has, or is returning, has lately had several bleedings of the lungs looks pale, and I believe in Some measure despairs, talks of making a Journey to Floriday or some other Southern Country, with the hope of regaining health. he was well fixed at Harpers ferry, attended to his official duties with promptitude, and maintained a respectable Character. Poor fellow, I fear all his hopes of Earthly enjoyments are Vanishing, as I believe he is thus again assailed by a disease that I have never yet known to be Cured.

Our Crops of wheat now are worse than I ever knew them there is Scarcely a farm in this ... will make its seed and bread & ... the district from Shepherds Town ... abundant Crops, our whole dependence is on Rye, of which there was unfortunately ... too little Sowed, and on our Corn now growing. For the last three years my Crops of wheat were Very short; but the present Crop is still more, Vastly more deficient. Those failures have greatly affected, both myself, and my immediate Neighbors, and is a Source of greater pressure or panic than Could be inflicted by the U. S. Bank, or any other banks of this country. tis well ascertained that money is more plenty in the Seaports than it has been for years. Yet we fail of the means of obtaining any of it, because we have not flour

[p. 265]
(that being our Staple) to sell. I find the people along the Scioto Canal are realizing fine prices for produce it seems wheat Sells at 80 Cts has been as high as $1.00, flour $5 and Corn above 50 Cts. Whether this is owing to Scarcity, or to whatever Other cause, the prices of bread stuffs, as well as of beef & pork, appear to me, to be extremely high. Our friends in Ohio as well as here enjoy good health generally. I had almost forgotten to tell you that Henry Bedinger our Brother Daniel's Second son, has Commenced the practice of law and bids fair to make a Conspicuous figure at the bar, that his first speech, made in defense of a Criminal cause, gained great applause; also that Edwin Bedinger is about to again Visit his lands in Ohio & will set out and proceed by the way of Bankaway in a week or two. God bless you my dear Brother, present us affectionately to your family.
    Henry Bedinger
Maj. Geo M. Bedinger
 Maj. George M. Bedinger
 Lower Blue Licks
 Kentuckey

[p. 266]
Political address
 It is no ordinary circumstance Fellow citizens, ... induce me aged and infirm as I am to attempt a ... of ... to attend a political gathering of the people, it is now. Tis more than sixty ... years

since with ... the ... <u>Liberty or Death</u> I shouldered my ... and became a soldier in the cause of Freedom and independance and was among the few who at the first call of this country became a rebel ... the cause of the legitimacy ... my all ... sovereignty of the people, and the indepenance of the ... united colonies, since that ... and have been ... by my country & my fellow citizens I can truly say that I have still ... by and devoted myself to the ... of the same ... which ... the call ... peaceable ... and mother to ... that the ... often ... to U. S. ... in death and I can truly say that the same love of liberty the same devotion to the cause of human rights which filled my breast with enthusiasm and moved my arm to exertion at the age of eighteen years, now ... and ... & ... of my heart at 84 for had my fellow-citizens during that ... many ... dismay but as the ... with whom ... all foreign and easily distinguished ... patient ... to be trodden was still plain and easy to be found.

Letter from George M. Bedinger
             Decmber the 16, 1842
Honereable Walker Reed Dear Sir
     I this day returned from Carlisle and hav been advised by our friend Lewis H. Arnold to lay the matter relalative to the condemnation of my land for the benefit of the turnpike road before you placing the most entire confidence in your abilities as a jurist and believeing you would not permit as far as you are conserned an act of such gross injustice taking my land by as I believe an unconstitutional act of the legislature without the posibility of my being heard in defence of my right, Mr Arnold Col Morgan and Mr. Norval are

all under the impression that you will stop the the procedings as ex party and unconstitutional.

My son Jos Bedinger is hearby empowered to act for me in any matter concerning the condemnation of my land by the Maryville Washington Paris and Lexington Turnpike road company.

Respectfully yours

George M Bedinger

Lewis papers

[p. 267]
Letter from D. P. Bedinger to Lyman C. Draper
Bourbon County Ky. September 13th 1847
Dear Sir

Your favor of the 17th Ultimo was received in due time; and whilst acknowledging the reciept of that I feel bound to acknowledge also the reciept of several other letters of earlier dates, under circumstances that prevented immediate answers: and so not being answered at the proper time were neglected altogether. I take therefour this opportunity of thanking you for all. And shall proceed to answer your last. It is with pleasure that I learn from your letter that you desire a better acquaintance with me. And from what I have heard my mother say of you, I doubt not, that I should enjoy your acquaintance much more than you could mine. And should on that account be your debtor. I however trust that when you pass this way again you will visit us, as I am sure that my mother would be much pleased to see you again. And as you say "I should rejoice to take you by the hand" at my house.

Agreeably to your request I saw Majr. John Edwards of this County and he promised that he would deposit in the Post Office for me a sketch of the early life and publick services of his father. But when I called at the office at the time appointed (last Saturday) I found nothing from him.

Immediately after receiving your last letter, I wrote to my brother Dr. B. F in Boone County and requested him at his earliest convenience, to call on Dr. Drake and get the deposition of Jesse Hodges, in relalation to Bowmans campaign.

[p. 268]
The aforesaid deposition (as I learn from my mother) has been loaned by my father to Benj. Drake Esq decd, and brother of Dr Drake who is the Executor of his deceased brother. But as the Doctor is now absent from home, and will not be at home for some weeks to come, I fear that the deposition can not be obtained for some time. If however it shall come to my hands I will cause it to be sent to you forthwith. My father was born december 10th 1756 and departed this life december 8th 1843.

Owing to my own sickness I was not able to visit him during his last illness, nor to be present at his burial. But I am informed that a large concourse of neighbors and friends from the surrounding country attended to offer their condolence, and to discharge their last sad duty to their departed friend and neighbor.

Mr. H. F. Wilson, merchant formerly of Paris has removed from this County I could not therefore learn from him whether or not his father is still alive. But I inquired of his son-in-law Mr. Henry C. Chiles and he told me since the receipt of your letter that the old gentleman is still living.

Hoping for your prosperity and the success of your labors I subscribe myself Respectfully

Your friend &c.

D.P. Bedinger.

Mr. Lyman C. Draper
    Mr. Lyman C. Draper
    Baltimore
    Md.

[p. 269]
Letter from Lyman C. Draper to D. P. Bedinger

Bourbon County Ky. April 2nd 1848
My Dr. sir

Your favor of the 24th Febry reached my hands I suppose in due time, but notwithstanding I determined to answer it the next day, in multitude of business it escaped from my memory and so has been neglected or rather overlooked until now.

I will probably see Majr John Edwards in a few days and will remind him of your request and his promise.

You wish to know something of Majr Jno Finley (the companion of Col D Boone.) I recollect to have seen when I was a boy Majr Jno Finley at the Upper Blue Lick. he was a particular friend and acquaintance of my father at that time. His son David still lives there and owns the salt spring and a large part of the property that formerly belonged to his father. But whether he was ever a companion of Col Boone or not I do not know, but as he was perhaps older than my father, I think it very probable that he may have been frequently in the Company of Col Boone.

But he is not I imagine the John Finley who first visited Ky. and who I believe accidentally met with Boone in the wilds of Ky as has been stated I think by Mr Marshall.

David Finley lives at the Upper Blue Lick, Fleming County and I know of no man in his neighborhood who is more capable of giving you any information in relation to his father's early life than himself. a post office was formerly kept by him at his own house, but I think it was discontinued because it was not on any regular mail rout. He lives within I think five miles

[p. 270]
of Elizaville Fleming County Ky. which I think will be the proper place to direct your letters to him.

Majr John Finley was a brother of Gen Saml Finley, formerly of Chillicothe Ohio, another old friend and perhaps a brother soldier of my fathers.

My mother still resides with me, and desires me to say give her respects to you, and desires to see you here if you shall again pass through these parts.

She says she would like very much to see your first volume before she dies.

I remain with much esteem your friend.
D. P. Bedinger

Lyman C. Draper Esqr
Baltimore, Md.

[p. 271]
Majr. G. M. Bedinger
Narrative
Indian Campaigns

Recollections of Maj. Geo. M. Bedinger taken down by B. Drake, Sept. 13, 1839, at the Lower Blue Licks

Geo. M. Bedinger, born in York County, Pa. the 10th of Decr. 1756; removed at 4 years to Shepherdstown, Berkely County, Virginia. Visited Kentucky in March 1779, coming out by the Crab Orchard Cinti. Went directly to Boonesborough. Had in company ten men & two negroes; object to see the country. Not more than 16 or 20 men at Boonesborough including his Party. About the 10th of April, went over to Harrodsburg when he saw Gov. Hamilton &

[p. 272]
and other prisoners, taken by Genl. Clark at Kaskaskia. Great excitement against Hamilton & many of the men disposed to kill him.

In the month of May, Col. John Bowman, commandant of the County of Kentucky, authorized by the Governor of Virginia, made a call for troops to go on an expedition against the Indians, at "New Chillicothe" on the head waters of the Little Miami, above Xenia. Some of these troops were collected at Harrodsburg & its vicinity. Some came from Boonesborough but not more than ten

[p. 273]
or twelve, and a Party came up from Louisville

and joined Bowman at the Mouth of Licking When Maj. B. joined Bowman at the Mouth of L.& the troops were all assembled, he formed 3 companies, commanded respectively by Ben. Logan, James Harrod & John Holder. The troops amd. in all to some 250 men. Crossed the Ohio between Cina. & the Little Miami in canoes & pirogues, swimming their horses. The day after crossing the Ohio Col. Bowman appointed Maj. B. Adjutant and Quarter Master of the troops in which capacity he

[p. 274]
acted throughout the Campaign. In going out there were but few of the men mounted, armed with rifles & tomahawks, carrying but small amt of provisions in order to travel with the more expedition. Saw no Indians until they reached their encampments at new Chillicothe, which occurred in the night. When a few miles from the place a Council of War was held, at which it was decided that Capt. Holder with his Company, should during the night, approach as near the town, on the side on which they were approaching it, as could be done, without discovery, & there rest upon

[p.275]
their arms. Capt Logan & Captain Harrod were to pass round the town with their commands, one on the west & the other on the east side, and lay in wait, so far apart, as to enable the Indians to pass between their companies. It was agreed that the period of the attack should be daylight next morning at which time Captain Holder, to whose company Maj. Bedinger was attached should

commence the action, & drive the Indians into the Pass between the other two

[p. 276]
companies, which were then simultaneously to attack them on the sides. Early in the night the three companies had attained their respective positions, and had rested a while, & the company of Capt. Holder, was preparing to lie down, when an Indian, quite out of breath, came running to the spot, where Holders Company were lying. He was evidently making his way to the Indian town to give the alarm. One of Captain Holder's company by the name of Ross shot him with his rifle, and another by the name of Stearns

[p. 277]
scalped him. Before the Indian was killed, he hollowd and gave the alarm to the Indians, when the Squaws cried out "Kentucke "Kentucke". This alarm occurred before midnight. In a few minutes six or seven Indians with their rifles & dogs came out toward Holders Company to make discoveries. When they had approached pretty near some of the company fired on them, but whether any were killed is not known; blood was discovered next morning. The Indians retreated to the center of the town, & Capt. Holder aware that he was

[p. 278]
now discovered, pursued them. The Indians were commanded by Black Fish a distinguished Shawanee. When the alarm was given, he addressed the Indians, urging them to be "strong", to "be

warriors." The Indians under his direction then retreated to a block house, standing in the village where they worked all night, cutting Out holes through which to shoot. At the moment, when Capt. Holder rushed upon the Indians, some of the troops in Logan and Harrod's company defeated the plan of the attack by

[p. 279]
violating orders & raising a shout. This prevented the Indians from retreating as it was expected they would, & thinking themselves surrounded, they had no alternative but to take post in the block-house. Some few shots were fired during the night, and a good deal of hollowing & boasting was heard from some of Bowmans men, he being with Logan and Harrod. A part of Capt. Holder's company approached during the night within 50 or 60 yards of the block-house. At daylight, however, Capt. Holder, & all of his company except Maj. B. & about 15 men, had

[p. 280]
withdrawn from this point, beyond the fire of the Indians, alarmed it is supposed by the statement of a negro woman, who came out from the blockhouse & stated that Simon Girty was at Pickaway with 100 Indians & was hourly expected. The woman then returned to the Indians, they no doubt having sent her out with a view of alarming the Whites. After day light, & in the course of the morning, eleven of the 15 men with Majr. B. were shot by the Indians. One man by the name of South, was killed touching Majr. B.

[p. 281]
on the right, and another by the name of Hickman, close on the other side. Many shots were fired by the Indians & some few by the whites under Majrd. B. but the latter shot without effect, for if their raised their heads above the logs, they were instantly greeted my the rifles of the Indians. At day light Bowman was not to be seen, nor any of the troops under his command, save the men with Majr. B. About nine Oclock, Bowman made his appearance, in the rear of Majr. B. and at such a distance, as to be safe from the balls of the Indians, & pering over the top of a hill, called

[p. 282]
called to Majr. B. & his men to make their escape, as he could bring them no assistance. He had been out scouting, & had caught a number of horses & found some Indian plunder. Majr. B. now found, as this statement of Bowman's was heard, it is supposed by the negro woman, that it would be certain death to remain any longer behind his breastwork of logs. He accordingly directed his men to make ready for a retreat, that all should jump at the same moment & run in a zig-zag course, until beyond the reach

[p. 283]
of the enemies fire. At the signal, agreed upon, none jumped but Majr. B. The consequence was that the whole of the balls of the Indians were fired at him, but being active, & jumping from side to side, & throwing his person into different positions, he escaped the balls whizzing in

numbers about his head. At the end of about 60 yards, Majr. B. treed, & looking back, saw his companions about to follow his example of running. They had evidently waited until the Indians had discharged their guns, at Majr. B. & then before there was

[p. 284]
time to reload, they jumped & run, & escaped without a gun being fired at them. When Majr. B. reached the top of the hill, from which he had been hailed by Bowman, he found all the troops belonging the expedition, assembled there and in much disorder. The Indians by this time had sallied out of their block house & were pursuing the whites & making an occasional shot. Bowman said he thought they had better fight the Indians. Accordingly, Majr. B. as the adjutant undertook to form the line, Col. Bowman & the Captains, manifesting a strong dispo-

[p. 285]
sition to permit him to assume the direction of the retreat. Majr. B. did form the line, but a few random shots broke it, & a disorderly retreat was commenced. The troops believed, or affected to believe, that Girty, with 5 or 6 hundred men, was close upon them. With great exertion, Majr. B. prevailed upon the 3 Captains to form their respective companies into single files, & take their positions a short distance from each other, & retreat in such manner, as to enable them to form three sides of an oblong square. In this manner, with Bowman

[p. 286]
and the Captains in front & Majr. B. in the rear, they marched about seven miles, and had just crossed a small branch, when Majr. B. perceived, from the motion of the weeds, that the Indians were close upon them. He immediately dashed to the front of the companies, and ordered a halt, and that the troops should form in an oblong square, which was done, instantly the yell was raised, by the Indians all round the Whites, and firing commenced. The Indians were screened, by trees & bushes. In the course of the day, but few were

[p. 287]
killed. The object of the Indians appearing to be to keep the whites in that position until they could get a reinforcement. The voice of Black Fish was frequently heard in the course of the day ... the Indians. About sun set, Majr. B. made an application to Col. Bowman to know what course he proposed stating to him that the troops, were becoming faint from hunger, and that the enemy were increasing in numbers. Col. Bowman stated he did not know what to do, & requested him to do what he thought best. Majr. B. at once decided that a charge must be

[p. 288]
made, with rifle & tomahawk in hand, upon that Part of the Indian line, at which Black Fish's voice was heard. Accordingly about 60 men, on foot, followed Majr. B. & forced their way through the line. In doing this, Black Fish was wounded and being placed on a horse was carried

off the field, and died as was afterwards ascertained, just as he reached his village. The command of the Indians now devolved on Yellow Hawk. So soon as it was perceived that Majr. B. & his following had broke the Indian lines the rest of the troops fol-

[p. 289]
lowed, on horseback, & commenced a retreat. Majr. B. & his sixty following, now returned on their tracks and having mounted their horses, also joined in the retreat, which was continued nearly all night. In the course of it, Majr. B. having dismounted lost his hat, which had been knocked off, his horse ran off, & was never recovered. He marched for some time on foot & finally got on a poor animal which was following the troops; this he rode without saddle or bridle. The retreat was

[p. 290]
continued without intermission until the troops reached the mouth of the Little Miami, there being a total want of food. When they reached the bank of the Ohio, & while Majr. B. was stationing sentries to guard the troops, while crossing Col. Bowman, & his three Captains, & indeed nearly all of the officers, except himself, jumped in the boat, & were the first to cross. It was sent back & in the course of the morning all the troops were crossed over, the horses swimming. No attack

[p. 291]
was made by the Indians, although one was momently expected. The entire loss of the Whites in

killed, on this campaign was 16 or 17 men. No officer was killed. But few Indians were killed. It is supposed that near three hundred horses were captured & brought in. These were animals that had mostly been stolen by the Indians from Kentucky. After the troops crossed the Ohio they took such routes to their respective homes, & they thought fit. There was an auction

[p. 292]
of the captured horses. The Indians, attacked on this campaign, were principally Shawanees. Majr. B. does not know that Col. Bowman ever made any official report of his campaign. The troops never received any pay for their services in this campaign. Bowman was about 35 years of age, a native of Virginia. Majr. B. thinks he was an honest man and not a coward, but that he was unacquainted with Indian fighting & the plan of attack failing, he seems to have been Name Struck & lost his self possession.

[p. 293]
After his return from this campaign, Majr. B. remained at Boonesborough, until Novr. when he returned to Virginia. He returned to Kentucky in 1783; was with Kenton in several Scouting parties. Was adjutant to Alexander Orr's company which went from Washington & Maysville up the Ohio on the Kentucky side about two miles above the mouth of the Sciota. Here the Indians had made an encampment & attacked all the boats that descended the Ohio. At this point they found 21 white persons, who had been killed by the Indians & left on the shore. There bodies the Com-

pany buried. Here Simon

[p. 294]
Kenton & Majr. B. crossed the Ohio in a perougue, where they found several bodies which they also buried. There was an appearance of some one having been burnt to death. After an hour or two the company of Capt Orr, consisting of some 150 persons, crossed the Ohio also, and set off in pursuit of the Indians, some ten or 15 miles up the Sciota, but did not find any, which Majr. B. thinks was a fortunate circumstance, as the appearances indicated that they were stronger than the Whites & would have defeated them. The company returned to the Ohio, crossed over and returned to Lewastone where it was disbanded.

[p. 295]
Majr. B. does not recollect the year in which this expedition occurred.

Majr. B. was with the army of St. Clair, having joined it at Wheeling, Va. In this Campaign, Majr. B. had command of the First Virginia Battallion of Levies, being the oldest Majr. & appointed by Washington. His Battalion consisted of 330 men. Darke was his Colonel. Descended the Ohio in boats to Fort Washington. At Fort Hamilton, Majr. B. was appointed President of a Court Martial, for the trial of some

[p. 296]
30 soldiers under arrest for different offences. The General approved of all the sentences. Three were hung, and the others whipped and punished

in various ways. All the way out from F. W. Majr. B. had rheumatism badly & 4 days before the defeat he was taken with a fever. Genl. St. Clair insisted that he should go no further, & he at length consented to take charge of some 10 or 12 invalids & return to Fort Jefferson. On reaching that place, he found no provisions & was compelled to come back to F. W. subsisting on the provisions scattered along the road by the Indians, who had captured them from the army. Among these invalids were Capt. Lewis & Lieut. Vance. They reached F. W. just before the army of St. Clair, which

[p. 297]
in the meantime had been defeated and was returning to the same place.

Majr. B. says that St. Clair anticipated a defeat and held conversation with him before the latter started for Fort Jefferson in which he seemed to be preparing his defence. St. Clair was in bad health, so much so that for some time before the battle he was carried on a litter. Majr. B. attributes the defeat to the lateness of the period when the Virginia horse arrived, to the fact that the first regiment was sent back to protect the supplies on the way out from F. W. etc. He considers St. Clair, a brave & ...mended man.

[p. 298]
In Wayne's campaign, Majr. B. was reappointed a Majr. by Genl Washington and joined the army at Pittsburg, having come directly from General Washington's House. When Majr. B. reached Pittsburg he found some difficulty was likely to

& did occur in regard to his command. Genl. Wayne decided that Majr. B. should command some other officers, whose commissions were older than his, although they had seen less service. Majr. B. had received his commission without solicitation & indeed preferred going to Kentucky to attend to business, to continuing with the army.

[p. 299]
Here Majr. B. remained drilling the troops for about two months. Having been placed in the 2d. Regiment under the orders of Genl. Knox, he was commanded by officers in the first, bearing younger commissions. Majr. refused to be thus commanded & threatened to leave the army. To prevent this, Genl. Wayne issued a Genl. order that Majr. B. should be respected as commander of all the infantry. This continued until new orders were received from Genl. Knox. Wayne was determined not to yield. To prevent his being brought into collision with the Secy. at War, Majr. B. asked leave to retire from the army until the question was settled. This Wayne granted and he accordingly descended the

[p. 300]
Ohio to Kentucky. The question not being satisfactorily adjusted, Majr. B. sent in his resignation, and left the service.

From this time Majr. B. continued to reside in Kentucky. He was in the first session of the legislature of Kentucky, & one of the electors for the first Governor. In 1803 he was elected to Congress & served four years. In 1804, he made a motion, for a committee to bring in a bill, to prohibit after 1808, the importation of Slaves into the United States. This measure was decidedly opposed. Majr. B. was the chairman of the Committee. Several times before he was elected to Congress, Majr. B. was a member of the Kentucky legislature. Before going to Congress, Majr. B. was appointed County Surveyor & Judge of the Court of Q. Sessions.

[p. 301]
Declaration by George M. Bedinger, Jan. 26, 1836
State of Kentucky} Set
Nicholas County

On this 26 day of January 1836 Personally in open before the court of Nicholas County now Sitting, being a court of Record, George M. Bedinger a resident of said County & state of Kentucky aged 79 years the 10 day of December last who being first duly Sworn according to law doth on his oath make the following declaration in order to obtain the benefit of the Act of Congress passed, June the 7th 1832 "That early in the month of June 1775 he entered the service of the United States at Shepherdstown Berkley now Jefferson County in the state of Virginia as a volunteer rifleman for the term of one year, in the company commanded by Captain Hugh Stephenson and that he marched ... well as he now recollects on the 10th or the 11 of the same month, in said Company to the siege of Boston, passing through Frederick Town, Little york, Lancaster and Bethlehem crossed the Susquehannah at Wrights Ferry, the Delaware at Easton, and passing through New Jersey and Hartford Connecticut, thence to Roxbury; continued there at the siege of Boston eight months. Early in March we left Roxbury, continued there at the siege of Boston eight months early in March we left Roxbury and took our station (in the night) on Dorchester point, near Dorchester heights, where we were not discovered by the enemy until next morning by which time it was not in their power to dislodge us from our position. We had during the night ... working party, and all other means in our power ... that little doubt existed but that the British fleet and army could not long be able to retain their station and possession of the harbor and town of Boston. Soon after this and a few days before Boston was evacuated Capt. Stephensons Company were sent to New York City. I think we remained there two or three weeks: from there to Staten Island where we remained in said Stephensons Rifle company until I had served out the full time for which I entered the service, to wit, one year, and was honorably discharged was not in any general engagement or Battle during the above time

[p. 302]
of service but was in frequent scirmishes in one of which 26 of us took 13 prisoners. My Lieutenants were William Henshaw Samuel Findley George Scott, and Abraham Shepherd, successively. We were generally under the immediate command of Gen. Washington. While we remaind at the Siege of Boston we were not attached to any particular Regiment or corps but were generally near head... came home to

make preparations to recruit a Regiment ... died soon after he got home. After ... volunteered and ... until driven thence by the enemy; they had already ... and were scouring it ... when Joseph Swearingen and ... in a small boat or skiff got safely to the Jersey shore but lost some of our clothes, blankets &c. Went thence to our army ... British army and navy ... by the two Hows and a general ... movement was along east ... weak, when ... powerfull ... the British, we were in great need of all the troops that could be raised, to think of leaving our army at so ... painful reflections and to stay much longer from a widowed mother with an almost helpless family of children ... anxiously looking for my ... gone home and many other family ... Yet I continued with the army three weeks ... my discharge then left the army arrived ... of July 1776 and got home to Shepherdstown I think ... 10th and 15th July.

And again, in the month of January 1777 I volunteered in a company of volunteer Riflemen Commanded by Capt. William Morgan of Berkley County Va. Ed. Lucas William Lucas and myself were the lieutenants all of said County, and each in said month we marched from Shepherdstown where I entered said com-

[p. 303]
pany by Philadelphia, crossed the Delaware at Trenton and joined the Army under Gen Washington near Morristown, our company joined the ... commanded by Col. Charles M Thurston of Frederic County, Va. We were that winter stationed at different places to guard

against the encroachments and plundering parties of the British Army by ...

Early in March perhaps the first day we fought the Battle of Piscataway served out our full time of three months when at the request of Genl. Washington to stay 3 days longer the commany who were then under my command the other officers being absent ... to them the request of the Commander in chief and ... and ... when the whole company with the exception of three or ... and were honorably dis... and allowed a tour of duty of three months & three days ... excepted.

... to wit a few days after having ... defeat of our army at Brandywine Benoni Swearingen ... left our homes at Shepherdstown Va. and went ... Army about 18 miles from Germantown and ... as volunteers in the company commanded by Captain Joseph Swearingen in the 12th Virginia regiment commanded by Col. James Wood, being in Genl. ... Adam Stevens's ... honorably discharged ... in said discharge that we B. Swearingen & myself had distinguished ourselves in the most brave & ... way ... on the day of the Battle of Germantown by the ...

From the time we joined said Regiment ... with several of whom we had been long & intimately acquainted most particularly with Captain Joseph Swerangen and General Stevens frequently ... In the many ... as soon as we got in sight of ... the enemies encampment next to us as we were going by ...

[p. 304]
from Chestnut Hill the Adjutant Genl addressed us thus Gentlemen Volunteers you will now have

an opportunity to distinguish yourselves you are not confined to any particular platoon or Corps. These were his words to the best of my recollection or words to that effect, when Benoni Swearingen and myself immediately advanced with such speed that we soon left our advancing Army behind us. Prepared to defend ourselves with our rifles and swords we got between the fire of the contending armies and it was believed by those who saw us advance that we should both be certainly killed but owing to the fog smoke and the mercies of God we both escaped unhurt, (the morning being very foggy and the day smoky. Before we left the army to return home we were both told we could have appointments in the Regiment, but as our mothers were Widows and as I had one brother who was then a prisoner with the British and another who had also been taken prisoner at Fort Washington and had just got home his life despaired of I returned home with my worthy companion and well tried friend Benoni Swearingen to Shepherdstown. for this service we never asked or received any pay altho our horses & traveling expenses were paid by ourselves and was sensibly felt by me as I was in low circumstances.

In the spring of 1779 on the 1st day of ... affiant in company with nine others left his home in Berkley County Virginia and arrived at Boonsborough in Kentucky on the 7th of April where we found Captain John Holder with only about 15 men under his command and the fort in great distress and eminent danger in consequence of a Mr. Starns and a party of 10 or 12 men having left the fort a day or two before our arrival and who as it afterwards appeared had nearly all fallen into the hands of the Indians. One of the party who made his escape got into the Fort about 2 hours after we did and gave information of the defeat of Starns & his party. Fortunately for us we had missed the path and at the time the Indians who killed Captain Starns and his party were passing on it we were in a thick canebreak near to it we had not traveled more than about half a mile

[p. 305]
before we got into the path again and were surprised to see a large trail that had just been made: and from a broken bow, the shape of the tracks of the feet, and particularly the pigeon great toe as some call it we were convinced that a number of Indians had passed and that providentially our lives had been saved by our missing the path at that place. We proceeded on in the path and that ... and got within six or 7 miles of the Fort and encamped for the night made a fire and laid by it until day break without a sentinel or spy to watch for the approaches of the Indians. This incautious conduct was occasioned by Col. William Morgan he was I think the oldest man except one in the company had been in Gen. Braddocks time an Indian was our Spy and Scout. Who when some of the young boys as three of us were called proposed going out from the path for greater safety observed "that we would not die until his time came." ... and it was believed that this apparently improper conduct induced another party of Indians who were seen that evening and had

chaced two spies to wit Col. Estil & anothers. The Indians came out on the path that we were on and it was believed they saw our fire, horses, etc. but that they suspected the fire to be made to deceive them and draw them into an ambuscade... they would be more ready to believe from the fact that the people of Boonsborough had but a short time before tied an old horse by the heel ... ambush but the Indians disagreed ... and tomahawks ... who escaped from them reported that the Indians ... White people should think Indians could be ... for fear of not giving the general circumstances of his services discovers that he has digressed too far by reminiscing ... he hopes the digressions will be excused and will now return to the main subject. When we arrived at Boonsborough the distresses of the Fort induced me to join Capt. Holders company who had the command of the fort at that time in which company and service I sered seven months. For part of the time, I acted as an Indian Spy, scout &

[p. 306]
Hunter always taking my turn with the other men of the Fort as Hunter. To this course I was impelled by the feelings of humanity and Sympathy for distressed women and children who were unable to leave the country and who if they had attempted it would have been sacrificed to the Indians who were constantly scouring the country around the Fort and would in all probability have taken it had we not joined it when we did. I have ever considered the service I performed at this place and during this time as the most dangerous difficult and at the same time most useful to my

country, as we were almost continually surrounded by Indians who were lying in wait for us and and as we had to supply ourselves and the inhabitants of the Fort mainly by the success of our hunting excursions to effect which he had to slip out at night retire to some distance from the fort, kill our game which was generally Buffaloes and pack it in in some succeeding night and by our exertions the possession of Boonsborough was retained and the lives of the inhabitants preserved. During the above term of service an expedition against the Indian Town then called New Chilicothe now old Chilicothe under Col. John Bowman was planned and executed in which expedition I was called on and acted as Adjutant and Quarter Master in which capacities I acted not less than two weeks. We proceeded by the way of the mouth of Licking River were detained some time waiting for other troops to join us then went on to the Town made an attempt to surprise and take the town but owing to one of our men stationed near the houses in the night firing his gun at and killing an Indian the Indians were apprised of our near approach went to work and by day light had so secured, reinforced and prepared themselves as to induce us to make a retreat the best way we could which we proceeded to execute were surrounded and so kept for about 9 hours when, as a last resort, we made a charge and broke through their forces and made our escape after having fought them about from 12 to 15 hours and came off from them about 300 horses and some trinkets. Many of the horses had been stolen by them from Kentucky. Our company returned to Fort Bonsborough where I remained to the end of my aforesaid term of seven months then returned to my home at Shepherdstown.

[p. 307]
I further state that in the month of May 1781 I took the command of a company of Militia in Berkley County Virginia under Col. William Darke and marched with them through different parts of Virginia to the seige of York. In addition to performing the duties of Captain I had also to act as Adjutant to the Regiment and occasionallly performed the duties of Major. We were the first who approached the enemy at York. was not at York at the surrender of Cornwallis, the time of service of my company having expired a few days before the surrender. During this time I served 5 months as captain of the company and all the time performed the duties of Adjutant to the Regiment and part of the time as Major.

I would further state that while I was at Boonsborough I acted for about 3 months as commissary in ... out salt & some provisions purchaced from hunters for the use of the fort. I do further state that I have not any documentary evidence in my possession which will go to prove my foregoing services except the deposition of Jesse Hodges if it would be considered of that character which I ... on the 7th instant and that I know of no person whose testimony I can procure except that of Henry Bedinger of Berkley County, Peter Fisher of Jefferson County Virginia & Daniel Bell of Jefferson County Kentucky... should they or either of them be still living.

I hereby relinquish every claim whatever to a

pension or annuity except the present and declare that my name is not on the Pension Roll of the agency of any state.

Interrogation by the War Department.
Int. 1st. Where and in what year were you born?
Ans. I was born in York county state of Pennsylvania on the 10th Dec 1753.

Int. 2. Have you any record of your age and if so where is it?
Ans. I have a copy of a record of my baptism, original is in Berkley County Virginia.

Int. 3. Where were you living when called into service. Where have you lived since the Revolutionary war and where do you live now?
Ans. I was living in Shepherdstown then Berkley County now Jefferson County Virginia

[p. 308]
when I entered the service. Shortly after the close of the Revolution I moved to Kentucky settled in Bourbon county near Paris, from thence I moved to the Lower Blue Licks then in Bourbon now in Nicholas County Ky. and have continued to live at the latter place and in the neighbourhood of it ever since and now live there. Since I ... to Kentucky I have been in several campaigns against the Indians was a Major under St. Clair & Waine both was engaged for some time after I first came as Surveyors of Military lands and subsequently served a session in Congress.

Int. 4. How were you called into service. Were

you drafted did you volunteer or were you a substitute and if a substitute for whom
Ans. I was always a volunteer.
Int. 5th. State the names of some of the regular officers who were with the troops such continental and militia regiments as you can recollect and the General circumstances of your service.
Ans. In addition to the officers named in the body of my foregoing Declaration I was well acquainted with Gen Washington, Lee, Gates the two Stevenses Wayne and indeed nearly the whole of the Generals Cols. & Majors in the regular and Militia Service who were at any time in command in the states of Virginia Maryland Pennsylvania New Jersey &c. as to the general circumstances of my service they are set forth in the body of my Declaration ... above campaigns that I have not taken any notice of in said declaration which I served during the Revolution and since.

Int. 6th. Did you ever receive a discharge from the service and if so by whom was it given and what has become of it.
Ans. As well as I now recollect I received a discharge from Capt. Hopkinson or rather from one of his Liutenants. I think the Captain had signed the discharges before he went home to raise his Regt. and ... them with one of his Liuts. to deliver to us when our time was out. I received said discharge on Staten Island about the 10 of June 1776 and it has long since been lost or destroyed. I also received a discharge from Col. James Wood of the 12 Va. Regt. (See body Decln.) which is also lost or destroyed. I do not

recollect of having received any other discharge.

Int. 6. Did you ever receive a commission and if so by whom was it signed & what has become of it.
Ans. I do not recollect of having a regular commission in my possession while in the regular volunteer service. The periods I served as an officer were short and commissions may or may not have been made out for me. I acted in obedience to orders from my superiors and believed that I was duly authorised either by appointment or commission or both to do so.

[p. 309]
Deposition of Jesse Hodges, Jan. 7, 1836
Be it remembered that I Jesse Hodges of the county of Madison State of Kentucky, aged 78 years ... 10 day of November last being ... but of sound mind having not been able to leave my farm for the ... 7 months and now at my own house do hereby certify ... 1836 That I am well acquainted with Major George M. Bedinger and have been since April 1779. In April 1779 George M. Bedinger now Major Bedinger came to Boonsborough in company with Col. William Morgan Major Thomas Swearingen and others and soon after they came to Boonsborough the said Bedinger & myself ... who was a commissioned officer under Morgan ... left Boonsborough to join Col. John Bowman's campaign and ... near the mouth of Licking on the Ohio River. As soon as he ... the said George M. Bedinger was appointed Adjutant and Quarter Master and was ... as such throughout the

campaign against the Indians. My impression is that the said George M. Bedinger remained in now Kentucky and ... about seven months before he left for Virginia. While under the command of Col. John Bowman we marched to Chilicothe and took about 300 horses from the Indians and soon after returned to Boonsborough. ... was ... George M. Bedinger ... in company with him and do with pleasure state that he was a willing and an efficient soldier and & believed by others and further sayeth not.

     Signed Jesse Hodges

Madison County

 ... foregoing deposition of Jesse Hodges was taken subscribed and sworn to by the said Jesse Hodges at the time and place ... stated before the undersigned an acting Justice of the Peace for the county aforesaid and I do further state that I have been acquainted with the said Jesse Hodges for the ... 30 or 35 years and from my acquaintance do believe that every reliance can be placed in his statements. Given under my hand this 7th day of January 1836.

    Signed E Bush J. P. Madison [i.e. probably Justice of the Peace, Madison Co.]

[p. 310]
State of Kentucky
Madison County Set

 I David Irvine clerk of the Courth of Madison County certify that Elkanah Bush is a Magistrate as above and one of the Justices of said Court and that the foregoing signature purporting to be his is genuine.

 In testimony whereof I have hereunto affixed

my seal of office and subscribed my name this 8th day of January 1836.

   David Irvine
   Clerk of the Court of Madison County

[p. 311]
Deposition of George M. Bedinger

 Int. State the names of persons to whom you are known in your present neighbourhood and who can testify as to your character for veracity & good behaviour your services as a soldier of the Revolution &c.

Ans. I will refer to the Rev. James G. Leach, Rev. John Rogers, Gen. Thomas, Gen. Wolfe, L... Arnold, Esq., Col. John F. Morgan, Andrew Couchman ... I might name the whole of my acquaintances in ... counties and who are very numerous. I will also refer ... to the following gentlemen now in Washington City ... Hon. H. Clay Hon. John Chambers Hon. R M Johnson Hon. ... Col. Jas. C. Picker and many others I could name who would testify to my character & standing were it necessary.

 ... to and subscribed the day and year aforesaid.

 ... residing in the town of Carlisle Nicholas County State of Kentucky and Oliver E. Houle residing in the same place hereby ... acquainted with Major Geo M Bedinger who has subscribed and sworn to the above declaration that we believe him to be 79 years of age that he is reputed and belived in the neighborhood where he resides to have been a soldier of the Revolution and that we concur in the opinion and further certify that the said Major Geo M Bedinger is a gentleman ...

standing and respectability and that he is the same person ... congressional district 4 years in the congress of the United States and that we believe his statement entitled to the fullest credit.

Sworn to & subscribed the day & year aforesaid.

[p. 312]
Map of the Blue Lick Battle Ground
Scale 200 rods to the inch.
References.
A. Battle Ground Hollow   }Ambushd. — a
       thick growth of timber
B. Indian Creek Hollow   }
C. Lower Ford
D. Middle Ford
E. Upper Ford
F. Harlan's Grave on an elevation of some 50 feet.
G. Rude Monument — "B. G." rudely carved for
       battle ground.
H.H. Where Indians were first seen
I. The tree where Todd died, is in the extreme upper fork of the old & new road
J.J. Salt Springs.
K. The fresh water Spring on rice-bank, where Indians camped night after action.

Between the Todd tree (oak) & the Monument, were scattered large quantities of bones for some years after the battle. Some 35 yrs. after the battle, the present Mr. Wickliffe & a large company of visitors gathered up bones, & made the rude stone pile. Boone, in the retreat crossed at the Lower Ford, & probably Patterson. There were some, tho not many crossed at the Upper

Ford. It is a trifle over a mile from the mouth of Indian Creek to the Middle Ford, & a mile from the Todd tree to the Mid. Ford.

Plat of the
<u>Blue Lick Battle Ground</u>

Copied from a plat in possession of Maj. G M Bedinger, in 1843, with additional localities designated by him.

<u>L.C.D.</u>

Blue Licks
<u>Plat</u>
<u>Bedinger</u>

The first 4 pages of the following document are unfortunately lost. I never had them.

<u>L.C.D.</u>

[p. 313]
Deposition of Robert Pogue

This affiant States that he was born in what is now called Rockbridge county Virginia about the month of october 1765 from the best information he can get: he has seen a record of his age and belivs it was about that date. he does not know where that record is, it is not now in his power to Controul; When he first enterd into the Service he resided in the fort at Haradsburg Kentucky and continued to reside there and in the vicinity of that place in the county of Mercer until the Spring of the year 1796 when he removed to Mason county, Ky where he has resided ever Since; He was calld into Service by being enroled as a militiaman for the defence of the fort at Harradsburg and by voluntary enggagement as a Spy and on Scouts & Comands.

He was acquainted and served with Gnl. Geo

Rogers Clark Capt Bowman Colonel Ben logan Coll John Logan Colonel Daniel Boone Colonel John Todd Colo Trigg Majr Harlan Col Harrod & Colo McGary, there was ne regular Regt. at Harradsburgh during his Service but what was calld the Illinoise Regt. and all that were at Harodsburg were considered part of & did duty in Said Regiment he never receivd a discharge from the Service.

He refers to Genl. John Adair Gen James Ray Colo George Thompson & Gen Robert B. Mcafee who were well acquainted with him during his residence in Mercer County; and to Judge Adam Beaty Colo Marshal Key and Majr Walter Lacy, who are his neighbours an have known him for many years where he now resides in Mason county Kentucky for avid as to his character for varacity and for his Services during the Revolutionary War.

Most of the facts in the declaration are Stated from the Knowlidge and recollection of the affiant and the others from the infomation of those on whom he can rely the dates are Stated principally from memory and from his best impresseons are correct he can not swear positively to all the Statements herein containd but to the best of his Knowledge belvs them to be true.

For the proof of his Services he refers to the annexed deposition of Gen James Ray and Mrs Elizabeth Thompson, and the reason he makes this declaration before the Mercer Courts is that he resided and was well known in that county for more than twenty years, that the Services were performd there, where the witnesses are to prove it reside, & who are too old & infirm to travle with conveneance to Mason county court where the affiant affiant resides, a distance of about 90 ninety miles.

He hereby relinquishes every claim what Ever to a pention or anuity except the present & declares that his name is not on the pension Roll of the agency of any State.

Sworn to and Subsribed the day & year aforesaid
          Robert Pogue

[p. 314]
Deposition of Gen. James Ray

Genl James Ray, of Mercer County Kentucky aged about 72 years came into Court and being duly sworn declares on oath that in the year 1775 he assisted in removing the family of William Pogue the father of Genl. Robert Pogue who has made the foregoing declaration, from Boonsburough to Harradsburg, that he resided in the fort at Harradsburg from the time it was first built in 1776 until sometime in the year 1779 and in the vicinity thereof ever since that in the year 1777 when his brother William Ray was killed at the Shawany Spring, this affiant was one of the party made his escape and got into the Fort by outruning the Indians. About this time Colo. McGary and Colo. Harrad, had had all the men and boys in the fort enroled, and they were all obliged to do duty by standing Guard, hunting & Spying. He was well acquainted with Genl Robert Pogue who subscribes this declaration at that time and ever Since and well recollects that the said Pogue was enrolled and did duty in

Standing Guard &c and towards the year 1779 & until 1782 he frequently hunted and acted as a Spy and went on Scouts. He has examined the foregoing declaration of sd Said Robert Pogue and believs the meterial facts therein Stated are true. Harradsburg was the principal Seat of the Indian war in Kentucky from the years 1777 til 1779 the fort was frequently attacked, and the troops there had many hard fights with the Indians, and every man woman and child were engaged assisting in in the defence & support of the Fort in some way. The applicant Robert Pogues Father was killed by the Indians in the year 1778 He was the oldest male of the Family was well acquainted with the use of a gun and ... but a boy was hardy and active and performed much Service in hunting Spying &c Sworn to and subscribed the day afore said.
    James Ray

Deposition of Elizabeth Thomas
 Elizabeth Thomas of Mercer County aged about 70 years came into court and being sworn declared on oath that she is the sister of the applicant Robert Pogue that she resided in the Fort at Harradsburg from the year 1776 till the year 1783, and in the neighborhood ever since; that she well recollects that the sd Bother was enroled about the year 1777 and did duty in the fort, standing Guard &c. and after the year 1778 did usuel duty as a Hunter Spy and on Scouts, for at least three years. She has heard the Statements in the declaration & and the deposition of Genl James Ray reads and the material facts therein Stated are true to the best of her Knowledge and

belief.

Sworn to and Subscribed the day & date aforesaid   Elizabeth Thomas

[p. 315]
We Samuel Morison & Isaac Chaplin residing in Mercer County Kentucky do hereby Certify that that we are well acquainted with Genl Robert Pogue who has Subscribed & swore to the above declaration, that we believe him to be 68 years of age that he is repeted and believed in the neighborhood whare he resides to have been a soldier of the Revolution and that we concur in that opinion.

Sworn to and Subscribd the day and date afore Said.
        Isaac Chaplin
        Saml. Morisonn

State of Kentucky
Mercer County

And the said court do hereby Certify and declare their opinion after the investigation of the matter and after putting the interrogatories prescribed by the War department that the above named applicant was a Revolutionary Soldier and servd as he States, and the Court further Certifies that it appears to them that Isaac Chaplin is a Clergeman and Samuel M'cown who have subscribed Signed that certificate are residents of Mercer County and are credable persons and that their Statements are entitled to credit.

I Thomas Allen Clerk of the county court of Mercer county do certify that the foregoing contains the original proceedings of the said Court in the matter of the application of Genl

Robert Pogue for a pension.

In testimony where of I have Set my hand and the Seal of sd County this 3 day of June 1833.

Tho Aallen Jr. Clerk
Mercer County Court

The Declaration
of My Dr Freind
Genl Robt Pogue
a Copy the
origional was
returnd to his Son

[p. 316]
SPEECH OF HON. A. R. BOTELER, OF VIRGINIA, ON THE ORGANIZATION OF THE HOUSE
DELIVERED IN THE HOUSE OF REPRESENTATIVES, JANUARY 25, 1860

Mr. BOTELER. I have, Mr. Clerk, no set speech to make. I have not come here to-day with that intention. I have sought the floor simply for the purpose of submitting a few suggestive remarks, which, I trust, will serve in some degree to promote the object which many here are sincerely desirous of accomplishing — of bringing this discussion to a close, and perfecting the organization of the House. Sir, I do not stand here to-day to make any appeals to the prejudices, the passions, or the sectional pride of those who represent that quarter of the Confederacy from whence I come. I have no desire to indulge in any pyrotechnic display of "glittering generalities," which, however much they may dazzle and amuse, are but little calculated to bring about any practical solution of the difficulty in which we are now involved — like summer lightning, they "play around the head but do not touch the heart." Nor is it my purpose to deal in any unjust, ungenerous, or unnecessarily harsh denunciation of those upon the other side of the Chamber, who, claiming to be conservative, are here in the exercise of their undoubted right as the Representatives of the country, entertaining sentiments utterly adverse from the sentiments held by my constituents and myself. I say I shall not indulge in any unnecessarily harsh denunciations of them. I recognize the fact that we who are assembled here to discharge the legitimate duties of legislation devolved upon us by our constituents, coming as we do from different and distant portions of this vast Confederacy, some of us from the rugged, rock-ribbed hills of the North, some from the ever-blooming plains of the South, some with the dust of the distant prairies on their feet, and others with the spray of either ocean on their brows, representing interests and opinions as variant as are the latitudes in which we live, must necessarily differ on many points; it is not to be expected of us that there should be perfect uniformity of sentiment, and especially in regard to those great questions of public concernment which, from time to time, stir up the depths of human feeling in our land. But, sir, it is expected, and our country demands, patriotism requires at our hands, that, coming here under these circumstances, we should remember, in the language of a distinguished citizen of my good old State,"that we have a country to serve, as well as a party to obey."

But, sir, what do we see? What is the spectacle which this House presents? On this side of it, with those with whom it has been my pride and my pleasure to act in good faith from first to last, what have we seen? Three organizations — a Democratic party, a southern Opposition party, and an anti-Lecompton party; for we must recognize the last named as a party, since, though insignificant in number, they are most potential in their influence. Well, sir, what have they been doing? They know, they feel, the country knows, that it is only by a union amongst them all that we can beat down the nominee of the Republican party. They profess to be honest in their desire to accomplish that, and I know they are honest in their opposition to that nominee. But yet, with the majority and with the power in their hands, they have never once exercised that power

[p. 317]
to secure the object which they profess to be anxiously desirous of attaining. And why? Because they have allowed

their party prejudices and their party pride to interfere with their patriotism. There has not been a ballot taken in which there has been a union of the different anti-Republican parties; and there will be no election resulting in the success of this side of the House unless there is such a union — a cordial and hearty union amongst us all.

Now, sir, let me illustrate our position here. We are all on board the same ship, the glorious old ship which our fathers built for us. They laid its keel; they fashioned its bulwarks; they forged the anchor of its hope; they launched it upon the ocean of national existence, and they gave us a chart by which to sail our ship. We have differed heretofore amongst ourselves; earnestly, sincerely, openly differed, as freemen should differ and will differ, in regard to the construction of that chart; we have differed amongst ourselves in regard to the best mode of working the ship. Some of us have been for sailing her upon this tack, some upon that tack; some have been for taking in a sail, others for shaking out a reef. We believe that, under Providence, our ship has been built to be the life-boat of the world; and throughout the progress of the voyage we have been constantly engaged in saving those who have come on board from the wrecks, the rafts, and rotten governments of the Old World. We have taken them into our vessel when they have been swimming for their lives. We have spread before them the table of our bounty; we have saved their lives and have given them an equal participation in the profits of our voyage; yet some of us (and I amongst the number) have seen, and seen with surprise and pain, that after they have been brought on board the ship, they have shown a propensity to interfere in the management of it, and we have said to them: "We have brought you here to save you, and to make you prosperous, happy, and free; but we are not willing that you shall take hold of the tiller and handle the ropes, until you have been here long enough to know one rope from another."

Well, sir, this has been a source of honest difference of opinion amongst those on board, whilst all of us have loved the old craft, from truck to keel, with all our hearts. Thus we have voyaged; and whilst thus differing, what has happened? We have been drifting towards the breakers, we have been insensibly drawn towards a lee shore, where no light-house sends it friendly ray! A storm has arisen upon us; we hear the spirit of the tempest shrieking in the shrouds; clouds of danger, difficulty, and doubt are dimming the heaven of our hopes, and threatening to burst in desolation over our heads! And not only that; but, sir, we see yonder "a band of mutineers" determined to take possession of the vessel; men associated together to dispossess us of our rights, and to deprive us of our property, who would thrust us down the hold, and batten the hatches over our heads. And yet, in the midst of all these imminent dangers which are threatening the destruction of the ship, we have been engaged here for weeks past in a disgraceful squabble upon theoretical points of political navigation!

Now, Mr. Clerk, I ask is it right, is it reasonable, can we answer to our constituents, and to the country, if we continue to allow these paltry, miserable differences to interfere with our duty, and to prevent cordial, united action among the conservatives of the House against those whom we recognize, and whom we are are bound to recognize as our common enemy.

Sir, I have no practical suggestion to offer; there are older heads than mine here to do that; but I do protest against the continuance of this most unnecessary discussion. For myself, the House will do me the justice to say that I have occupied my seat upon this floor in silence during the seven weary weeks we have been in session, while this exciting discussion has been going on, and whilst the infamous Abolition outrage upon the district I have the honor to represent has been the fruitful inspiration of almost every gentleman who has risen to address the House. Now, sir, I was present at that horrible Harper's Ferry raid; I was a witness to that abominable outrage; I saw the blood of my friends

[p. 318]
shed in the streets of Harper's Ferry; and if there is a man here who has a right to discuss that subject, it is myself; and yet I have forborne. I have remained silent for various reasons, not the least of which is, that the distinguished Senator before me (Mr. Mason) is engaged in the investigation of the facts connected with the whole affair, and will present them fully and fairly, at the proper time, before

the country, to leave it judge of them, after which I shall avail myself of a suitable opportunity to mention some circumstances to the House concerning that foray which I wish the country to know, and which justice to my constituents requires that it shall know from me.

There is another reason which, I must confess, has also influenced me in this matter. I know (and I have been painfully conscious of it whenever my mind has reverted to that dark day) that when the heart feels most, the tongue refuses to perform its wonted task.

And, sir, when I have heard gentlemen on the other side of the floor stand up and derisively refer to that infamous outrage, I have been hardly able to retain my seat and refrain from the expression of my indignation in terms which might not have sounded parliamentary. My mind, sir, has again and again, during this discussion, gone back to that gloomy October evening, when I stood by the side of a friend, and laid my hand upon his brow where the death damp was gathering, while the blood was gushing from his noble heart, and I have been often disposed to say, in apology for my forbearance:

"Oh! pardon me, thou bleeding piece of earth,
That I am meek and gentle with these butchers!"

For I tell you, sir, that in my opinion, the leaders of the Abolition party, which is seeking to control the organization of this House, and to obtain possession of the Government, are as much the murderers of my friends at Harper's Ferry as were old John Brown and his deluded followers; and I think that the committee engaged in the investigation in my State, and the investigation on the part of the Senate, will prove that the agitation of the slavery question by the great leaders of the Republican party has been the direct cause of the Harper's Ferry invasion.

I tell you further, sir, that the Commonwealth of Virginia has come to the determination that this shall be the end of it; that this slavery agitation shall cease, so far as she is concerned; that her territory shall be protected from a repetition of that bloody raid. She has taken some indemnity for the past and means to have security for the future. And, sir, to make her determination good, she has buckled on her armor, and her borders are now bristling with bayonets, for she feels compelled to take the guardianship of her rights and her honor into her own hands. Heretofore she has trusted to the tie of consanguinity; heretofore she has relied upon the linked shields of all the States for her protection; but, sir, at a moment when she dreamed not of it, she has been smitten upon the cheek. Our honored old mother has been struck a blow which has roused her children from their false security, and rallied them to her rescue. We now discover that we must depend upon our own right arm to protect our State from further outrage, so long as there remains a "Republican" organization in Congress and the country. Why will you persist, men of the North, in maintaining that organization? What good do you expect to effect by it? You formed it, so you have said, for the sole purpose of making Kansas a free State. You have Kansas, and when she comes into this Union, she will come in "free." If there be any other purpose that you expect to accomplish by it, it must be to transfer your "irrepressible conflict" from the Territories to the States.

But, gentlemen of the other side, I know there are some among you who profess to be conservative, and are conservative, as compared with the moving spirits of your party. The distinguished gentleman from Ohio (Mr. Corwin) who sits before me, and who has entertained us and held this House for two days in listening admiration, by his intellectual efforts, claims to be — I wish he

[p. 319]
were so in reality — the leader of the Republican party; but
how few are they who gather round him, who will recognize him as their leader, and will indorse the sentiments he has uttered here yesterday and the day before. When I look at him, when I see him there amongst them — a triton amongst the minnows — when I see him there, sir, my mind goes back to the literature of my boyish days, and I remember how it was that once upon a time Gulliver, in his travels, laid himself down to sleep in the country of the Lilliputians; how the pigmies climbed upon his person and wound their tiny chains about him; how they bound his hands, and so led him, a spectacle of wonder, through the land. Oh, sir, if I could

but make such an appeal to that distinguished gentleman as would awaken a responsive feeling in his heart, its patriotic throbs would burst the bonds which bind him to the earth, he would stand erect in the frightened presence of his diminutive associates, and would march forth with a firm tread from the low miasmatic marshes of sectionalism and join us here upon the high ground of nationality, where the flag of the Union floats "with not a stripe erased or polluted, or a single star obscured." [Applause from the Democratic benches and in the galleries.] And the leader, (Mr. Sherman,) whom they recognize, the leader who bears their banner, I listened to his explanation, or rather his attempt at explanation, made a few days since, with sincere sympathy for him. In my very soul I pity him. And it is with wonder and amazement that I behold a gentleman with the traits which that gentleman is said to have — for he must have noble traits who, during so many weeks of conflict, can keep friends around him in unbroken ranks, persisting in their efforts to place him in the third position under our Government — to see such a gentleman permit himself to remain for one hour more before the country, as he is, according to his own account of himself, and the account his friends have given of him, in connection with the Helper Book.

What has he told the House? What has his friend who nominated him (Mr. Corwin) told this House? That he signed the recommendation of the Helper book at the solicitation of a friend who came to him and asked him to sign it; that he took the precaution to inquire of the friend whether there would be anything objectionable in the compilation, and was assured that there would not; that the book would be prepared by a committee, &c. Well, sir, what has that committee done? They have put forth a book under the sanction of Mr. Sherman's name, which is everywhere denounced as objectionable, and which is, unquestionably, a most infamous publication; a book which he himself intimates his objection to, and, as I understand, desires an opportunity to denounce as it deserves. They have deceived him; they have betrayed him; they have made him their victim, their dupe, ay, their tool; and he submits to it all! Yes, sir, it is admitted that they have deceived him, for he allows the inference to be made that he does not indorse this most infamous Helper book. I am told, indeed, that gentlemen on the other side — if the gentleman from Missouri will withdraw his resolution — one after the other, will rise and denounce that book. That is what they say in private. They are ready to denounce it now, and well they may be; for, sir, I would like to see a man in the American Congress who would rise in his place and indorse the sentiments of that book, after all that has occurred within the last three months. If any man should do so here in our presence, we would see a traitor standing in our midst.

Mr. Clerk, the gentleman from Ohio still occupies his position. Week after week he has occupied it, and Heaven only knows how long he will continue to hold on to it. But his chance is gone. I tell him, in all candor, that he cannot be elected to the Speakership, and is not fit for the position; not meaning, however, to say that his private virtues and personal graces would not fit him to fill that chair. From his association with this infamous Helper book, and the manner in which he has been persistently pressed at this particular time, *he never can be Speaker*, and never should be called upon to preside over the deliberations of this body. To be elected at all, it must be by means of the plu-

[p. 320]

rality rule; and a vote upon the plurality rule, it is understood, must be a sneaking vote for Sherman. Now, sir, that plurality rule never can come to a vote. I do not hesitate to say that I was one of those, after the discussion arose in the House the other day, who sought out the paper referred to by the gentleman from Indiana, (Mr. Colfax,) and that I placed my name to it, pledging myself to stand here day and night to oppose by all lawful means the adoption of the plurality rule; and I will stay here in this Hall, eat here, drink here, live here, and, if necessary, die here — before I give my sanction, as a Representative from Virginia, to that rule, when I am satisfied that its adoption will result in the election of John Sherman as Speaker of this House.

Mr. Colfax. Will the gentleman allow me to ask him a question? I do not wish to interfere without the gentleman's consent.

Mr. Boteler. Certainly.

Mr. Colfax. Suppose any number of gentlemen, after it was organized, were satisfied that an appropriation bill reported by the Committee of Ways and Means contained an appropriation of money which would probably be used by the Federal Administration for corrupt purposes — I do not say that would be; I only put the case as a supposititious one: would you justify us in signing a written agreement, binding ourselves to each other, that we would, by a factious opposition, prevent any vote ever being taken upon it, and thus prevent a majority from adopting it? If so, all legislation could be thus arrested.

Mr. Boteler. You have to meet your own responsibility to your constituency, and I am responsible to mine. I can go back to mine, and hold up my head, with the full assurance in my heart that the position I have taken during this protracted struggle for the Speakership will be indorsed by every one of my constituents whose good opinion is worth an effort to retain. You can do the same.

But I have yet to learn that that is a majority side of the House. I am going upon the premises that *this* is the majority side of this House, and that the factious course is pursued by the other side. That is the factious side. True, it is a side with seventeen States represented by it; but I see not a single southern man affiliating with them — not one. I look upon the flag they carry, and I cannot recognize upon it the escutcheon of a single State south of Mason and Dixon's line.

But, Mr. Clerk, I am sorry I have been betrayed into these extended remarks. I assure gentlemen I rose not to bring the torch of discord among the members of the House, but to offer the olive branch of peace. I rose to make an appeal to gentlemen upon this side; to make an appeal to my distinguished friend from Ohio (Mr. Corwin) before me; to my friends from Pennsylvania and New Jersey, some of whom were old college-mates, and whom I had not met before for twenty years, but whom I see now, to my great regret, upon that side of the House, voting and acting against the interests of my State. I came here, sir, to stand by those gentlemen from Pennsylvania and New Jersey in their rights and interests. I came here a tariff man; though not a protective man for protection's sake; not in favor of a high protective tariff, yet ready to lock my shield with theirs, and fight out the great question of protection to their interests. But I see them arrayed against my interests and the interests of my constituents; and how can they expect that I shall be found fighting zealously with them for their interests? Sir, I have said that I am in favor of protection. I desire that every man in this country of ours, from the Aroostook to the Gulf of Mexico — no matter what his occupation may be, whether he shoves the plane or throws the shuttle, whether he works in the mine, or, like myself, belongs to the great agricultural interests of the country — shall feel that his Government is with him and not against him. I would have every farmer throughout the land feel, as he scatters the golden grain in the furrows, that, next to the Providence of Almighty God, who sends the sunshine and the shower, the seed time and the harvest, that the Government discriminates for his interests and not against them.

[p. 321]
I came here to vindicate that principle side by side with those whom I believed to be conservative men from the great States of Pennsylvania and New Jersey, (that old battle-ground of the Revolution, where my fathers stood with theirs, shoulder to shoulder, in the snows of Trenton and the hot sands of Monmouth,) to vindicate that great principle of protection to American industry, in accordance with the necessities of the times. But I find you rallying behind a sectional banner, and giving aid and comfort to that intolerant sectional organization of the North, the fundamental principle of which is opposition to slavery. I cannot, therefore, expect that any appeal I may make to you will be listened to.

Mr. Hale. Will the gentleman from Virginia allow me to ask him a question?

Mr. Boteler. I certainly will permit the gentleman to ask me a question?

Mr. Hale. You say you find us arrayed against your rights and interests, and that you came here to endeavor to promote the interests of Pennsylvania. I would like to know what rights or interests of Virginia the Pennsylvania members have attacked on this floor, or what rights they propose to attack? We have stood by you, as I understand. In your Harper's Ferry foray, as you call it, Pennsylvania acted the part of a sister State, according to the testimony of Governor Wise himself, and returned your fugitives from justice. Pennsylvania, sir, has always done her duty to her sister

States; and I defy any gentleman from Virginia, or any other gentleman upon this floor, to show that in any respect Pennsylvania has failed in her duty to any sister State in any manner whatever. When gentlemen deal in general charges like these, they ought to specify wherein we are interfering with their rights.

Mr. Boteler. I recognize the fact — and it is a fact which affords me pleasure, a fact of which every Pennsylvanian may well be proud — that her Governor did his duty fully, fairly, faithfull, in returning to Virginia the fugitives from her justice, and that he was sustained by the people of Pennsylvania in that patriotic act; and, sir, I came here prepared to testify to the State of Pennsylvania my grateful appreciation of the conduct of her Governor. I am still grateful to the people of Pennsylvania, who, I believe, are misrepresented upon this floor by those who have from first to last acted with the other side, to whom, however, there may be some exceptions. (Referring to those who voted for Mr. Gilmer.)

The gentleman asks me when he had acted contrary to the interests of Virginia? You have done it, sir, on every ballot in which you have given your vote for a sectional candidate, whom the people of Virginia must regard, if elected to that chair, as having been forced upon the country against their interests, against their wishes, and against the protestation of every man, woman, and child, within her borders.

Now, sir, a word to Massachusetts.

Mr. Hale. I would ask the gentleman if we are not the best judges of what our constituents desire?

Mr. Vallandigham. I rise to a question of order. I object to this interruption.

Mr. Hale. Has the gentleman the right to say —

(Loud cries of "Order!" from the Democratic benches.)

Mr. Hale. Has the gentleman the right to say —

(Cries of "Order!" "Order!")

Mr. Vallandigham. I insist upon the point of order.

Mr. Boteler. The election which returned these gentleman here took place a month before the John Brown raid. The people of the North know, they must know, they cannot fail to see, what is the inevitable tendency of this slavery agitation. They have been told by you, the politicians, you the leaders — and we have allowed ourselved to be deluded by the syren song sung in our ears — that you do not intend to interfere with slavery within the States. Personally, I believe you do not. Personally, there is not a leader among you all — not even Fred Douglass — who can be found with courage enough to come into

[p. 322]

the southern States and interfere with slavery there. But, from year to year, you have beaten the drum of abolitionism in all the highways and byeways of the North. From your pulpit and press and forum, in season and out of season, you have preached to the rising generation that slavery is a curse; and that anti-slavery sentiment has stimulated others, less careful of their personal safety, to come amongst us with a hostile intent, to steal our slaves and incite them to insurrection.

I can illustrate this by an incident which occurred in my own county the other day. That poor wretch, Coppie, a week or two before his execution, stood at the window of his prison, pressing his brow against the iron bars across it, looking out intently in the street at the happy groups of negroes assembled there, and after some time, he turned away and sobbed. A friend asked why he sobbed. "Sir," said he, "I have seen, day after day, the negroes in your streets, and they are better clad than the laboring people of the northern States; they are well cared for in every way, and see, oh! see how happy!" Said my friend, "What did you expect? "Oh," said he, "I have been taught to believe that they were downtrodden and oppressed, and were ready to cluch at liberty; but they refused it when we offered them the boon."

Now, Mr. Clerk, who is responsible for this? On whose head is the blood of Coppie? There was not a man amongst the Harper's Ferry insurgents except John Brown, who was not born since 1830, and who did not grow up under the influence of abolition preaching. This sir, is a significant fact, which I commend to the thinking portion of my countrymen. There was not one of them who had not breathed the atmosphere of abolition, and who had not his mind poisoned against the South by such teachings. You do not care for the negro. You admit the fact. It is a most miserable hobby upon which you have ridden into power. Now, in the name of our common country, I demand that you disband your anti-slavery party and take down your piratical flag!

When sir, I have heard the name of a gentleman called here, day after day, first on the roll — a great, historic name, (Mr. Adams,) I have been reminded of Massachusetts in her prouder day in the heroic age of the Republic. I have been reminded of a historical incident connected with the county in which I live — that county selected by John Brown for his bloody raid; and feel that I have a right to appeal to the Massachusetts delegation here, if they are not deaf to the voice of consanguinity, and if they are, I appeal from them to their people on this question; I demand of *them* to come up to the rescue of the country now as they did in the good old times of their revolutionary fathers.

The district which I represent, and the county where I live — that county made famous by the raid of Brown — was the first, the very first in all the South, to send succor to Massachusetts in the time of her direst necessity! In one of the most beautiful spots in that beautiful county, within rifle shot of my residence, at the base of a hill, where a glorious spring leaps out into sunlight from beneath the gnarled roots of a thunder-riven oak, there assembled on the 10th of July, 1775, the very first band of southern men who marched to the aid of Massachusetts. They met there, then, and their rallying cry was, "a bee-line for Boston." That beautiful and peaceful valley — the "valley of the Shenandoah" — had never been polluted by the footsteps of a foe; for even the Indians themselves had, according to tradition, kept it free from the incursion of their enemies. It was the hunting range and neutral ground of the aborigines. The homes of those who lived there then were far beyond the reach of danger. But Boston was beleagured! The hearths of your fathers were threatened with pollution, and the fathers of those whom I represent, rallied to their protection:

> "They left the plow share in the mould,
> Their flocks and herds without a fold,
> The sickle in the unshorn grain,
> Their corn half-garnered on the plain,
> And mustered in their simple dress,

For wrongs of *yours* to seek redress."

[p. 323]

Thus they mustered around the spring I speak of, and from thence they made their "Bee-line for Boston." Before they marched, they made a pledge that all who survived would assemble there fifty years after that day. It is my pride and pleasure to remember that I, though but a child then, was present at the spring when the fifty years rolled round. Three aged, feeble, tottering men — the survivors of that glorious band of one hundred and twenty — were all who were left to keep their tryst, and be faithful to the pledge made fifty years before to their companions, the bones of most of whom had been left bleaching on your northern hills.

Sir, I have often heard from the last survivor of that band of patriots the incidents of their first meeting and their march; how they made some six hundred miles in thirty days — twenty miles a day — and how, as they neared their point of destination, Washington, who happened to be making a reconnoissance in the neighborhood, saw them approaching, and recognizing the linsey-woolsey hunting-shirts of old Virginia, galloped up to meet and greet them to the camp; how, when he saw their captain, his old companion-in-arms, Stephenson, who had stood by his side at the Great Meadows, on Braddock's fatal field, and in many an Indian campaign — and who reported himself to his commander as *"from the right bank of the Potomac"* — he sprang from his horse and clasped his old friend and companion-in-arms with both hands. He spoke no word of welcome; but the eloquence of silence told what his tongue could not articulate. He moved along the ranks, shaking the hand of each, from man to man, and all the while — as my informer told me — the big tears were seen rolling down his cheeks.

Ay, sir, Washington wept! And why did the glorious soul of Washington swell with emotion? why did he weep? Sir, they were tears of joy! and he wept because he saw that the cause of Massachusetts was practically the cause of Virginia; because he saw that her citizens recognized the great principles involved in the contest. These Virginia volunteers had come spontaneously. They had come in response to the words of her Henry, that were leaping like live thunder through the land, telling the people of Virginia that they must fight, and fight for Massachusetts. They had come to rally with Washington to defend your fathers' firesides, to protect their homes from harm. Well, *the visit has been returned!* John Brown selected that very county, whose citizens went so promptly to the aid of the North when the North needed aid, as the most appropriate place in the South to carry out the doctrines of the "irrepressible conflict;" and, as was mentioned in the Senate yesterday, the rock where Leeman fell was the very rock over which Morgan and his men marched a few hours after Stephenson's command had crossed the river some ten miles further up.

May this historical reminiscence rekindle the embers of patriotism in our hearts! Why should this nation of ours be rent in pieces by this irrepressible conflict? Is it irrepressible? The battle will not be fought out upon this floor. For when the dark day comes, as come it may, when this question, that now divides and agitates the hearts of the people, shall be thrust from the forum of debate, to be decided by the bloody arbitrament of the sword, it will be the saddest day for us and all mankind that the sun of Heaven has ever shone upon.

I trust, Mr. Clerk, that this discussion will now cease. I trust that all will make an effort, by balloting, and by a succession of ballotings, to organize the House. I trust that we will go on in our efforts, day after day, until we do effect an organization, and proceed to perform the duties which we were sent here to discharge; that the great heart of our country will cease to pulsate with the anxiety which now causes it to throb; and that we will each, in our appropriate sphere, do what we can to make ourselves more worthy of the inestimable blessings, which a good God has given us, and which can only be enjoyed by a *free,* a *virtuous,* and *united* people. (Applause.)

[p. 324]
Letter from Henry Bedinger
Sir   Washington March 16th 46

... your letter of the 17th Jany ... in due course of mail but it ... mislaid and I did not find it until yesterday. If you will address a letter to N. W. Manning Esqs. Charles Town Jeff County Va, I think he will ... write everything of importance concerning the history of Genl. Wm. Darke as he is the grandson of Genl. D. For the history of Capt. Abraham Shepherd I refer you to Edmund J. Lee Esqr. Shepherds Town Jeff Coty Va, and for that of Genl. Wood to Robt. Wood Esqr. Winchester Va. I have none of the writings of my father except the "Cassue Celebration" I believe he destroyed them all before his death. If you will write to Col. Braxton Davenport Charles Town, Jeff. Coty Va. he can probably furnish you with some interesting particulars of the history of Maj. Henry Bedinger my fathers brother and possibly some of his papers. There are many incidents in the History of my fathers life which would be interesting but I have not time to write them out just now. Michael Bedinger another brother of my father was one of the earliest Kentucky pioneers and his early life was filled with adventures & interesting incidents. I refer you to his son Doct. Benj. F. Bedinger of Cincinnatti O. for an account of them. It will afford me pleasure to afford you any aid in my power in the prosecution of your work.

        Respectfully
        Henry Bedinger

Hon. Henry Bedinger
March 14th 1846
References.

[p. 325]
Letter from George W. Ranson

        Blue Lick Springs Ky
        May 3d 1887

Lyman C. Draper Esq.
Madison Wisconsin
Dear Sir

    As the representative of my friend and kinsman Honorable Danel P. Bedinger who was the representative of his father Major Geo M B-edinger. I write to enquire if you have any papers belonging to either of the gentlemen just named. There has never been any account published of Majr. G. M. B.'s life. I am endeavoring to write a short statement made of the leading events in his history, and will thank you to send to me at this place any information you have or any papers in your possession belonging to these parties. I am the administrator c. t. a. of Mr. D. P. B. and his brother in law, and the grand nephew of Majr. G. M. B. I have seen a letter or two from you to these gentlemen which lead me to infer that you may have the means of throwing light on some events which are now obscure.

        Very Respectfully
        George Wm. Ranson

[p. 326]
INTERESTING JUBILEE.

    A party of ladies and gentlemen met on the 10th June at the spring of Daniel Morgan, Esq. near Shepherdstown, Va. to celebrate the day, pursuant to an arrangement made fifty years ago. It appears that in the spring of 1775, two volunteer companies were raised, one in Winchester, the other in Shepherdstown, as the quota Virginia had been required to furnish. They turned out for twelve months, furnished their own rifles and equipage, and marched to Boston in twenty-one days. They were commanded by Hugh Stevenson and Daniel Morgan, (afterwards Col. Stevenson and Gen. Morgan.) On the 10th of June, 1755, and previous to their departure, Col. Wm. Morgan gave a barbecue to Stevenson's company at the spring above mentioned; and the heroes of the company made an engagement "that the survivors should meet at that spring on that day fifty years to come; which agreement has thus been fulfilled. But of the ninety-seven who composed the company, *five* only are living, and of the five, only two were present, the others being prevented by old age and infirmity. Those present were: Maj. *Henry Bedinger*, of Berkely, Va., and Maj. *Michael Bedinger*, of Kentucky. The other three are *Judge Robert White*, of Winchester, Va.; Gen. *Samuel Findley*, and *William Hulse*, Esq. of Ohio. Two patriotic songs, the same that had been sung there fifty years ago, were sung. *"Auld Lang Syne"* was played, and before breaking up, the company agreed that the survivors should celebrate the day at the same place twenty five years hence. *Luminary.*

THE END

INDEXING NOTE

Page numbers used as locators in the index refer to those stamped on the pages of the original manuscript, which appear in the microfilmed edition of the manuscript of Volume 1A. These numbers also correspond to the page numbers appearing in brackets in the transcript.

Every occurrence of all personal names appearing in Volume 1A is indexed, using last, first, and middle names when available. When only a last name is used in the manuscript, the first name is supplied in brackets when it can be determined with reasonable certainty from other sources. Titles such as military rank, academic degree, or political office are used with personal names only if no given name is provided in the manuscript. If neither given name nor title is available, the person is indexed as e.g. Mr. or Mrs. at the surname.

The original spelling of personal and place names is preserved in the transcription. In the index, spellings of these names are normalized to the most commonly occurring variants of the full names, with cross-references from other variants if these sort elsewhere in the alphabetically arranged index. Word-by-word sorting has been employed in ordering the index headings.

INDEX

A

abolitionism preached in Northern states, 322
Adair
    Maj. [John], 250
    John, 313
Adams
    [Charles Francis], 322
    [John Quincy], 259
adventure stories
    exploration of Green River country, Ky., 32, 37, 39, 45-53, 55
Afro-Americans. See Negroes; Slavery; Slaves
agriculture
    apple orchards, 19
    crop failures (1835), 264, 265
    products, prices of (1835), 265
Alexander, Dr. [Ashton], 71
Allen
    Mr., 262
    Thomas, 145, 146, 160, 315
Alsace (Alsatz), ancestral home of Bedinger family, 2
Amboy, N. J., George M. Bedinger military service at (1776), 11, 87, 93, 101
Anecdotes. See Narratives
animal stories. See Narratives, animal
Anti-Lecompton Party, 316
apple trees, planting of, 19
appointment of George M. Bedinger in militia, doubts concerning, 118
archaeology, mammoth (mastodon) bones at Big Bone Lick, 20

army
    positioning of
        in siege of Yorktown, Va. (1781), 144
        in St. Clair's defeat (1791), 133
    provisioned by George M. Bedinger
        at Santee Hills, S. C. (1780), 31
        at Valley Forge, Penn. (1777), 128
    training of, by George M. Bedinger, 61, 118
    Twelfth Virginia Regiment, 93, 102, 256, 303
    weakness of American (1776), 86, 90, 108, 127
Army stories. See Narratives
Arnold, Lewis H., 266, 311

B

Bankman, John, 69
    killed and scalped by Indians, 18
bankruptcy of canal company, 263
Banta family, 148, 154, 241, 243
barge, travel by, 72
Barnett, [Joseph], 211, 222
Bathe, James, 69
battle of Blue Lick, Ky. (1782), 312
battle of Germantown, Penn. (1777), 11, 12, 68, 93, 94, 101-103, 110, 111, 118, 126, 127, 139, 256, 260, 303, 304
battle of Piscataway, N. J. (1777), 11, 87, 88, 93, 96, 109, 129, 303
bear
    in cherry tree, killed for meat, 56
    George M. Bedinger encounter with, in cave, 38
    jerky, preparation of, 35, 38

bear *(continued)*
   meat, for food, 41, 45, 46
Beatty (Beaty), Adam, 255, 313
beaver, hunting of, 37, 38, 40
Bedford, Betsy, 258
Bedinger. *See also* Biedinger
   Anna Maria, 2
   Benj. F., 267, 324
      distress over inability to pay debts, 131, 132
   Christian, 2
   Christina, 2
   Daniel, brother of George M. Bedinger, 2, 115
      agreement for surveying military bounty lands, 135
      confined on British prison ship, 10, 31, 127, 128
      military service, 118
      scholastic aptitude, 3
   Daniel P., son of George M. Bedinger, 121, 262, 325
      contracts smallpox, 264
      letters from, 267-270
   Edwin, 265
   Elizabeth, 2
   George M.
      ambushed by Indians (1779), 18
      ancestry, 2
      attends Ralph Morgan's wedding (1783), 69
      avoidance of Indians near Boonesborough, Ky. (1779), 14
      in battle of Germantown, Penn. (1777), 11, 12
      birth, 2, 268, 307
      in Bowman's expedition (1779), 20
      British prisoners taken by, on Staten Island, N.Y. (1775), 9
      burial, 268
      cares for brothers while prisoners of war, 10
      at commemoration of farewell barbecue (1825), 326
      commissary at Boonesborough, Ky. (1778), 19
      death of wife (1787), 57
      election to Kentucky legislature (1792), 1
      encounter with bear in cave, 38
      escape from Indians (1778), 15
      expedition to Boonesborough, Ky. (1779), 130
      journey to Boonesborough, Ky. (1779), 12
      legislative service of, 300
      marriages, 2, 5, 57, 61
      military career, 75-125, 254, 256, 271-299
      origin of first name, 83, 136
      in Orr's campaign (1791), 64, 65
      patriotism, 121
      pursuit of Indian horse thieves (1791), 64
      request for papers of, 325
      role in Estill's defeat (1779), 4
      role in retreat from Shawnee Indian village (1779), 22-28
      in trespass suit, 253[2]
   Henrietta, 2
   Henry
      agreement for surveying military bounty lands, 135
      brother of George M., 2, 115-117, 123, 131, 307
      affidavit on military career of brother George, 260
      at commemoration of farewell barbecue (1825), 326
      death, 1
      enlistment in Stephenson's company of riflemen (1775), 81, 82
      imprisonment by British, 10, 122, 127, 128
      view on expedition to Pacific coast, 65, 66
      letters from, 256-265, 324
      recruitment of soldiers by (1776), 137
      scholastic aptitude, 3
   father of George M. Bedinger, 2
   son of George M. Bedinger, 257

Bedinger *(continued)*
  Jacob, 2
  Jos., 266
  Nancy, 2
  Rachael, 2
  Sally, daughter of Henry Bedinger, 263
  Sarah, sister of George M., 3
  Sarah (nee Rutherford), sister-in-law of George M., 2
  Solomon, 3
Bedinger's Branch of Muddy Creek, Madison Co., Ky., 152, 167, 180, 191-193, 195, 196, 198-200, 207-209, 215-217, 221, 223, 227, 228, 232, 238, 241, 244, 246
  naming of, 151, 157, 159, 166, 206
Bell, Daniel, 123, 307
  at siege of Yorktown, 117
belting of trees to identify land claims, 151, 162, 182, 183, 185, 234
Benton, [Thomas Hart], 259
Berry
  George, 37, 38
  Jack, 37, 38
  James, 69, 235
    ambushed by Indians, 18
    deposition in land claim lawsuit, 201, 202
    wounded at Estill's Defeat, 4
  William, 201, 202
Bethiah, Elisha, escape from Indians (1779), 27
Bettinger, Nicholas, 122
Biedinger. *See also* Bedinger
  Adam, 2
  George Michael, son of Adam Biedinger, 2
  Henry, father of George M. Bedinger, 2, 3
  Magdalene, 2
  Nicholas, 2
  Peter, 2
Big Bone Lick, Ky., mammoth or mastodon bones at, 20
Big Muddy Creek, Madison Co., Ky., naming of, 224
birds. injured paroquet befiended by George M. Bedinger, 47

Bittinger, Nicholas, 87, 93, 101
Black Fish (Indian), 278, 287, 288
  address to Indian warriors, 22, 26
  death, 27, 133
"blackberry campaign" against Indians (1791), 65
Blackford, Joe, Capt. Nation murdered by, 53, 54
blacks. *See* Negroes; Slavery; Slaves
Blue Lick battleground, map, 312
Blue Licks, Ky., history, 70
Boles family, 154, 157
Boone
  Daniel, 19, 74, 171-173, 218, 269, 313
    at battle of Blue Lick, 312
  Jacob, 74
  Squire, peace talks with Indians, 19
Boonesborough, Ky.
  besieged by Indians (1779), 112-114, 306
  defense of (1779), 94, 145, 254
  expedition to (1779), 104, 150, 304, 305
  George M. Bedinger service at (1779), 260, 307
  hunting parties during Indian siege of (1779), 17, 18, 95
  repair and provisioning of fort at (1778), 19
Boston, Mass., siege of (1775), 9, 75-77, 81-83, 85, 89, 92, 99, 107, 260, 301, 302
  march of Virginia troops to, 256, 262, 263, 322, 326
Boteler, A. R. speech (1860), 316-323
Boughman family, 243
bounty lands,agreement for surveying of, 135
Bowman, John, 313
  assessment of, 292
  expedition against Shawnee Indian village (1779), 19-31, 75, 97, 105, 106, 114, 132, 139, 256, 260, 272-291, 306, 309
Brady, Sam, capture by British, 63
Bridge, Mr., land claim on Muddy Creek, Madison Co., Ky., 157, 231

bridle made from pawpaw bark, 38
Briscoe, William, 159, 160, 168, 169
Brissot de Warville, [Jacques Pierre], letter on invention of steamboat, 73
broadsides and handbills, in Kentucky congressional campaign (1829), 254, 255
Brooks, Thomas, 243
Brown, John, in raid at Harper's Ferry, 318, 321, 322
Buck, Capt. (Indian), 42
buffalo
    hide of, use as food, 36
    hunting, during siege of Boonesborough, Ky. (1779), 17, 18, 95, 114, 306
    jerky, preparation of, 35
    killing of
        heroic, 19
        for meat, 48
        shooting of, by George M. Bedinger, 39
Bulgon, John, 132
Bullock
    Dina, 175, 177
    John, 175, 177, 243
Bush, Elkanah, 132, 309, 310
Bush's Settlement, near Boonesborough, Ky., 4
Butler, Gen. [William], 61

C

Calamees, Marcus, 57, 59, 60
Calaway. See Calloway
Caldwell
    Geo., 63
    R., 202
Calloway
    Col. [Richard], 19, 243
    Fanny, 69
    John, 69, 243
    Mr., role in Estill's Defeat, 4
campaign for Congress by George M. Bedinger, 254, 255
canal company, financial affairs of, 263
canals, popularity of transport by, 264

cap of goose skin, 46
Capline, Capt., 63
Carrington
    Edwd., 247, 248
    Joseph, 247
    Mayo, 39
cave, Geroge M. Bedinger encounter with bear in, 38
celebrations
    anniversary of march of Stephenson's company of riflemen to Boston, 8, 323, 326
    pioneer wedding, 69
chain carriers for surveying, 39
Chambers, John, 123, 124
    of U.S. House of Representatives, 115, 116, 311
Chaplin, Isaac, 315
Chiles, Henry C., 268
Chillicothe (Shawnee village on Little Miami River), attack on (1779), 20-25, 97, 98, 105, 106, 114, 306
cholera
    contracted by Col. Miller, 263
    epidemic of (1832), 257
chopping of trees to identify land claims, 162, 164, 183, 212, 225, 234, 236
Christian, Wm., 74
Clark
    George Rogers, 53, 74, 272, 313
        desire for peace with Indians, 41, 43
    John, 63
Clay
    Green, 170-173
    H., role in land case involving Blue Lick estate, 70
    Henrietta, 2
    [Henry], 259, 311
clothing of hunters, description of, 46
Cobbs, John, 74
cold bath as rheumatism treatment, 47
Colefoot, John, 211, 223, 242, 243
Colfax, [Schuyler], 320
Collins
    Henry, 74
    Wm., 243

commerce, steamboat role in, 72
commission of George M. Bedinger in militia, doubts concerning, 118
conciliation
   George M. Bedinger desire for, of competing factions in federal government, 254
   George Rogers Clark desire for, with Indians, 41, 43
Constant, John, 146, 155, 174, 189, 243
   in defense of Boonesborough, Ky. (1779), 69
   journey to Boonesborough, Ky. (1779), 12, 166
constitution of Virginia, revised, 255
Cooke, John R., 262
Coppie, Mr., view on treatment of negroes in South, 322
Cornwallis, Charles, capture at Yorktown, Va. (1781), 138, 141, 143, 256
Corwin, [Thomas], 318-320
Couchman, Andrew, 311
court martial, George M. Bedinger presides over, 295
Court of Quarter Sessions, Nicholas Co., Ky., George M. Bedinger as judge of, 62, 300
Cowan, John, 74
Cox
   Henry, 211, 222, 245
   Mr., 236
Cradlebaugh
   John, 16, 17
   William, 69, 166-169
Crawford, Col. [William], possible contribution of Monongaheleans to defeat of (1782), 31
Crewe (Crewse), Mr., land improvement by, 154, 157
crimes
   of army officers (1792), 250
   military, court martial for, 295, 296
   murder
      of Capt. Nation, 53, 54
      massacre of Indians, 69, 70
      of Walker Daniel, 56

theft
   of George M. Bedinger's personal effects, 136
   of horses by Indians, 63, 291, 306
Crooke, John, 219, 220
   surveyor of Madison Co., Ky., 164, 235, 240
crop failures (1835), 264, 265
Cumberland River, settlement of lands near mouth of, 247, 248

D

Daniel, Walker, killed by Indians, 56
Danville, Ky., road to Tillico, Tenn., survey for (1815), 74
Darke, William, 31, 61, 119, 133, 295, 324
   agreement for surveying military bounty lands, 135
   in battle of Germantown, Penn. (1777), 118
   in campaign against Pennsylvania insurgents (1794), 1
   military career of, 68
   at siege of Yorktown, Va. (1781), 114, 141, 143, 256, 260, 307
Davenport, Braxton, 1, 264, 324
Davis, Thomas, 253[2]
Declaration of Independence, George M. Bedinger present at proclamation of, 10, 137
deer
   jerky, preparation of, 35
   killing of, for food, 18
Dibans Run, Madison Co., Ky., naming of, 224
discipline, George M. Bedinger instruction of troops in, 61
diseases
   cholera, 257, 263
   fever, 296
   fits, 55
   nervous fever, 80, 131, 141
   rheumatism, 39, 45, 47, 61, 121, 123, 126, 134, 296

diseases *(continued)*
    smallpox, 264
    snakebite, 20, 33
dog, value to backwoodsmen, 52
Doniphan (Donathan, Doniphen), Joseph, 146, 155, 189, 243
    moves to Boonesborough, Ky., 69, 125, 150, 166
Doniphen, George, 125
Dorchester Heights, Mass., capture and fortification of (1775), 9, 76, 77, 81, 99, 107, 301
Dorschell, Liechtenstein, Alsace, ancestral home of Bedinger family, 2
Douglass, Fred, 321
Drake
    Benj., 268, 271
    [Daniel], 267
Draper, Lyman C., letters to, 267-270, 325
duel of James Marshall and Charles Vancouver, averted, 60
Duncan, James, 12, 69
Dunmore's War, 3
Duree
    Dina (Winey), 175, 243
    Peter, 175
    Samuel, 69, 146, 152, 153, 157, 174-176, 182, 189, 228, 231, 243
    journey to Boonesborough, Ky. (1779), 12, 150, 166

E

economy
    protectionism, defended, 254, 320
    U.S., progress of, 254
education
    escheated lands designated for schools, 74
    of George M. Bedinger, 3
    German schools in Virginia, 3
Edwards
    John, 267, 269
    [John], campaign against Indians ("blackberry campaign", 1791), 65

elector for governor of Kentucky, George M. Bedinger as, 62
electoral college, George M. Bedinger in favor of abolition of, 254
elk jerky, preparation of, 35
Elliott, John, 57
emigration of Biedinger family to America, 2
Estill
    James, 15, 69, 112, 171, 183, 185, 211, 214, 219, 223-226, 237, 242, 243
    character of, 190, 199, 201
    killed by Indians, 4, 236
    Samuel, 69, 146, 233, 240, 243
    in defense of Boonesborough (1779), 104
    deposition in land claim lawsuit, 203-210
    narrow escape from Indians, 15
    Wm., 235
Estill's defeat, 4, 219
Estill's Station, history of, 184, 199, 210, 211, 214, 222, 223, 242
European immigrants, 317
Evans, John, 160, 236
exploration
    of Kentucky, 32-53, 56
    of western America, 60, 61, 65

F

farm
    estimate of crop yields, 140
    sale by George M. Bedinger to assist brothers in prison, 128
Farrow, Thornton, 28
federal government, growth of, 254
fever, nervous, George M. Bedinger loss of memory due to (1787), 80, 131, 141
Fields, Lewis, 32-37, 126
Findley (Finley), Samuel, 8, 270
    agreement for surveying military bounty lands, 135
    in capture of British soldiers on Staten Island, N. Y. (1776), 85, 89, 92, 100, 108

Findley (Finley), Samuel *(continued)*
   in siege of Boston (1775), 77, 83, 302, 326
Finley
   David, 269, 270
   Jno., 269
fish
   shooting of, 34
   use as food, 37
Fisher, Peter, 123, 260, 261, 307
   military career, 140-143
   testimony on military service of G. M. Bedinger, 138, 139
Fitch, [John], 73
fits, rattlesnake heart as cure for, 55
Fleming, Wm., 74
Floyd, John, 74
food sources
   apples, 19
   bear, 35, 38, 41, 45, 46, 56
   beaver tail, 37, 38
   buffalo, 17, 18, 35, 36, 48, 95, 114, 306
   elk, 35
   fish, 34, 37
   rye, 264
   terrapin, 36
   venison, 18, 35, 37
   wheat, 264
   wild hogs, 19
   wolf, 51
Fort Hamilton [at site of Hamilton, Ohio], threatened by Indians (1792), 251
Fort Jefferson [near Greenville, Ohio], George M. Bedinger accompanies company of invalids to (1791), 61
Fort Washington, N.Y., Daniel and Henry Bedinger taken prisoner at (1776), 10, 121, 122, 137
fossils, mammoth (mastodon) bones at Big Bone Lick, Ky., 20
Foudnee (Indian), 42
Fulton, [Robert], 71, 72
furs, beaver, 37

G

Gaithers (Gaither), Latham (Nathan), 259
Garison, Samuel, 179
Gass (Gess, Goss, Guess, Guest)
   David, 15, 146, 183, 218, 219, 242-244
      character, 190, 199, 201
      in defense of Boonesborough, Ky. (1779), 69
      in peace talks with Indians at Boonesborough, 19
   John, 69, 183, 235
Gates
   Horatio, 66
   James, 145, 147, 148, 154, 157, 211
   Lee, 308
Gather, Maj., 133
Georgia Settlement in Logan Co., Ky., 74
Germantown, battle of. *See* battle of Germantown, Penn. (1777)
Gess. *See* Gass
Gilbert, Samuel, 152, 167-169, 171, 191, 220
Gilmer, [John Adams], 321
Girty, Simon
   gun and vest found in Shawnee village, 22
   rumored to come to aid of Shawnees during Bowman's raid (1779), 24, 280, 285
given name of George M. Bedinger, origin, 126
goose skin cap, 46
Goss. *See* Gass
Green River country (Ky.), George M. Bedinger trips to, 5, 31-53
Greens, Elihue, 154
Gregg (Grey), Squire, 131
grist mills on Licking River, Ky., 3
Grugell, John, 187
Guess. *See* Gass
Guest. *See* Gass
gunpowder stored in magazine at Williamsburg, Va. (1775), 80

guns, squirt, Fort Boonesborough, Ky., defense with (1778), 19

H

Hacket (Hackett), Peter, 223, 227, 233
Haines, Peter, 8
Hale, [James Tracy], 321
Hall, Horatio, 64
Hamilton
   [Henry], taken prisoner at Kaskaskia (1779), 271, 272
   James, 211, 223, 242
   William, 211
Hampton, Andrew, 70
Hancock, Stephen, 235
handbills in Kentucky congressional campaign (1829), 254, 255
Harlan, Maj. [Silas], 312, 313
Harper's Ferry, Va., raid at (1859), 317, 318, 321, 322
Harpes, Mr. Tully assassinated by, 73
Harris, Overton, 178
Harrod
   James
      in Bowman's expedition against Shawnees (1779), 97, 132, 273, 275, 279
      role in attack on Shawnee village (1779), 20, 21
   William, 20, 313, 314
Harrodsburg, Ky., defense from Indians (1777), 313, 314
Hart, Nathaniel, 175, 176
Haweson, John, 17, 69
Haynes, Jacob, 261
Helper Book, 319
Henderson, Samuel, 147
Henry, Richd., 262
Henshaw (Henshew), William, 77, 83, 85, 89, 92, 100, 108, 302
Hickman, Wm., 22, 23, 281
Hickory Lick, Madison Co., Ky., naming of, 199, 224
hide, buffalo, use as food, 36
Hocker, Nicholas, 160, 168, 186, 234, 236
Hodges, Jesse, 69, 267

provisioning of Fort Boonesborough with buffalo meat by, 18
role in escape from Indian village at Chillicothe, 22
testimony on military service of George M. Bedinger, 309
hogs, wild, killed for meat, 19
Holder (Halder)
   Fanny, 69
   John, 56, 74, 146, 155, 174, 189, 243
      in Bowman's expedition against Shawnees (1779), 97, 132, 273, 274, 276-278
      commander at Boonesborough, Ky. (1779), 13-15, 69, 94, 104, 105, 111, 113, 304, 305
      troops for Bowman's campaign against Shawnees recruitment by, 19
holidays and celebrations
   anniversary of march of Stephenson's company to Boston, 8, 323, 326
   pioneer wedding, 69
Hopkinson, Capt., 308
horses
   capture of
      during attack on Shawnees (1779), 291, 292, 306, 309
      by George M. Bedinger, 38
   prices for (1835), 264
   sale by Bowman's party (1779), 29
   theft by Indians, 63, 291, 306
Houle, Oliver E., 311
House of Representatives (U. S.)
   George M. Bedinger campaign for (1829), 254, 255
   George M. Bedinger service in, 62, 300, 311
   debate on organization of (1860), 316-323
   John Sherman as candidate for speaker of (1860), 319, 320
Howard's Creek, near Boonesborough, Ky., 4

Howe
- Adm. [Richard], of British navy, 9, 82, 86, 90, 100, 108
- Gen. [William], of British army, 82, 86, 90, 100, 108

Hubbel, Mr., 64, 65

Hudson, Rh. C., military land office of, 37

Hughs, Andrew S., 253², 253³

Hulse, William, 8, 326

human rights, George M. Bedinger devotion to, 266

humor, practical jokes, 16, 17, 62

Hunter
- Mr., husband of Adam Stephens' daughter, 68
- R. M. T., 68

hunters, clothing of, described, 46

hunting parties
- from Estill's Station, 194
- during Indian siege of Boonesborough, Ky. (1779), 17, 18, 95

I

imitation of owls and ravens by Indians in ambush party, 58

immigrants from Europe, 317

importation of slaves, bill prohibiting, 62, 254

improvements. *See* Land claims

Indians
- ambush of George M. Bedinger and party by, on Little Sandy River, Ky. (1788), 58
- burial of, by Orr's company (1791), 65
- danger from
  - around Estill's Station, Ky. (1780's), 194
  - at Boonesborough, Ky. (1779), 13, 18, 94
- oratory, battle oration by Black Fish (1779), 22, 26, 98, 278
- peace talks with
  - at Boonesborough (1778), 19
  - by George M. Bedinger (1785), 40, 41
- Samuel Estill's narrow escape from, 15
- stories about. *See* Narratives
- war with, urgency of (1792), 61, 65

Inning Corday (Indian), 42

intestine, battlefield surgery on, 68

inventors, of steamboat, James Rumsey as, 66, 71-73

Irvin, Christopher, 235

Irvine
- David, 178, 310
- Will, 173, 195, 202

Irwin, Mr., injured at Estill's Defeat, 4

J

jerky
- bear, preparation of, 38
- buffalo, preparation of, 35

Johnson
- Dr., 61
  - ridicules posting of sentinels at camp, 62
- R. M., 311

judge, George M. Bedinger as, in Nicholas Co., Ky., 62

K

Kearsley, John, 66

keelboat, travel by, 72

Keene, Nancy, wife of George M. Bedinger, 2, 5

Kelly, William, 84, 108

Kenton
- Philip C., 253²
- Simon, 64, 65, 293, 294

Kentucky
- exploration, 32-53, 56
- legislature, George M. Bedinger as member of, 1, 300
- wildlife. *See* Wildlife

Kemey, James, 66

Key, Marshal, 313

King, Mr., survey of Green River country by (1781), 37, 38

Kings Branch, Muddy Creek, Madison Co., Ky., naming of, 224

Kirtley, Mr., killed by Indians, 56

Knox, Gen. [Henry], 299

L

Lacy, Walter, 313
Lamb, Thomas, 167-169
land
   condemnation for turnpike, 266
   military bounty, agreement for surveying, 135
land claims, of George M. Bedinger and others, 145-248
land papers, hidden from Indians, 39
Lauck
   Isaac S., 256
   Peter, 256
law
   military court proceedings, 295, 296
   military service claims, 82-97, 99-133, 256-261
   to prohibit importation of slaves (1808), 62, 300
lawsuits over land, 145, 146, 150-246, 253^2, 253^3, 266
Leach, James G., 311
leaves, moccasins stuffed with, 46
Lee
   Charles, 172
   Edmund J., 324
   Henry, 74
   Mr., financial dealings of (1835), 263
Leeman, [William Henry], 323
Lewis, Capt. [Meriwether], 61, 62, 296
Liberia, transport of free blacks to, 254
Lichtzstein (Liechtenstein), Alsace, ancestral home of Bedinger family, 2
Licking River, Ky., mills built by George M. Bedinger on, 3
Liechtenstein (Lichtzstein), Alsace, ancestral home of Bedinger family, 2
Lipscomb, Squire, 154
Little Muddy Creek, Madison Co., Ky., naming of, 199, 209, 224
Lockhart, Charles Edward, 69, 243

Log Lick Branch, Muddy Creek, Madison Co., Ky., named, 224
Logan
   Benjamin, 313
      in Bowman's expedition against Shawnees (1779), 97, 132, 273, 275, 279
      role in attack on Shawnee village (1779), 20-22
   [Benjamin], expedition against Shawnee Indians (1786), 74
   John, 67, 313
Love stories
   courtship of George M. Bedinger, 5
Lower Blue Licks, Ky., history, 70
Lucas
   Edward
      in battle of Piscataway, N. J. (1777), 129
      joins army at Morristown, N. J. (1777), 87, 93, 101
      in Morgan's company of volunteer riflemen (1777), 109, 116, 118, 137, 302
      reelection to Congress, 262, 263
   Robert, 116, 129
   William, 118, 129
      joins army at Morristown, N. J. (1777), 87, 93, 101
      in Morgan's company of volunteer riflemen (1777), 109, 116, 137, 302
Lynch. See Lyntch
Lynn's Station, 55
Lyntch, David, 160, 168, 169, 199, 211, 220, 229, 233-235, 240
   deposition in land claim lawsuit, 160-166, 182-186, 222-227, 236-240
   escapes uninjured at Estill's Defeat (1779), 4

M

McAfee, Robert B., 313

McCabe, Josiah, 253[3]
McClure, Parson [Andrew], 69
M'Cown (Morison), Samuel, affidavit to military service of Robert Pogue, 315
McGary, Hugh, 74, 313, 314
McIntire, Capt. [William], 119
McKee, Alexr., escheated lands of, 74
McKenzie, Rob., escheated lands of, 74
Madison, James, role in revision of Virginia constitution, 255
Magary. *See* McGary
mammoth (mastodon) bones at Big Bone Lick, Ky., 20
Manning
    Mrs., daughter of Wm. Darke, 118
    N. W., 324
manual skills of George M. Bedinger, 3
manufacturing, tariffs for protection of U.S., George M. Bedinger in favor of, 254
map of Blue Lick battleground, 312
Mark, John, 66
Mark (negro owned by Estills), apple nursery planted by, 19
marking
    of land claims, 188, 204, 211-213, 219, 220, 228, 229, 232, 242, 244
    of trees to identify land claims, 16, 151, 161, 162, 165, 166, 175, 185, 225, 235
Marshall
    [Humphrey], history of Kentucky written by (1824), 75
    James, 57, 59, 60
    Thomas, 32, 313
Martin
    John, 69
    Tyra (Tyree), 167, 171
    William
        defendant in land dispute, 130, 150, 152, 160, 164, 166, 167, 170, 179, 180, 183, 187, 203, 205, 209, 210, 217, 221, 228, 230, 233, 237, 240

land claim on Muddy Creek, Madison Co., Ky., 204
Mason, Sen. [James Murray], 318
massacre of Christian Indians by Williamson's company (1781), 69, 70
Massie, Peter, 228, 230
mastodon (mammoth) bones at Big Bone Lick, Ky., 20
May, John, 74
Maysville, Ky., proposed road to, from Nashville, Tenn., 254
meat
    bear, curing of, 38
    jerky, method of preparing, 35
medicine. *See* Diseases
memory of George M. Bedinger
    ruined by nervous fever, 80, 131, 134, 141, 257
    weakness of, 116
Meriwether, Geo., 74
Meyers, Jacob, 125
Michel, John, 242
Middle Fork, Muddy Creek, Madison Co., Ky., naming of, 177, 180, 194, 231
military career
    of George M. Bedinger, 254
        enlistment (1775), 5
        resignation (1793), 1
    of William Darke, 68
    of Peter Fisher, 140-143
    of Robert Pogue, 313-315
    of Adam Stephen, 68
military records
    commission of George M. Bedinger in militia, doubts concerning, 118
    George M. Bedinger loss of, 124, 126
Military stories. *See* Narratives
militia, training of, by George M. Bedinger, 118
Miller
    Charles, 232
    Col., suffers from cholera (1835), 263, 264
    Ellen Augusta, 263
    Jacob, 241
    John, 261

Miller *(continued)*
  Lt., blamed in Estill's Defeat, 4
  Robert, 170, 196
  Will, 195
mills of George M. Bedinger, 57, 124, 135
mimicry of owls and ravens by Indians in ambush party, 58
Mitchel, John, 211
Mitchell, Joseph, 66
moccasins stuffed with oak leaves, 46
Monongaheleans
  poor military discipline of, 30
  role in battle at Shawnee Indian village (1779), 24
  sale of Indian horses by, 29
  slaughter of Moravian Indians by, 31
Montgomery, Wm., 74
Moore, John, 211, 222, 236, 245
Morehead, Mr., Indian trader, 60
Morgan
  Abel, 2, 5, 264
  Abraham, 2, 129
  Anna Maria, 2
  D., nephew of George M. Bedinger, 263
  Daniel, 6, 9, 75, 117, 326
  Elizabeth, 2
  George, 80
  Jacob, 262, 263
  John F., 311
  Jos., 257
  M., in battle of Piscataway, N.J. (1777), 96
  Olivia, 257, 262
  Ralph, 56, 146, 152, 161, 164, 174, 186, 189, 222, 236, 245
    deposition in land dispute (1816), 130, 179-182
    in hunting party at Boonesborough, Ky. (1779), 17
    journey to Boonesborough, Ky. (1779), 12, 150
    role in escape from Shawnee village (1779), 24
    truthfulness of, when sober, 155
    wedding of (1783), 69
  Thomas, 129, 264

William, 56, 69, 87, 93, 118, 146, 189, 243, 305, 323
  in battle of Piscataway, N.J. (1777), 96, 129
  company of volunteer riflemen commanded by (1777), 109, 116, 128, 137, 256, 260, 302
  George M. Bedinger service under, 1, 11, 144
  joins army at Morristown, N.J. (1777), 101
  journey to Boonesborough, Ky. (1779), 12, 104, 112, 150, 166, 309
Morison (M'Cown), Samuel, affidavit to military service of Robert Pogue, 315
Morrow
  Charles, 66
  John, 66
Mud (Indian), 53, 54
Muddy Creek, Madison Co., Ky.
  George M. Bedinger land claim on, 1, 145-246
  naming of branches of, 180, 192, 194, 199, 209, 224, 231
Mulberry Fork, Muddy Creek, Madison Co., Ky., naming of, 224
music, "That seat of science, Athens," Revolutionary War song, 6-8
Myers, Jacob, 32

N

Narratives
  adventure
    exploration of Green River country, Ky., 32, 37, 39, 45-53, 55
  animal
    bear in cave, 38
    bear in cherry tree, 56
    beaver dam, 40
    capture of horse, 38
    capture of wolf, 50, 51
    paroquet, 47
    wounded dog, 51, 52

narratives *(continued)*
- crime
  - death of Capt. Nation, 53, 54
  - death of Walker Daniel, 56
  - massacre of Indians, 69, 70
- historical
  - James Rumsey's steamboat, 71
  - 60th anniversary barbecue, 262, 263
- humorous
  - David Zeigler cheated out of wine, 67
  - polecat story, 16
  - practical joke, 16, 17
- hunting, 17, 18
- about Indians
  - hostilities
    - Bowman's campaign to Shawnee village (1779), 20-31, 97, 98, 272-294, 306
    - defeat on Little Sandy River, Ky. (1788), 57-60
    - John Bankman killed, 18
    - on journey to Boonesborough, Ky. (1779), 304, 305
    - Orr's campaign (1791), 64, 65
    - over horse theft, 63, 64
    - siege of Boonesborough (1779), 12-15, 19
    - peace mission of Piankeshaws, 54, 55
    - peace mission to Capt. Whitenday, 40-45
    - Tom Swearingen lives with Indians, 64
- military
  - battle of Germantown, Penn. (1777), 102, 123, 303, 304
  - battle of Piscataway, N. J. (1777), 87
  - battlefield surgery, 68
  - dispute at Pittsburgh over command, 298-300
  - Estill's Defeat (1779), 4
  - **journey to Boonesborough, Ky. (1779), 111-113**

  - ruse at battle of Germantown, Penn. (1777), 68
  - siege of Boonesborough, Ky. (1779), 4-6, 8-12
  - siege of Boston, Mass. (1775), 76-79, 99, 301, 302
  - St. Clair's campaign (1791), 61, 62
- romantic
  - courtship of George M. Bedinger, 5

Nashville, Tenn., proposed road to, from Maysville, Ky., 254

Nation, Capt. (Indian), murder of, 53, 54

national roads, construction of, 254

negroes. *See also* Slavery; Slaves
- transport of free, to Liberia, 254
- treatment of, in South, 322

Nelson
- Edward, 243
- Mr., survey of Green River country by (1784), 37, 38

nervous fever, George M. Bedinger's memory ruined by (1787), 80, 131, 141

New York, N. Y., Hugh Stephenson's company of riflemen stationed at (1776), 77, 107

Ney, Marshal [Michel], Michael Rudulph as, 67, 251, 253[1]

Nolin (No-Linn) Creek, 37, 55

No-Linn Hill, 55

Norval, Mr., role in condemnation of land for turnpike (1842), 266

O

oak leaves, moccasins stuffed with, 46

O'Bannon, John, 39
- land papers of George M. Bedinger taken by, 57

Oldham
- Conway, 75
- Wm., 25, 75

Opposition Party, southern, 316

Orr, Alexander D., 64, 65, 293, 294

owls, imitation of hooting of, by Indians in ambush party, 58

P

Pacific coast, intended trip of George M. Bedinger to, 60, 61, 65
parakeet (paroquet), injured, befriended by George M. Bedinger, 47
Parks, Hen. G., 253[3]
paroquet (parakeet), injured, befriended by George M. Bedinger, 47
patriotism, discussed, 254, 316, 317
Patterson, Mr., at battle of Blue Lick (1782), 312
pawpaw, use of bark in fabrication of bridle, 38
Peck
   John, 123
   [Peter, Sr.], in siege of Yorktown, Va., 117
Pendleton, Philip, 66
Pennsylvania insurgents, campaign against (1794), 1
pension application of George M. Bedinger, 82-133
pension office, regulations regarding evidence of service, 117
Perth Amboy, N. J., George M. Bedinger military service at (1776), 11, 87, 93, 101
Philadelphia, Biedinger family landing at, 2
Piankeshaw Indians, peace talks with Gen. Clark, 54, 55
Picker, Jas. C., 311
Piomingo (Indian), actions after St. Clair's defeat, 70
pioneer life
   Indian troubles, 12-15, 18, 19, 32, 33, 39, 40, 42-45, 57-59, 62-65, 94, 104, 105, 111-113, 145, 175, 194, 236, 251, 293, 304-306, 314
   wedding celebration, 69
Piscataway, N. J., battle of. *See* battle of Piscataway, N. J. (1777)
plat of Blue Lick battleground, 312
plurality rule, opposition to adoption of, in U. S. House of Representatives (1860), 319, 320
Pogue
   Robert, military service of, 313-315
   William, 314
politics, national, 254, 255, 316-323
Powder (Indian), 42, 45
preemption warrants for land, 145, 148, 149
President of U.S., election by direct popular vote, George M. Bedinger in favor of, 254
Price, Richard, 211, 222, 236
prison ships, Daniel and Henry Bedinger held on British, 10
Proctor
   Joseph, 69, 168, 169, 217, 227, 235
      deposition in land claim lawsuit, 150-155
      residence at Estill's Station, 157, 158, 211, 223, 242
   M., 243
   Mr.
      in peace talks with Indians (1778), 19
      role in escape from Shawnee village (1779), 22
   Nicholas, 69, 187, 211, 242
   Reuben, 69, 211, 228, 242
pronunciation of Bedinger and Biedinger surnames, 3
protective tariff
   George M. Bedinger in favor of, 254
   A. R. Boteler position on, 320

R

railroad, speed of travel on, 263, 264
Ransom, Mrs., 262
Ranson, George Wm., 325
rattlesnake
   heart, as cure for fits, 55
   man in Bowman's party bitten by, 20
ravens, imitation of croaking of, by Indians in ambush party, 58

Ray
  Capt. [James], in Wabash expedition (1786), 74
  James, 313, 314
Reed, Walker, 266
Republican Party, abolitionist intentions of, 318
Revolutionary War. *See also* Siege and specific battles
  George M. Bedinger enlistment in (1775), 5
  Bedinger surname changed during, 3
  William Darke service in, 68
  Peter Fisher service in, 140-143
  Adam Stephen service in, 68
rheumatism
  cold bath as treatment for, 47
  George M. Bedinger afflicted with, 39, 45, 61, 121, 123, 126, 134, 296
Rhoades, Henry, 55
Rice
  Edward, 43, 44
  Samuel, 211, 222, 236, 238, 245
Riley, Wm., 79
roads
  construction by federal government, George M. Bedinger in favor of, 254
  Danville, Ky., to Tillico, Tenn., survey for (1815), 74
  Maysville, Ky., to Nashville, Tenn., proposed, 254
Robertson (Robison), George, 222, 245
Rogers, John, 311
Rolins, Col., 137
Romantic stories
  courtship of George M. Bedinger, 5
Root, George, 80
Ross, Mr., shoots Indian in ambush of Shawnee village (1779), 21, 98, 276
rotation in office, George M. Bedinger in favor of, 254, 255
Rout, Wm., wounded in expedition against Shawnees (1786), 74
Rowan, Andrew, 55

Roxbury, Mass.
  George M. Bedinger stationed at (1775), 79, 81, 85, 86, 89, 92, 99, 301
  Stephenson's company of riflemen at (1775), 75-78
Rudulph, Michael, 249-253, 253[1]
  as Marshal Ney, 67
  service in Revolutionary War, 67
Rumsey, James
  planing and grooving machine designed by, 57
  steamboat invented by, 66, 71-73
Russel, Edward, 148
Rutherford, Sarah, 2

S

saddle, fabrication from tree bark, 38
safety of travel by boat, 72
Sagwell, Mr., quarrel with [Henry] Clay, 259
St. Clair, Arthur, 61, 133, 260, 308
  campaign against Indians, 295-297
  defeat of (1791), 70
  saved by Wm. Darke, 68
Salt Springs, Ky., 70
Santee, S.C., George M. Bedinger trip to (1780), 31
sawmills built by George M. Bedinger on Licking River, Ky., 3
Schlegel (Slagle)
  Christopher, 2
  Henry, 262
  Magdalene, 2
  surname changed, 3
schools
  escheated lands designated for, 74
  German, in Virginia, 3
Scott
  Gen. [Charles], 256
    in battle of Germantown, Penn., 93, 101, 102, 110
  George, 77, 83, 85, 89, 92, 100, 108, 302
sectionalism
  A. R. Boteler opposition to, 321
Shaner, George, 261

Shawnee Indians
   Bowman's expedition against
      (1779), 19-31, 75, 97, 98,
      105, 106, 130, 132, 256,
      273-290
   [Benjamin] Logan's expedition
      against (1786), 74
Shepherd (Shepard), Abraham
   (Abram), 77, 83, 85, 89, 92,
   100, 108, 135, 302, 324
Sherman, John, candidate for speaker
   of U. S. House of Representatives (1860), 319, 320
Shields, Mr., wounded in battle of
   Piscataway, N. J. (1777), 11,
   88, 96
siege
   of Boonesborough, Ky. (1779), 112-
      114, 306
   of Boston, Mass. (1775), 9, 75-77,
      81-83, 85, 89, 92, 99, 107,
      260, 301, 302
   of Yorktown, Va. (1781), 114, 140-
      144, 256
skin, buffalo, use as food, 36
skunk, encounter with recruit, 16
Slagle. See Schlegel
slavery
   agitation over (1860), 318
   George M. Bedinger views on, 254
   opposition to, in North, 322
slaves, bill to prohibit importation of
   (1808), 62, 300
smallpox contracted by Daniel
   Bedinger, 264
Smith, Mr., escape from Indian
   ambush near Boonesborough,
   Ky. (1779), 4
snakebite, 20, 33
songs, "That seat of science, Athens,"
   Revolutionary War song, 6-8
South
   John, 243
   John Jr. (Jack), 69
      role in escape from Shawnee
         village (1779), 22, 23
   John Sr., 69
      wounded at Boonesborough,
         Ky. (1778), 19
   Samuel, 259

Thomas, 69, 243
   killed in attack on Shawnee
      village (1779), 22, 23,
      98, 280
speeches, battle oration by Black Fish
   (1779), 22, 26, 98, 278
squirt guns, Boonesborough, Ky.,
   defence with (1778), 19
Stanberry, [Henry], 259
Stams (Stearns)
   Capt. [Frederick A., Jr.], 243
      abandonment of Boones-
         borough, Ky. (1779), 13
      killed by Indians, 94
      massacre of party of, by Indians
         (1779), 15, 104, 105,
         111, 112, 304
   Jacob, 69, 243
      escapes Indian massacre, 15
      scalps Indian in ambush of
         Shawnee village (1779),
         21, 98, 276, 277
Staten Island, N. Y.
   George M. Bedinger escape from
      British troops on (1776),
      79, 86, 87, 90, 91, 93, 122
   George M. Bedinger stationed on
      (1776), 82
   British soldiers captured on (1776),
      9, 77, 81, 85, 89, 92, 100,
      108, 301, 302
   Stephenson's company of riflemen
      stationed on (1776), 75, 78
steamboat invented by James
   Rumsey, 66, 71-73
Stearns. See Stams
Stephen. See also Stevens
   Adam, 256
      in battle of Germantown, Penn.
         (1777), 11, 12, 93, 101-
         103, 110
      service in Revolutionary War, 68
   Robt., 68
Stephenson
   A., 261
   Hugh, 123, 134
      friend of George Washington,
         78, 89, 90, 100, 323
      George M. Bedinger military
         service under, 144

Stephenson, Hugh *(continued)*
   led company of riflemen from Virginia to siege of Boston (1775), 5, 6, 9, 75-77, 81-83, 85, 89, 92, 99, 107, 136, 256, 260, 301, 326
   military receipt book of, 127, 136
Stevens. *See also* Stephen
   Edward, 1, 31
Stevenson. *See* Stephenson
Stinson's (Stephenson's) Spring (near Shepherdstown, Va.), rifle company formed at (1775), 6, 8, 136
stirrups, fabrication from tree bark, 38
Stories. *See* Narratives
Stovall, John, treacherous character of, 45-53
Strassburg, Alsace, ancestral home of Bedinger family near, 2
Strode
   John, 69
      arrival in Kentucky, 31, 150
      journey to Boonesborough, Ky. (1779), 12
   Rachael, 2
Strode's Station, Ky., 31, 57, 63, 69
Stronge, Mr., 119
Stubbs, Robert, 66
surgery on intestine on battlefield, 68
surveyors
   George M. Bedinger as, 300
   in Green River country, Ky., 5
   of Nicholas Co., Ky., 62
   of military bounty lands in Green River country, Ky., 125
   types of personnel needed as, 39
surveys. *See also* Land claims
   of Green River country, 32
Swan, J., 248
Swearingen
   Andrew, 63, 64
   Benoni, 69, 88, 146, 174, 189, 220, 243
      in battle of Germantown, Penn. (1777), 11, 12, 93, 101, 102, 110, 111, 126, 127, 303, 304

Swearingen, Benoni *(continued)*
      brother-in-law of George M. Bedinger, 3
      death, 1
      exploration of South Elkhorn country, Ky., 56
      in hunting party at Boonesborough, Ky. (1779), 17
      journey to Boonesborough, Ky. (1779), 12, 150, 166
      land claim of, 16, 145, 147, 157, 158, 163, 164, 170-173, 176, 179, 181-184, 193, 203, 207, 209, 210, 212, 213, 215-219, 226-229, 231, 236, 237, 239, 241, 242, 244
      raised near Shepherdtown, Va., 63
   Joseph, 63, 127, 147, 256, 303
      agreement for surveying of military bounty lands, 135
      in battle of Germantown, Penn., 93, 101, 102, 110
      death and burial, 1
      escape from British on Staten Island (1776), 79, 86, 90, 101, 108, 122, 302
   Lydia, 56
   Sarah, 3
   Thomas, 56, 69, 124, 146, 152, 153, 174, 189, 198, 199, 244
      character and competence of, 201, 231
      in hunting party at Boonesborough, Ky. (1779), 17
      Indian woman saved by, 63
      journey to Boonesborough, Ky. (1779), 12, 150, 166, 309
      land claim of, 157, 163, 164, 170, 171-173, 176, 179, 180, 184, 185, 203-205, 207-209, 212, 213, 215-220, 223, 225-229, 243, 245
   Thomas Jr., life with Indians, 64

T

tariff
  A. R. Boteler position on, 320
  George M. Bedinger views on, 254
Taylor
  Edmund, 74
  John, 69, 146, 155, 189, 243
    exploration of South Elkhorn country (1779), 56
    journey to Boonesborough, Ky. (1779), 12, 166
terrapin, use as food, 36
"That seat of science, Athens," Revolutionary War song, 6-8
Thomas, [John], 311
Thomas (Thompson), Elizabeth, 313, 314
Thompson
  Elizabeth, 313, 314
  George, 74, 313
  Laurance, 69, 174-178
Thornsburg, Mrs., 124
Thruston, Charles M., 1, 87, 88, 101, 303
  in battle of Piscataway, N. J. (1777), 96, 109, 129
  military service in N. J. (1777), 11, 139, 260
Tillico, Tenn., road to Danville, Ky., survey for (1815), 74
Todd
  John, 74, 313
  [John], death in battle of Blue Lick (1782), 312
  Levi, 74
Townsend
  Joshua, 233
  Oswald (Oswell), 196-200, 202
  Thomas, 232-234
training of Virginia troops by George M. Bedinger, 61, 118
transportation
  canals, 264
  railroads, 263, 264
  roads
    Danville, Ky., to Tillico, Tenn., survey for (1815), 74
    Maysville, Ky., to Nashville, Tenn., proposed, 254
    national, 254
  steamboat, invented by James Rumsey, 66, 71-73
trapping of beaver, 37
travel
  Eastern states, 263, 264
  Virginia to Boston, Mass., 9, 76, 77, 81, 85, 89, 92, 99, 107, 301
trees
  belting of, for identification of land claims, 182, 183, 188
  inscribed, for identification of land claims, 175, 185
Trenton, N. J., attack on ferry house near, 137
Trigg, Col. [Stephen], 313
Tully, Christiana, land grant to, after husband's assassination, 73
Tunison, Garrit, in Hugh Stephenson's rifle company (1775), 8

V

Vallandigham, [Clement Laird], 321
Valley Forge, Penn., George M. Bedinger military service at, 128, 144
Van Meter, Jacob, 36, 53
Van Swearingen. See Swearingen
Vance, Lt., among invalids at Fort Washington (1791), 61, 62, 296
Vancouver, Charles, 57, 60
venison, 37
Venus, Thomas, 211
Vice President of U.S., election by direct popular vote, George M. Bedinger in favor of, 254
Viney Fork, Muddy Creek, Madison Co., Ky., naming of, 199, 224
Virginia
  Joseph Swearingen as candidate for legislature of, 1
  revision of constitution of, 255

W

Wabash, expedition to (1786), 74
wages for military service, 136
wagon-making business of George M. Bedinger, 3
Walker, Joel
    defendant in lawsuit over land claim of George M. Bedinger, 130, 210
    heirs of, as defendants in lawsuit over land claim of George M. Bedinger, 150, 174, 187, 196, 203, 207, 217, 228
    land claim on Muddy Creek, Madison Co., Ky., 145, 147-149, 160, 204
Walton
    Edward, 211, 224
    Ned, 236
    Robert, 211, 222, 224, 245
    Thomas, 222, 245
Warren, Thomas, 168, 169, 209, 222, 227, 235, 240, 242
    deposition in land claim lawsuit, 150-155, 210-219
Washington, George, 86, 93, 303, 308
    George M. Bedinger appointed to command Virginia troops by (1790), 61
    confidence in George M. Bedinger, 119
    as friend of Hugh Stephenson, 77, 89, 90, 100, 323
    meets army at Boston (1775), 9
    reviews troops at Cambridge, Mass. (1775), 78
    reviews troops at Germantown, Penn. (1777), 102
    in siege of Boston, Mass. (1775), 108
water moccasin bites Lewis Fields, 33
Watson, Evan, 167-169
    deposition in lawsuit, 159
Wayne, Anthony, 260, 308
    commander at Pittsburgh, Penn. (1793), 61, 298
Weber, Mr., land claim by, 157
Webster, Daniel, 133
weddings, pioneer, 69
West, Thos., in campaign against Indians (1791), 64
White
    Aquilla, 69, 234
        deposition in lawsuit, 228-232
    Mr., 16, 159
    Robert, 8, 326
    Thomas, 66
Whitenday, Capt. (Indian), gift of horse to, 41-44
Whitley, Wm., survey for road by (1815), 74
Whittamore, William, 253^2, 253^3
Whorton, Mr., land claim of, 171, 172
Wicklif, Mr., 241
wildlife. *See also* Food sources
    bear, 38, 56
    beaver, 37, 40
    birds, paroquet, 47
    buffalo (bison), 18, 39
    skunk, 16
    snake, 33
    wolf, 35
Wilkinson, Gen. [James], 249, 250
    cleverly obtains wine from Maj. Zeigler, 67
Williams
    John, 240
        deposition in lawsuit, 221, 222
    Otho H., 9
Williamsburg, Va.
    George M. Bedinger stationed at, in siege of Yorktown, Va. (1781), 141, 143, 144
    gunpowder stored in magazine at (1775), 80
Williamson, David, in slaughter of Moravian Indians on Muskingum (1781), 31, 69, 70
Wilson
    Capt., wounded in battle of Piscataway, N. J. (1777), 11, 88, 96, 129
    H. F., 268
    [Moses], 243
Winrot, Maria, 262
Wise, Gov. [Henry Alexander], 321

wolf
    George M. Bedinger encounter
        with, 35
    meat, as food, 51
Wolfe, Gen. [James], 311
Wolwind, Philip, 256
women
    frontier, 5, 55, 314
    Indian, 63
    Negro, 22, 280, 282
Wood
    Gen. [Solomon], 324
    Dick, 245
    James, 256, 303, 308
        in battle of Germantown, Penn.,
            12, 93, 101-103, 110
    Robt., 324
Woods
    Archibald, 230, 233
    John, 224, 230
    Mr., mill belonging to, 154
Woods's Lower Fork, Muddy Creek,
        Madison Co., Ky., naming of,
        209, 224
Woods's Upper Fork, Muddy Creek,
        Madison Co., Ky., naming of,
        199, 209, 224

Y

Yellow Hawk (Indian), 288
Yorktown, Va., siege of (1781), 114,
    140-144, 256
    George M. Bedinger at, 31, 117,
        138, 260, 307

Z

Zane, Col. [Ebenezer], 248
Zeigler, Maj. [David], conduct in army
    in Revolutionary War, 67
Zingg, Stephen, 74

www.ingramcontent.com/pod-product-compliance
Lightning Source LLC
Chambersburg PA
CBHW050831230426
43667CB00012B/1960